THE NEWS MEDIA:

A JOURNALIST

LOOKS AT HIS PROFESSION

BOOKS BY JOHN HOHENBERG

The Pulitzer Prize Story: An Anthology
The Professional Journalist
Foreign Correspondence: The Great Reporters
    and Their Times
The New Front Page: An Anthology
Between Two Worlds: Policy, Press and Public Opinion
    in Asian-American Relations
The Professional Journalist: A Guide
    to Modern Reporting Practice

THE NEWS

MEDIA:

A JOURNALIST

LOOKS

AT HIS

PROFESSION

JOHN HOHENBERG

HOLT, RINEHART AND WINSTON, INC.
New York   Chicago   San Francisco   Atlanta
Dallas   Montreal   Toronto   London

Still Another for Dorothy

The First Amendment presupposes that right conclusions are more likely to be gathered out of a multitude of tongues than through any kind of authoritative selection. To many this is, and always will be, folly; but we have staked upon it our all.

JUDGE LEARNED HAND
(U. S. v. Associated Press—
52 F. Supp. 362)

PREFACE

There are excellent reasons for all the attention that is being given to the journalist in the United States during these declining years of the twentieth century. It is primarily because of his efforts that the United States has developed the most powerful and pervasive concentration of news media that has ever existed in an open society. He, too, has set off the massive information explosion that bursts with dismaying regularity from the wire services and newspapers, radio and television, the weekly news and picture magazines, and the journals of intellectual comment and criticism. Nothing comparable in scope has ever occurred before in any nation that has aspired to world leadership, basing itself on the proposition that its people could learn enough and absorb enough to govern themselves.

The journalist's role in these disorderly and changing times has thus become one of the most sensitive in American life. How well he is able to inform over 200 million Americans each day is a matter for continuing debate. To what extent he is able to influence them is open to argument. But certainly, what he says, writes and photographs, how and why he does it, and what methods his media use to project his work deserve far closer scrutiny inside and outside the profession. The working journalist himself seldom has time for introspection.

This book seeks, first of all, to undertake a selective examination of the principal problems of the news media in the United States. But far more than that, it considers values that are rarely discussed by journalists themselves because they have so moralistic a sound—the ethics of the journalist, his outlook on society, his duties to the nation. Such values are difficult to measure except where specific cases have provided a guide, and even these may under certain circumstances prove contradictory.

The judgments presented herein are therefore highly personal and subjective in the main—the product of my own observation and beliefs after a quarter-century as a working newspaperman and some seventeen years as a teacher of journalism. They are offered as an accounting to the public and the rising generation of journalists of the mores of a business that was once just a trade—a trade that became a profession during x the wars, depressions, and revolutionary upheavals of this century.

If there is any caution I have to offer, it is that American journalism is enormously diverse and represents a tremendous variety of media, people, and points of view. Call the roll of the fraternity of journalism and you must include James Reston of *The New York Times* and Mel Ruder of the *Hungry Horse News* of Montana, E. B. White of *The New Yorker* and Tony Escoda, the Manila correspondent of the Associated Press; Pauline Frederick, the United Nations correspondent of the National Broadcasting Company, and Walter Cronkite, the managing editor of the news service of the Columbia Broadcasting System. To generalize about such people is dangerous; to classify them, impossible.

My debts for this book are heavy. So many in every field of journalism have contributed to my knowledge and background with full and frank discussions of their own situations. They may be assured that I have, throughout, respected their confidences while drawing on their background and experience. And this goes for present and former officials of American and foreign governments as well.

My thanks, in particular, go to Dean Theodore Peterson of the University of Illinois College of Journalism and Communications for having encouraged me to do this book and—quoting him—"to speak for yourself, John." I have tried. I am also indebted to Dean Edward W. Barrett of the Columbia University Graduate School of Journalism and to the School's Research Committee headed by Professor Frederick T. C. Yu for a grant. For the time that gave me an opportunity to redraft pertinent portions of the manuscript in the summer of 1967 after discussions with my colleagues at the East-West Center in Honolulu, where I was a senior specialist, I am grateful to Chancellor Howard P. Jones. As always, the ever-knowledgeable J. Montgomery Curtis, former director, and Walter Everett, his successor, at the American Press Institute were generous with their assistance whenever I had need of it, which was often. But without the patience, good humor, and wise counsel of Dorothy Lannuier Hohenberg, whose task it was once again to help me with my research and to read and criticize what I wrote, I am sure that this book would never have been completed.

As is customary, let me absolve all these of responsibility for what follows. Whether the reader's interests are general or professional, he is asked to consider these observations as those of a life-long journalist who thinks well of his profession, for all its frailties, and has a healthy respect for the character, ability, and resolution of both the new generation of journalists and his own colleagues.

John Hohenberg

New York
February 1968

CONTENTS

PREFACE   ix

PART 1   GROWTH OF THE MEDIA: Problem
          and Promise

    1. The Limits of Power   3

    2. A Question of Purpose   17

    3. Interlocking Media   28

    4. New Times for Newspapers   42

    5. Magazines and the News   58

    6. Trends in Television   71

PART 2   OF MANNERS AND MORALS:
          Truth or Consequences

    7. The Meaning of the News   87

    8. The Credibility Gap   107

    9. War, Truth, and Vietnam   132

    10. Coverage by the Herd   153

    11. Junket Journalism   167

    12. Underdeveloped Journalism   178

    13. The American Cultural Revolution   194

    14. The Ills of Photo Journalism   207

PART 3   THE SHAPING OF PUBLIC OPINION:
          The Endless Struggle

    15. Polls and Pollsters   221

    16. Free Press and Fair Trial   234

    17. Right to Know vs. Need to Know   256

    18. Many Voices, Many Media   269

    19. The Basis of Public Service   279

    20. The Future of the Journalist   293

NOTES AND COMMENT   307

PART 1

GROWTH

OF THE MEDIA:

PROBLEM

AND

PROMISE

THE LIMITS

1

OF POWER

The American news media on the whole have seldom been more affluent, and more on the defensive, than they are today. The better newspapers and magazines have been inclined to place a large share of the blame for this peculiar state of affairs on the follies of television. The electronic media, in turn, have pointed with angry righteousness to some of the more reprehensible practices of their printed opposition.

When areas of lamentable public ignorance in the news have been disclosed, both have been accused of under-

4   informing and even misinforming the people. In return, the more despairing among The Journalistic Establishment have tended to question the intellectual competence of a public that has seemed too often to be more devoted to soap opera, packaged sex, and animated comic strips than to the necessity for accumulating information to advance the slow and sometimes painful process of self-government.

It has been the kind of distressing situation in which an ancient Quaker once observed to a friend at the Village Meeting House: "Everybody here is crazy except thee and me, and even thou art a little queer."

THE STATE OF THE PROFESSION

Nevertheless, the concern that many responsible journalists feel over the state of their profession in the United States is very real and it is soundly based in the main. Not since the era when 80 percent of the American press unsuccessfully opposed Franklin Delano Roosevelt during his four campaigns for the Presidency has the serious journalist felt less like a leader of public opinion and more like a follower. The strictures of the United States Supreme Court in the cases involving free press and fair trial, the frustrations of the Vietnam War and its coverage, and the lingering public resentment of the journalists' role in the Lee Harvey Oswald television murder all have played a part in this slump in news media prestige.

But the trouble goes somewhat deeper. There is demonstrably little public enthusiasm for the undoubted rights of the news media, for their perennial crusade for freedom of information and more than a little suspicion of the noble postures of the American journalist. When James Reston observes, "The credit of the American newspapers with the American people for accuracy and good judgment is not high," [1] it is not necessary to draft a questionnaire and take a public opinion poll to conclude that he is right. There is also little doubt that the credit of television ranks considerably lower with the well-educated viewer, no matter how enthusiastic the kids are over the animated comics and the housewives over the soap operas and tenors.

This is, of course, not a blanket indictment. Anybody who is a part of American journalism, and I have been for most of my life, has his own pet list of both organizations and journalists who are highly esteemed, mine being considerably longer than most. The point is that the bulk of the news media and a large section of the public are not on the same wave length for the diffusion of all but the most immediately important news, and have not been for a long time. There are few open signs of displeasure; instead, there is ample evidence of a prevailing skepticism and lack of enthusiasm that creates concern over the lack of public empathy for its news media as a whole.

Earlier in the century, when the country was smaller and the news much simpler, the situation was markedly different. A less affluent and a less educated public was far more inclined to embrace its newspapers and magazines with a fanatic loyalty or damn them with shrill invective. There was precious little apathy then, for it was the time of Joseph Pulitzer and William Randolph Hearst, of Adolph S. Ochs and the good grey *New York Times*, of Jacob Riis and Lincoln Steffens, and the rest of the muckrakers who fought many a good crusade. Everyone could find a hero or a villain in such a company; some, like Upton Sinclair, even cried out that the whole thing was a miserable capitalistic conspiracy.

In many an immigrant home, the favored daily newspaper was second in importance only to the Bible and was read with great care. I remember that when my father read aloud from his favorite editorial page, my mother and I were dutifully silent. Nor are my memories as a child unique; many another, coming from such an environment, will agree that a favored newspaper occupied a place of respect in the home. It was the communicator, teacher, moral force, and even the intellectual leader at times of a whole generation of new Americans. Their children, for the most part, have come to take much of the press for granted and to look at television for amusement plus a little news.

Ironically, the press as a whole is much better in the latter part of this century than it was at the beginning. Many more of its leaders take their public responsibilities with the utmost seriousness. They print more news and offer a greater diversity of opinion. While a monopoly position in all but a few cities has killed off a choice among newspapers, it has also caused many surviving newspapers in metropolitan centers to make substantial improvements.

Whatever gains the press as a whole has made in these areas, however, has been offset in the public mind to a considerable extent by the development of the electronic media

6 as the first source of breaking news. In addition, the rise of the weekly news magazine has given millions of Americans access to explanations of national and foreign news that are either omitted or sketchily published by many small and medium-sized dailies.

Finally, and this is most important of all, the essential character of the audience for the news media has changed. It is far better educated. Nearly 60 million Americans are in school today, more than half our high school graduates go to college and our enrollment in higher education will soon be 8 million, double that of a generation ago. As might be expected, this is essentially a young audience. Very soon, more than half the nation will be less than 25 years old, a public less oriented to the old-time newspaper than to the electronic media. Quite naturally, it will be argued that the older half of the nation and the better-educated younger people alike will turn in increasing numbers to good newspapers and away from sketchy television reportage.

Perhaps so, but that is not really the answer. For if the image of the news media is not one that provides general joy and satisfaction within the republic, it is far worse abroad where feelings range from professional jealousy to uncritical but emphatic dislike. To the world at large, the American press is a fat and luxurious varicolored jumble of newsprint, much of it wasted on irrelevancies, which reaches the stupendous proportions of a five- or six-pound advertising throwaway on Sundays. American wire services, despite the care with which they are edited for foreign consumption, are regarded as vehicles of American policy even by sophisticates in foreign governments. American news magazines, tartly and tightly written, often are resented when they produce unfavorable accounts of foreign lands and are accordingly charged with putting the American panorama in softer focus. As for American radio and television, they are the repositories of all the historic complaints first registered against American movies—crass, crude, money-grabbing representatives of a nonculture.

This exaggerated catalogue of journalistic shortcomings is largely accepted by the American intellectuals who have great respect for foreign opinion. But it would be a mistake to dismiss the impatience, even the outright dislike, of the news media by the intelligentsia as the built-in prejudice of a small number of inveterate critics. There is no doubt of the blindness of the prejudice, nor of the tremolo of scorn with which the very word, "Journalism," is uttered in the classroom; yet, such attitudes are an important part of the foundation of mistrust and doubt of the purposes of the news media that exist in the United States.

It is not enough to hold up a few great newspapers, magazines, or television programs as exhibits to prove the virtues of American journalism; nor can the work of the wire services be justified by showing how many million words are transmitted each day to thousands of outlets all over the world. Unlike the physician, the scientist, the lawyer, clergyman, or engineer, who are judged by their noblest works as a rule, the journalist is generally assessed by his worst performances. This may be unfair, but it is true. The youngest and greenest journalist knows, almost instinctively, that there will be latent hostility to his every inquiry even if he tries to learn who stole the cake at a Sunday school picnic. Somebody will always turn up who has an interest in delaying, twisting, or suppressing the news.

The suspicion of the journalist's intentions is, of course, not particularly new; it also is not confined by any means to the United States. Even in closed societies, where the journalist is supposed to be the mindless creature of the State, there have been instances in which government officials have been unduly annoyed by inquiries from their own press people. There should be little cause for wonder, consequently, that in the scant two centuries of independent journalism, mainly in the English-speaking nations of the world, the journalists have tended to cluster together for mutual effort, a kind of faltering semisupport, habitual professional shop talk, and the pleasures of social diversion. While they have never been able to present a solid front on very many issues, they have chosen to live for the most part in a self-imposed pale inhabited almost exclusively by other journalists, congenial news sources, and a few carefully chosen outsiders.

It has been observed in consequence by those who despair of the journalist and ridicule his profession that he prefers, and indeed, often enjoys his own company during leisure hours. He has also been accused, sometimes with justice, of gathering his ideas from his fellows and sometimes promoting his own wrongheaded notions, instead of departing from the herd for a cold, lonely, painful search for the truth. Nobody can determine, of course, the extent to which news and ideas are

8 shuffled and reshuffled instead of being independently reported and assessed. However, the sameness with which the news is reported, even by correspondents who are completely out of touch with each other, is one of the less pleasing aspects of American journalism today. Outside the confines of most metropolitan communities, news tends to be what the wire services say it is because the individual local newspaper and electronic media sometimes have no other quickly available resource to challenge the wire service file.

Nevertheless, it would be a mistake to place exclusive blame for these shortcomings on the publisher, the broadcast executive, or the responsible editor. Of the 600,000 people employed in all forms of journalism in the United States, perhaps 60,000 are engaged in news gathering, writing, editing, and commentary. Scattered as they are throughout the land, and working at all hours around the clock, these editorial staff members would be difficult, if not impossible, to control by any central source in American society. The Russians may not believe it; but then, the Russians are suspicious even of *Pravda* and *Izvestia* (and with better reason, too). The sameness of the product, in too many instances, may be accounted for only by the identical processes of training, news assessment, and operational techniques.

The truth is, quite baldly, that whether a journalist's professional beginnings are in the print or broadcast media or in a university or college newspaper or journalism school, the root of what he learns is still based on the newsroom techniques of the newspaper. It has been so for a hundred years or more and is likely to continue, unless more great universities in the land join the few that already have pioneered in a broader journalism education that breaks cleanly with the tradition of techniques. Until this happens, the man of ideas, with only a few exceptions, will inevitably be overshadowed in journalism by both the technician and the manager. Consequently, there will continue to be more concern over form than substance in the news media as a whole, with resultant public boredom over much of the routine end product.

It will not do to blame the advertiser for this static position in the development of a consequential news report. The journalist, conveniently overlooking his own weaknesses, customarily argues that the advertiser and his powerful agencies are at the bottom of most of the ills of journalism. He is often

singled out as the real culprit for the wave of press consolidations, the death of mass circulation magazines of some importance, the flourishing state of the fluffier side of television, and
the relatively hard struggle that is waged by marginal magazines
and newspapers of high intellectual quality.

This is quite an indictment; however, to accuse is
one thing and to provide convincing proof is quite another. Certainly, as the great patron of the news media, the advertiser
bears his fair share of responsibility for his part in the proceedings. But this scarcely excuses the journalists for producing so
much indifferent fare for the public. No advertiser, in short, can
be blamed because a newspaper is a poor shadow of what it
should be. And however great the influence of advertising on
television programming may be, it has less to do with the substance of news shows than the timidity of its editors. As Chet
Huntley once conceded, "In our sometimes zeal for shooting film
with interesting façades and lovely landscapes, and in our fear
of dullness and the low rating, we arbitrarily rule out a long and
imposing list of awesome subjects and conclude that they were
just not meant for television and radio. What an incredible
confession of weakness!" [2] Editors in the other media, who cannot hide behind lovely landscapes, could well make the same
confession.

It follows that the journalist, with the obtuseness of
a Brutus, too often has looked everywhere except within himself
to excuse his faults. He can no longer pretend that he is a poor,
raffish wretch, a hostage to uncertain fortune, to be batted this
way and that by the forces that contend for primacy over him. It
is an illusion that has no validity today, and probably had a lot
less than Upton Sinclair imagined at the turn of the century. For
the journalist in the declining years of the twentieth century,
despite his fluctuating influence, has won recognition as a substantial force within himself and very often is counted upon as a
valued member of local, regional, and national establishments.

THE RECORD OF THE NEWS MEDIA

Consider the record of the American news media:

The United Nations Educational, Scientific, and
Cultural Organization has reported that more newspapers, magazines, and other periodicals are published in the United States
than in any other country, that the growth of American television is greater than elsewhere, and that American radio audi-

10   ences are the largest on earth. The two American global news agencies, Associated Press and United Press International, are credited with having the widest domestic and foreign distribution in their field. In the American communications complex, only the film industry is said to be losing ground in the world market although American films still account for 55 percent of all showings abroad.[3]

As for profits, particularly in the long bull market of the 1960s, they have been substantial although there is no guarantee that this pleasant state of affairs will go on indefinitely. Television, of course, has been the most publicized beneficiary. However, prosperity also has been general among radio stations, news magazines, the newspaper groups that are geared to aggressive expansion, and the stronger newspapers everywhere regardless of size. The principal exceptions, as always, have been the chronic sick ones among metropolitan newspapers, battered by strikes and mergers, and the continuing losers elsewhere, plus some of the wavering magazines of general circulation.

Outwardly, the newspapers appear to have shared generously on the whole in the prosperity that has come to the news media. The circulation of 1,754 daily newspapers reached a record 61,397,000 in 1966. They carried $4.8 billion in advertising and took in another $2 billion in circulation sales (some of which went to carriers and agents). The 9.4 percent advertising increase over the previous year almost brought total newspaper advertising equal with the total $5 billion advertising of television, radio, and magazines. It was shown that daily newspapers with more than 100,000 circulation had increased in size from an average of 27 pages in 1946 to 53 pages in 1966, that editorial content spread from 12.3 to 20.3 pages in the same period and that advertising jumped even more from 14.7 to 32.7 pages. Newsprint consumption, at more than $140 a ton, was 9.077 million tons in 1966 and industry-wide employment was 353,800, an increase of 42 percent since 1947.

Of 111 daily newspapers that participated in a cost analysis survey, net profits ranged in 1965 from $22,007 before taxes for the smallest dailies to $1,021,011 for those in the 75,000–140,000 circulation group. Advertising provided more than 70 percent of the revenue for all papers in the survey, with local display advertising accounting for 50 to 58 percent of the total. And that, naturally, was what helped the successful newspapers; in a virtual monopoly situation most local advertisers—display and classified—have been obliged, up to now at least, to turn to the newspapers and national advertisers seeking bigger local sales have had to do the same.

The newspapers are fretting, however, over the drop of their share of total advertising from 37 to 29 percent between 1949 and the mid-1960s due to the growth of television. Yet, some profit margins have ranged from 8 to 20 percent; indeed, one daily with 246,000 circulation was said in a recent year to have made a 19 percent profit of $2.5 million on a gross of $13 million. The small newspapers, as Lord Thomson of Fleet said during his campaign to latch onto more of them in the United States, became his "little cash boxes." And that happy term may also cover the leaders in the overcrowded field of more than 8,000 weeklies.

For the great newspapers, profit margins have not been as large but they have continued to be substantial. *The New York Times*, for example, reported its consolidated revenues at $172,920,301 for 1966, with a consolidated net income of $9,355,469, or $4.28 per common share. The newspaper chains, for the most part, did better; moreover, most of the profitable newspaper and news magazine enterprises continued to develop educational and other sidelines in a determined move to diversify their holdings. Time, Inc., even bought the *Newark News*.

Despite this record, however, thoughtful newspaper people have continued to worry. To them and to others, it is obvious that the newspaper is confronted with the threat of greater losses of advertising to television, monumental problems of rising costs and perennial shortages of quality personnel. Yet, for those critics who continually dwell on the decline in American dailies from 2,200 in 1910 as if it would go on to the vanishing point, the downward trend should not be the whole story. Actually, there is reason to believe that the period of press consolidation is now slowing down except for some of the marginal metropolitan properties and some weaker units elsewhere. In the past twenty years, it is true, 403 newspapers have suspended publication, but almost as many new ones have begun interesting histories.[4] More consolidations and suspensions are to be expected, but not at the alarming rate of the period since 1950. After a long period of inertia, the leaders in the newspaper industry are beginning to stir; if their response to the technologi-

12   cal revolution thus far has been minimal, some at last have seen new opportunities in the growth areas of the nation and tried to grasp them. That, at least, is something.

In the magazine field, too, the woes of the failures and the advertising declines have distracted attention from the prosperity in which so many have shared in the 1960s. While there were spectacular deaths in the nonnews and nonpicture group, most news magazines have prospered. *Newsweek,* after a long struggle, has turned the corner and shown a profit, with 2 million circulation and gross revenues of $43.5 million in 1966. The McGraw-Hill industrial group, headed by *Business Week,* produced a net income of $8 million in 1966, up $2 million over the previous year. But the undoubted earnings champion of the magazines has been Time, Inc. When the founder of news magazines, Henry R. Luce, died on February 28, 1967, it was calculated that the $86,000 in borrowed capital with which he started *Time* in 1923 had increased to $690 million, of which he owned $109 million. In the decade before Luce's death, Time, Inc., (*Time, Life, Fortune* and associated ventures) had doubled its revenues and tripled its profits. In 1966 alone its report for operations disclosed record revenues of $503 million and net earnings of $37.3 million,[5] with magazines forming some 65 percent of the company's diversified revenues. For any realistic assessment of the financial status of news magazines, it should be noted that *Life,* the picture magazine, was the biggest earner and *Time* was second, with 3.5 million circulation and twice the gross revenues of its nearest competition, *Newsweek.*

Any consideration of the fortunes of television in general and television news, unlike that of the newspapers and news magazines, runs at once into the basic difficulty that they are not at all the same. General television, in the main, is show business with a thin layer of culture and public affairs to top it off. Television news is a merger of wire services, newsreels, theatre, and some of its own built-in peculiarities which, despite an audience that reaches 35 million a night for two big programs (Huntley-Brinkley and Cronkite), actually accounts for a comparatively small share of programming.* It takes a Presidential election, a war, a visit of Pope Paul VI to the United States, or an

---

* The last of the great newsreels, Universal News, surrendered to television and went out of business December 26, 1967, closing down what was once a major activity of journalism.

important space shot to make television go all-out with audiences that reach 150 million.

The television and radio industry, with revenues of $2,750 million annually from 773 television and 5,657 radio stations, concentrates its news efforts in the three big networks. While they have boosted their news budgets by 200 percent in five years, the total outlay for news is not commensurate with total profits for the networks. To be fair, it should be pointed out that from 1961, when news costs of the three networks were estimated at $50 million, they went to an estimated $125 million in the Presidential year of 1964, or about 20 percent of the total network expenditures. For 1964, with total expenses of $772.2 million, the three networks and the 15 stations they own took in $928.7 million for a pretax profit of $156.5 million. For the television industry as a whole, this profit amounted to $415.6 million before taxes based on total revenues of $1.8 billion, with 102 individual television stations showing individual profits of more than $1 million each.

PROFITS AND PURPOSES

The profit outlook for television continues to be good. For 1965, the three networks and their 15 stations earned $161.6 million before taxes, which one authority estimated to be more than a 100 percent rate of return on broadcasting property and 165 percent on the undepreciated part of tangible broadcast property. The median revenue of profitable VHF stations for the same year was estimated at nearly $1.5 million.

For 1966, television by itself took in a record $2.2 billion and its pretax profits increased by 10 percent to $492 million. The 15 network-owned stations earned $108 million before taxes, 41.2 percent of the gross, while 593 other stations included in the FCC report showed a pretax profit of 29.6 percent of the gross. The three networks, for a variety of reasons, netted 8.7 percent of the gross, or $79 million. Thus, while the estimated expenditure of $150 million for news that year by the three networks was impressive, it had to be measured against the profits that television on the whole had been making. Thus, while NBC and CBS talked of spending $500,000 each for Vietnam War coverage, the AP alone was spending $750,000.[6]

There was reason, consequently, for the dissatisfaction of television people with their news coverage. "The net-

14   works, including my own, do a first-rate job of disseminating the news," Walter Cronkite said, "but all of them have third-rate news-gathering organizations. We are still basically dependent on the wire services. We have barely dipped our toe into investigative reporting." [7] To this, David Brinkley added, "On a story like a convention . . . or an inauguration . . . something that is planned in advance . . . on that kind of thing, nobody can touch us. But when it comes to covering the news in any thorough and detailed way, we are just almost not in the ball game." [8] Yet, NBC kept trying, and planned a once-a-month news show of two hours for 1969.

The deep feeling of unease among journalists was best expressed by Turner Catledge, executive editor of *The New York Times*, when he gave this altogether realistic analysis of the position of the American press in the midst of the most prosperous period in its history:

"The criticisms which embarrass us most are those which find newspapers lagging behind the general evolution of society. I'm embarrassed because I have to confess it's true . . .

"Healthy though the economic substructures of many, or even most individual newspapers may be, common sense tells us that unless the newspaper business as a whole evolves with evolving technology, it cannot indefinitely survive in a competitive free economy. The newspaper competes as a dispenser of information, and a purveyor of advertising, with other very efficient and alert enterprises—notably television, radio and the national news magazines . . . It can be conservatively predicted that unless newspapers—and this includes not only newspaper management, editorial employees, mechanical workers but everyone else associated with this great profession—unless we can intelligently and swiftly resolve the conflicts which are holding off the introduction into general newspaper use of modern automation, the newspaper as we know it today will surely decline in significance if not, indeed, eventually disappear from the scene. It will surely be and will deserve to be replaced by some other medium more in tune with modern needs." [9]

Thus, a very considerable segment of the news media, for all its current prosperity, is approaching the limits of its power. Even without a full-blown recession, there is a point beyond which mere expansion of itself is useless unless the end product is improved. And if technology and the long-range effect of the competition for the advertisers' dollar worry newspapers today, it is equally possible that they will be of even greater concern to television and the news magazines tomorrow. In journalism in an open society, always so dependent on the ability of a news organization to maintain financial independence, nobody is likely to retain a privileged competitive position indefinitely. Big journalism is big business today, with proprietors in a constant struggle to meet rising costs, higher taxes, increasing union demands, and the intricacies of automation.

These are the symptoms of the malaise that affects the news media, but they are not the basic cause. Even if the most complicated electronic gadgets could be hooked up to the news engine tomorrow, making it completely automated, someone would still have to find and present the news which is, in effect, the fuel that makes it run. No gadget has been invented so far that can do this sensitive and difficult job, and it is unlikely that one will ever be perfected.

It is hard enough these days for a journalist to figure out sometimes what the news is and what it means without trying to program it into a supercomputer, then test it for high and low truth content. Because, of course, there has never been any guarantee to the trustful citizen (if any there be) that the news and the truth are identical, and this goes for everything from party campaign platforms and speeches at the United Nations to a review of a new play.

This state of affairs is due in considerable part to the continued operation of the news media on the historic principle that they will distribute news of enough interest to a sufficiently large body of solvent citizens to attract advertisers, who in turn will support the organization at given rates in order to vend their wares to its clients. If this formula has produced some news media of undoubted excellence, it is purely coincidental. The maintenance of excellence, or even common sense, is no part of the contract. Consequently, both solvent and unsolvent citizens in many metropolitan areas are asked to struggle with more undigested and unexplained facts about highly complicated matters than they can possibly absorb. However, in more isolated places, their fellow-citizens often find it difficult to keep in touch with daily events outside their immediate community.

Clearly, what is needed more than anything else is a new definition of purpose for the news media to fit the circumstances of the latter part of the twentieth century. With it, in this

16   rapidly changing world, the citizens of this republic are entitled to a far broader and more realistic concept of news, and the explanation of the news, than most news organizations are now able to provide. It is all very well to say that the people of the United States are better served today by their news media than any others in the world and very probably it is true. But the evidence also indicates that the service is not good enough, that the rate of profit is generous in many instances and that the time for boldness and innovation in journalism is long overdue even if it costs a lot more to put into effect. Certainly, if we go on letting journalists use yesterday's methods to produce today's news on tomorrow's devices, we can scarcely blame a large part of the public if it ignores the whole confusing business and switches on the latest television diversion.

A QUESTION

2

OF PURPOSE

There is a tendency in the higher echelons of government to believe that the purpose of the journalist generally is to stick his nose into affairs that are none of his business and, specifically, to interfere with the higher considerations of domestic and foreign policy. Without doubt, some of the framers of the Constitution would have agreed with this uncharitable assessment. However, on the assumption that the journalist on balance would turn out to be more of a benefit than a nuisance, he was recognized as a very special person and protected in the Bill of Rights under its free press guarantee.

18   This does not, of course, relieve the journalist of the responsibilities of citizenship common to all in the Republic, although he sometimes does not act like it. He is, among other things, subject to the laws of libel and slander (which he does not like to talk about), as well as those covering obscenity and contempt of court and such newer statutes as the imposition of atomic secrecy. While some of his critics may not believe it, he also takes very seriously the accepted standards of good taste but, like almost everybody else, must be given allowance for slippage now and then. With perfectly good reason, as the legal profession has recently rediscovered, the journalist has a traditional suspicion of such things as press councils and codes of conduct on the natural assumption that somebody may eventually use them to infringe on his Constitutional protection.

THE JOURNALIST AS A PERSONAGE

Just how well the journalist has justified the faith reposed in him by the Founding Fathers was not a matter of wide and profound discussion in this particular era until recently. Whereas the journalist earlier in the century had been scrutinized primarily by the bartender, bookmaker, stereotyper and pressman, night watchman, and an occasional feminine patron in the corner saloon near the news office, he now has become socially significant. Among others, he has attracted the attention of the sociologist, psychologist, political scientist, and even the historian, plus an occasional university president and foundation executive. Since this had happened only to a limited extent previously in the two-century history of the newspaper on this continent, the sour conclusion generally reached in the newsrooms of the nation is that this, like comic strip serials, has been motivated by television.

Having become a personage, the journalist can scarcely fend off a friendly inquiry into his whys and wherefores. He likes to think of himself romantically as living on the knife-edge of events and, save for such sedentary characters as editors and copyreaders, it is very largely true. But, with the perverseness of his breed, he does not really like to be thought of as a journalist and he despises the term, news media, although he cannot think of anything better. He wants to be known as a newspaperman, a radio reporter, a television newsman or correspondent, or a wire service deskman, with suitable variations thereof, which is obviously difficult in a general discussion. Unlike his American colleague, the European journalist is much more sensible about the small business of nomenclature.

It was, incidentally, a good European, Theophraste Renaudot, who stated both the principal purpose and the principal dilemma of the journalist more than 300 years ago when he founded the *Gazette de France* (Cardinal Richelieu, publisher; Louis XIII, editorial page editor):

"In one thing only will I yield to nobody—I mean in my endeavor to get at the truth. At the same time I do not always guarantee it, being convinced that among five hundred dispatches written in haste from all countries it is impossible to escape passing something from one correspondent to another that will require correction from Father Time." [10]

There have been similarly high-minded statements of purpose from many of those who molded both the form and the substance of American journalism, two of which are worth mentioning here. The first is Adolph S. Ochs's declaration of principle on August 19, 1896, when he became publisher of *The New York Times*, "to give the news impartially, without fear or favor, regardless of any party, sect or interest involved." [11] The second is Joseph Pulitzer's platform for the *St. Louis Post-Dispatch*, written on his retirement April 10, 1907, pledging "that it will always fight for progress and reform, never tolerate injustice or corruption, always fight demagogues of all parties, never belong to any party, always oppose privileged classes and public plunderers, never lack sympathy with the poor, always remain devoted to the public welfare, never be satisfied with merely printing the news, always be drastically independent, never be afraid to attack wrong, whether by predatory plutocracy or predatory poverty." [12]

While all journalists will approve of these noble sentiments, today and in the future, translating them into practical terms is something else again. I am sure that my first city editor on the *Seattle Star* was quite as idealistic as any, whenever it mattered to him. And yet I still remember, as a $20-a-week reporter, that he instructed me to cover my first out-of-town assignment, a State Federation of Labor convention, by watching for fist fights among the delegates and skipping the speeches. It was my introduction, however rough, to the theory of conflict in the news, which still has some basic appeal for both *The New York Times* and the *St. Louis Post-Dispatch*, in common with all other news media in the land. Small wonder, then, that the

20   journalist who writes with ease about the difference between the real and declared policies of great nations finds it difficult to account for subtle differences in his own profession, when he is able to think about them.

THE IMPOSSIBLE ART

It is not often that anybody in journalism is able to afford the luxury of philosophical contemplation. In addition to the mastery of his own calling, the journalist is expected to be knowledgeable in politics, economics, science, law, religion, medicine, art, education, agriculture, history, geography, mathematics, and the rarefied atmosphere of outer space, not to overlook many other fields. As if that were not enough, he is also called upon to write from time to time on the pangs of young and old love, the pleasures of family life, sports, fun and games, and the varying problems of foreign peoples from North Cape to Patagonia.

Within a single cycle of a wire service report, an edition of a newspaper or magazine, or a newscast of 30 minutes or less, he must make his contribution of news and try to tell what it means, if he is given the chance. At any given hour, this may vary from the parade of the expected to the shock and surprise of the unexpected, including such themes as an emergency in the community, an announcement from the White House, a new law enacted by the Congress, a fight at the United Nations, a war, a crime, a judicial decision, a birth, a marriage, a divorce, a death, or a scandal of fluctuating interest.

In such matters and others, the journalist may assume a variety of roles—an eyewitness or narrator, a guide or counsellor to the perplexed, a watchdog over the public and private sectors of the nation, or an advocate and defender of the public interest. The catalogue has been presented at perhaps longer length than necessary to make a point: If politics is the art of the possible, then journalism without doubt is the art of attempting the impossible. It is done almost every day, including Sunday.

This is not to excuse the shortcomings of the journalist, but to account for them. He seldom bothers to do so himself, being otherwise occupied as a rule. If he is asked to define his own purpose, he will usually say, with disarming simplicity, "I cover the news," as if it were a finite quality like milk, butter, or eggs. Nor will he appear very often as the bumptious caricature of reality that is seen on the stage, screen, and television.

Generally, the higher he rises in the rather steep scale of journalistic values, the more he will insist that he is, essentially, just a reporter (or writer or editor) in a profession whose power and influence are vastly overrated. The defense mechanism is a good one, for these are attributes that defy measurement. It is in large part responsible for the tendency today to underrate the journalist's power and influence, which is quite as serious a fault as the turn-of-the-century findings of the muckrakers—Upton Sinclair, Will Irwin, and others—that the press is an oligarchy. Neither the seraph nor the devil theories really apply to this complicated and diverse institution.

In any discussion of the purposes of the journalist and his media, two other characteristics must be considered. One is his rather vague definition (to outsiders, at least) of what he considers to be news, and the other is the adversary complex that motivates some of his work. Whenever the two are in harmony, the effect can be profound. If, for example, a public official builds a fine new home in a wealthy neighborhood, the average citizen usually does not concern himself about it. But a reporter with a generic suspicion of officialdom quickly discovers that the new structure is beyond the means of its owner and presto!—it becomes news.

The trouble with both the adversary complex and the varying definitions of what constitutes news is that they are applied with almost equal diligence against matters affecting the national security and a school bond issue in Riverhead Town, Suffolk County, New York. Moreover, while the combative tendencies of the press have accounted for much of its deserved reputation as a watchdog of the public interest, the blast of the editorial trumpet sometimes has not been heard in the land when it was needed most.

Consider the case of Senator Joseph R. McCarthy of Wisconsin. For a hundred years, the standard definitions of news in American newsrooms referred to events that affected large numbers of people and were told in accord with the ancient verities—accuracy, interest, timeliness. Few ever bothered to mention the word truth, since it was presumed to be covered under the term, accuracy. But many a reporter of an older era remembers, as I do, that "objective" city editors would dismiss

22   early attempts at interpretation as follows: "Just tell me what the man said and don't try to tell me what he meant. The reader will figure it out for himself." It was made to order for McCarthy; as it turned out, the reader *could not* figure out what he had said because the truth content in his charges of Communist penetration of the American government was abysmally low. But under the cult of objectivity, his untruths were accurately reported.

It was not until a small number of newspapers and a resolute and courageous television attack by Edward R. Murrow challenged McCarthy's statements that the much-heralded adversary complex began to show again, actively encouraged by a few public-spirited proprietors. But eventually, it was McCarthy who destroyed himself and undermined his own credibility with the public in his long television appearances during the Army-McCarthy hearings. Thereafter, the enthusiasm for interpretive and analytical journalism flourished and an influential segment of the media sponsored a spirited revival of investigatory reporting. True, the self-interest of the press, in seeking a field in which its superiority to television could be demonstrated, had something to do with this welcome development; yet, basically, the movement could not have grown without a certain amount of unadmitted idealism. It was not talked about very much but, to anybody who knew something about reporters, it was there. A few editors and publishers, too, gave evidence of a devotion to principle over commercial interest, particularly in the long civil rights struggle of the 1960s. It even existed to some extent in television, as Murrow's partner, Fred W. Friendly, demonstrated when he quit as president of CBS News over the network's failure to televise in full an important Senate hearing on the Vietnam War.

WHAT IS NEWS?

Yet, the objection persists, particularly among government officials at all levels, that the news media too often emphasize negative rather than positive elements of the news. As in the case of adversary-minded journalists, it would be easy to dismiss the complaints of officialdom by assigning them to crass self-interest. But if it is conceded that journalists occasionally are motivated by idealism and other higher virtues, these qualities can scarcely be denied to the elected and appointed officials in government. On both sides, there is a continuing agreement that a certain amount of tension between press and government is

both necessary and desirable in an open society and nobody of   23
importance advocates a great thaw.

In stating the case of officialdom in general, Secretary of Labor Willard Wirtz once argued during the Johnson administration's period of conflict with the press that isolated incidents were blown up out of context to discredit worthy organizations, such as the Peace Corps and Job Corps. He contended that the emphasis on draft card burners during the Vietnam War, as well as narcotic addicts, juvenile delinquents, and lovers of four-letter words tended to discredit a hard-working younger generation. He protested the practice of what he called "leading a story with some little sick fact that infects everything that follows." [13]

This goes to the heart of the problem of what news is. If every editor decided to offer only news that he could certify as true, unslanted, and properly balanced, he could scarcely claim perfection for his daily news report. For one thing, he would have to consider seriously J. Montgomery Curtis's famous unpublished lead: "While 1,286 students of Metropolitan High School pursued their studies quietly this morning, another student murdered the principal in his office." For another, he would have to indulge in the sickening practice, found today in television as well as in the press, of finding a favorable quote to balance an unfavorable quote in every news account.

This being an imperfect world, its imperfections must be reported and properly emphasized. Otherwise, the free press fails in one of its major functions—the presentation of the world as it is and not always (except maybe Sundays) as we would wish it to be. Any jury of twelve good men and true must consider the lies and half-truths and self-deceptions and self-serving claims and counterclaims that are a part of any legal case if they are to render a judicious verdict. In life itself, the same privilege cannot be denied to a larger public if it is to govern itself in accordance with democratic theory. Thus, the ingredients of conflict belong in the news just as much as balance, and the exposition of all sides of an issue is as necessary as an interpretation of its meaning.

If it is argued that such diversity and volume in the reporting of news in today's complicated world only confuses the public and makes the news so complicated that it cannot be absorbed, the answer is not to present pure, certified news in bite-sized chunks that can be quickly digested and will not make

24   the head ache, either. If, by any stretch of the imagination, that
was possible. While humanity has not abandoned sin, and some
have proclaimed the death of God, this has not caused any
perceptible decline in the volume, complexity, and sometimes
the dullness of sermons. And people still seem to be going to
church. Nor has the stubborn resistance of a large part of the
very young in the routine of the classroom led teachers to abandon hope in the mysterious processes of education, for all its
modern complications.

The news media are not solely to blame for the areas
of ignorance among the populace. Every institution in American
life that has an educational function shares the responsibility. It
simply will not do to contend that less news, larger type, colored
pictures, simple films suitable for the nursery, and a jolly-
good-fun press will suddenly make everybody want to know all
about NATO and the movement of the rediscount rate. Such
things are of interest primarily to specialized publics and students. The public at large has all it can do to inform itself on
matters of immediate importance and is highly selective in what
it will absorb.

THE ENGINE OF THE NEWS

If the problem of public communication is to be understood in all
its complexity, there must be some initial assessment of the
efficiency of the vast engine that gathers and transmits the news.
The fundamental machinery—the great twin turbine—consists
of the two American global wire services, the Associated Press
and United Press International, which gather, transmit, and
distribute a remarkably accurate file of news inside and outside
the United States. They are the main suppliers of events to the
bulk of the press and the electronic media. The AP, as a news
cooperative, and the UPI, a business engaged in the sale of news,
work on annual budgets of $55 and $47 million respectively and
blanket the nation with news, pictures, features, columns, and
special articles. If the form and presentation of the news are a
prime influence on the public, then the wire services have an enormous daily impact on opinion. It is the nation's good fortune that
they are close rivals, fiercely independent and controlled only by
the desires of their members or clients, who form a broad spectrum of political beliefs that automatically bars a fair degree of
special pleading.

Radio is generally first to break the wire service

bulletins to the public, although television is sometimes just as   25
fast. While the networks have their own correspondents in key
spots such as Washington, New York, and abroad, and can count
on the news staffs that are slowly being built up by member and
affiliated stations, they cannot dispense with the wire services
any more than the press can. Often, on big news, a radio or
television correspondent can be first; generally, however, the
networks must depend initially on the broader wire service coverage.

Since the great days of radio just before World War
II, when its brilliant commentators did so much to inform and
even influence the nation, its impact on the public has become
secondary to television and the press except in isolated instances. But it is still the fastest of all the media, even if its
hourly reporting is generally fragmentary and its all-day news
grind (on a growing number of stations) is wearing.

As for television, the primary problem is illustration. It almost seems sometimes that if there is no newsfilm,
there is no news to be displayed on the box in the corner of the
living room. The format—like that of radio—is still based on the
brief wire service bulletin with a few lines to each item and a
quick cut to some newsfilm or the inevitable string of commercials. Yet, despite the wealth of news that is displayed in a good
newspaper, the average 30-minute telecast has trouble covering
more than the equivalent of the news on Page 1 and there are
many complaints within the electronic media that the time is too
long. The frequent showing of long stretches of feature film on
the prime telecasts would seem to indicate that the television
format, as it is presently laid out, does not lend itself to the
reporting of even 30 minutes of concentrated news. The point is
important because it means that, no matter how many people
hear the news first on the electronic media, they have to turn to a
good newspaper for a complete report and that is what generally
happens.

It would be a mistake to consider the American
press as a great monolithic institution. Actually, many different
considerations shape it. The country is far too big and too diverse
to be able to support the kind of national newspapers that exist
in the United Kingdom and Japan.* *The New York Times,* which

* *The Economist*'s 1966 survey showed national newspapers in London were having trouble, too, with only three out of eight making a profit. In Japan, it is generally believed that the "Big Three" in Tokyo are kept going by their diversified
activities.

26   tried and failed to make a go of its West Coast edition and had to merge its Paris edition,[14] still comes closest of all newspapers of general circulation to the concept of a national press. Among the specialized newspapers, the *Wall Street Journal* has an enormous following in the numerous centers in which it is published. By contrast, the *Christian Science Monitor*, with its respected coverage in depth of national and international news, has to depend on a subsidy from its church to make both ends meet. It is one of the inflexible facts of geography and the time zones that the newspapers of Washington, New York, Philadelphia, and Baltimore are more or less closely read in the nation's capital, while those no less important in Chicago, Detroit, St. Louis, and Los Angeles generally have a smaller impact. And this despite the prestige of the *Los Angeles Times* on the Pacific Coast as a result of its national and foreign correspondence, and the influence of the *St. Louis Post-Dispatch* on Midwest opinion.

      Intermingled with the national leaders are the regional and state newspapers of the stature of the *Minneapolis Star* and *Tribune*, the *Des Moines Register* and *Tribune*, the *Louisville Times* and *Courier-Journal*, the *Atlanta Constitution* and *Journal*, the *Providence Journal* and *Bulletin*, the *Miami Herald*, and the newspapers of Boston, Kansas City, San Francisco, and other metropolitan centers. While most of them have their own Washington bureaus and a few maintain foreign correspondents to a limited extent, this is primarily a regional press and faithfully represents its area. In general, such newspapers subscribe to the syndicated news of *The New York Times*, *Washington Post*, *Los Angeles Times*, and other news organizations. More than 60 buy the great British news agency, Reuters, and some of the British newspaper syndicate services as well.

      But far larger than either the national and regional press in number, total circulation, and general affluence are the basically suburban and local newspapers. They range in size from *Newsday*, of Garden City, N. Y., which has grown with suburban Long Island, to such representative publications as the *Hutchinson* (Kansas) *News*, the *Santa Barbara* (Calif.) *News-Press* and the *Allentown* (Pa.) *Call-Chronicle*. Here is the heart of the American news complex, consisting of hundreds of newspapers that very often are the main dependence of their communities for news and public service. To the unthinking, these may appear to be mere provincial sheets; however, it deserves to be said that the State of Kansas achieved legislative reapportionment because of a stubborn, four-year campaign by the *Hutchinson News* and the ominous nature of the John Birch Society was first exposed by the *Santa Barbara News-Press*. Even the smallest of newspapers can exercise a certain amount of power, if it has the will and the opportunity.

THE COMPETITIVE URGE

Whenever a weakness appears in the local press, it is mercilessly exploited by the powerful combination of local radio and television stations and the news and picture weeklies. On a national level, this kind of warfare is more evident and its casualties are more spectacular. But at the ground roots, the continual fight for public attention and, with it, the advertising dollar is no less earnest and even more bitter.* One has only to visit a community of modest size, where the electronic media and periodical press are battling a single small newspaper, to understand the reality of the conflict and the stakes of victory. It is understandable, in these circumstances, that group newspapering has expanded rapidly and that a number of corporations have developed to cover both newspaper and electronic outlets.

Despite its many flaws and the unevenness of its coverage, this system of public communication is without an equal in the world for efficiency, speed, factual accuracy, and depth of penetration on major events. When there is public involvement, as in a Presidential election or a space shot, there is an almost compelling public eagerness and open-mindedness to understand the nature and character of events. But it is not a quality easy to achieve with so much pressure from so many media to attract public attention even momentarily. The public service character of the news media therefore deserves more emphasis than it habitually receives and the combative nature of the reporter, far from being deplored, is to be encouraged even at the risk of disturbing the operations of government. As the framers of the Constitution decided, it is a risk that must be taken in a nation that is devoted to the democratic process.

* For 1967, while total newspaper circulation reached a record 61,560,952, the total number of dailies declined from 1,754 to 1,749, and over-all circulation losses were evident in 13 states.

INTERLOCKING

3

MEDIA

The attitudes of journalists toward each other must be regarded with a certain amount of poetic license. If the galloping white knights of television such as Marshall McLuhan are to be believed, then newspapers will one day wither away at the touch of a detergent-tipped lance and a clean little magic news box will replace them. Their fellow-romantics, the old newspapermen of the Hildy Johnson school, are just as stubborn in their conviction that radio and television need not be taken seriously as dispensers of the news.

This kind of posturing is essentially harmless because two of the parties that have a considerable stake in the journalistic process, the public and the proprietors of the media, do not take much stock in it. Nor do the highly realistic news sources inside and outside government.

When there is a strike, a power failure or a storm that interferes with local newspaper publication, the public turns to the electronic media, the out-of-town papers and the news magazines without much ado. Interruptions of television and radio service, similarly, cause the public to make whatever adjustments are necessary to keep itself minimally informed. And when all else fails, there is a powerful body of evidence to indicate that word-of-mouth news transmission—the fabled "bamboo telegraph" of the Chinese mainland—is still a factor in passing news along in the highly industrialized United States.

As for the proprietors, the wealthiest and most powerful of them are making increasing efforts to diversify their interests in the operation of all types of media inside and outside journalism. Few of the great ones, whatever their motives, are standing pat on just one newspaper, or one magazine, or one electronic outlet. The risks in journalism are spread across the board as rapidly as possible by those who can best afford to do so. In the print and electronic media, chain operations are on the rise; indeed, the current fashion to diversify has led some of the most eminent into association with everything from book publishers to baseball clubs.

Certainly, the managers and the journalists who are most in demand operate on the assumption that it is often necessary, even imperative, to work in two or more parts of the media at the same time. It is not unusual, for example, to find James Reston expounding his views on television as well as in print or to read what Eric Sevareid has to say in a column as well as to listen to him. And those who seek influence over the news—whether they are in government or private industry, the professions or labor, or the civil rights movement—for years have acted on the assumption that the news media are integrated parts of a single powerful communications system.

Under these circumstances, it is asking a great deal of the innocent bystander to absorb without question the poetic views of the rival Hildy Johnson–Marshall McLuhan schools. One could just as easily enlist for the duration with Omar Khayyam, and possibly with somewhat more relevance, for it

30   does not take a great deal of originality to perceive that we have interlocking news media today that are often interdependent in spreading news and opinion to the nation and beyond its borders.

THE PROGRESS OF TEAMWORK

One of the most significant results of this new dispensation has been the News Election Service, in which the Associated Press and United Press International share responsibilities with the three networks in bringing national election results to the country. Up to 1964, there was ruinous competition between them which did not always serve the nation well. In that year, the newspaper-controlled news agencies (each of which service more electronic outlets than newspapers) agreed to share the work of covering the country with the networks.

Necessarily, all those involved—and the clientele as well—had to be on their guard against that endemic ailment of the journalist, overenthusiasm. However, in both 1964 and 1966, some races were inaccurately reported by components of the system and the early projections of results did not always work out as predicted. Looking toward the 1968 Presidential elections, there was a great deal of concern over the effect of the announcement of completed voting in the Eastern time zone on the polls in the Pacific zone states that close three hours later. This was magnified by the pell-mell rush of some of the television experts (and some in the press, as well) to announce an instant winner based on projections of the early vote sampling. It was for this reason that the National Governors' Conference approved a proposal for a uniform, 24-hour National Election Day which would in effect prevent the news media from announcing results until all polls closed.[15]

It is a testimonial to the good sense of the media managers that these and other shortcomings have not interfered with continued teamwork among the media—a kind of unadmitted public partnership. The network vote sampling and projection systems have been subscribed to by a number of newspapers. Some of the most important newspapermen have graced television with both their knowledge and prestige. In addition to printing the weekly television program listings, a well-nigh indispensable feature today, most newspapers have discovered that a surprisingly high quotient of their news (particularly on Monday mornings) originates with television interviews or other television enterprise. It goes almost without saying that much of the backgrounding and interpretation that first appears in the better newspapers also turns up on television eventually in one form or another. Nor are television's news analysts ungenerous in their appreciation of the work of their newspaper and news magazine colleagues.

Allowing for the normal rivalry in getting at the breaking news and the sometimes murderous competition for the advertisers' dollar, the outlook in the United States is for further teamwork among the news media on set events where it is difficult for anybody to have an advantage and costs may therefore be reasonably shared. There are those who question the morality of such proceedings; in fact, they also object strenuously to a traditionally Democratic newspaper sharing mechanical and building costs with a strong Republican rival. Yet, there is no indication that such minimal cost-sharing has softened the fierce rivalry between, for example, the *St. Louis Post-Dispatch* and the *St. Louis Globe-Democrat*. Nor, for that matter, have the joint ventures of the AP and UPI in stylebooks and other measures to standardize operations led to any letdown in their lively competition. In an age in which the United States and the Soviet Union can back rival sides in the Middle East and Southeast Asia and yet attain limited agreements on other important matters, it is to be expected that the far less potent privately operated news media will try to accommodate each other when it is in their interest to do so.

Thus, cost-conscious managers are always seeking means of sharing the work—and the expense—on such spectacles as space shots, conventions, major news conferences, and other events that bring out hordes of newsmen and technicians. The little fellows among the print and electronic media invariably tend to be squeezed out when the giants agree, whether it is on news coverage or absorbing weaker competitors. Hence, the cry of "Monopoly!" is heard with increasing frequency in the land, and the Department of Justice is growing more critical of news combines.

Yet, the trend is clear. The pattern of interlocking media is spreading. Whether it will last or not depends almost entirely on whether the weaker newspapers are able to change quickly enough with the times during an era of national prosperity. For assuredly, newspaper economies cannot depend in the long run on the cooperation of the rival media; the adjustment to

32   automation will have to come with far greater speed, even for the successful newspapers, if it is to have the desired effect. For once the steam goes out òf the boom, or economic conditions become less favorable for other reasons, it will be too late even for diversification and cooperative intra-media cost-cutting to save chronically ailing newspaper properties. To this limited extent, McLuhan may well be right with his doleful outlook for printed journalism. But it is sheer nonsense to contend, even for purposes of a "probe" that is intended to arouse discussion, that newspapers as a whole are either dying or already dead. This kind of thinking distracts attention from the very serious situation in which the press finds itself today in trying to modernize under the pressure of competition from what is, potentially, the most powerful of all news media, television.

THE PROBLEM OF QUALITY

It is far more important from the standpoint of the public interest to examine the effect of interlocking communications on the quality of the news than on the ultimate fate of what may be, at worst, a minority of daily newspapers. Historically, public concern has focused primarily on the steady reduction of newspaper competition until today only 4 percent of communities with newspapers can count on competition among them by reason of separate ownership.[16] Yet, it is equally significant to note that there is a radio monopoly in 44 percent of the cities that have local media of any kind and that radio stations in the United States outnumber daily newspapers by more than 3 to 1 and television stations by more than 7 to 1.[17]

It may be heartening to some that there is competition in 1,418 of 2,947 cities with news media and that, in 88 percent of the cities in which newspapers operate without competition from another newspaper, there is opposition from the broadcast media.[18] One could also observe, with justification, that both neighboring newspapers and broadcast media and the weekly news magazines provide a diversified diet of news and opinion. Yet, it is not precisely the same thing because the local broadcast media seldom exceed the local newspapers in the quality of their news presentation and often fall below them. Nor is this, by any means, a testimonial to the excellence of local newspapers in general.

The problem is basic in independent journalism in the United States. Because the American public rarely has a clear-cut opportunity to make known its feelings about the quality of the news it receives, and therefore is thought to be apathetic, it becomes the responsibility of the media managers and editors to make certain that all points of view are expressed in a community. And that, of course, has particular relevance to minority points of view. Where the proprietary interest is self-serving, a monolithic point of view is all that the public can expect. But where there is some consciousness of the public responsibility of the news media, its components may—and often do—serve as important links between the contending elements in an open society.

Only a particularly obtuse proprietor or media manager is likely to proceed for very long on the assumption that he is dealing with a complaisant public. It has been shown on numerous occasions that the public's response to events can sometimes be a major factor in the level of public comprehension of the news. During the big power blackout that paralyzed the northeastern United States on November 9, 1965, for example, New Yorkers and others generally were able to keep themselves informed by radio even though competing media were out of action.[19] In fact, voluntary reporting by the public proved to be an important element in the assessment of the situation as broadcast by radio. Once the emergency was over, of course, people went on about their business.

In equally dramatic tests of the news diffusion process by the public itself, researchers checked the first source of knowledge of respondents in a representative city in the Middle West of the removal of Nikita S. Khrushchev from power in the Soviet Union on October 15, 1964 and the arrest of Walter Jenkins, a Presidential assistant, on a morals charge on October 14, 1965. These were the results: [20]

FIRST SOURCE OF KNOWLEDGE

	RADIO	TV	PRESS	WORD OF MOUTH
Khrushchev	34	35	12	19
Jenkins	25	22	50	3

While there were variations in tests conducted elsewhere, and while the time of day had something to do with the diffusion process (the Jenkins story broke very late), it is evident that the public takes its news from the first available news medium and helps pass it along. Thus, if it had not been for the

34   newspapers, a very large segment of the public would not have been aware of the Jenkins case at the height of a Presidential campaign until some time had elapsed. Similarly, if it had not been for the electronic media, the fall of Khrushchev would not have become so widely known in such a short time. And if it had not been for radio, the power blackouts of 1965–66–67 in the United States could have created much more uncertainty and even fear in the areas directly affected.

Too much, therefore, is being made out of the supposed public apathy toward the American news media. Actually, the public response is often quite dramatic when its vital interests are affected on a very large scale. It is, perhaps, a sorry commentary on the nature of big city life that this kind of mass concern does not carry over very often into individual cases. There is no way to forgive the refusal of 38 witnesses to call for help when Catherine Genovese was being stabbed to death on the night of March 13, 1964 outside her home in Kew Gardens, N. Y.[21]

Yet, the highly publicized refusal of people to become involved in police cases, from time to time, can scarcely negate the far larger body of evidence of public concern with the news in which its interests are more immediately engaged. Any reporter who has ever covered a natural disaster, a train or airplane wreck, a riot, or other civic disturbance can testify to the depth and even violence of public feeling sometimes over the course of events. In such instances, people are far from neutral. More often than not, they hold their news media accountable for their performance long after the event. No one who saw Lee Harvey Oswald murdered on television will ever forget the wave of public revulsion that resulted. And no one who remembers the Sheppard case can brush aside the stiff rebuke the Supreme Court administered to the press in reversing a finding of guilt.

WHO'S FIRST—AND WHY

If it is thus so difficult to measure public apathy in judging such performances of the news media, it follows that the often wearisome argument over whether the public takes its news primarily from the newspapers, radio, or television is very largely irrelevant. An enormous amount of time, effort, and money has been devoted to proving the obvious: that newspapers have not been the primary medium for informing people of the big news as it is breaking for more than 40 years, that radio and television can present bulletin-type news much quicker than the press, that newspapers can give much better coverage in depth except for occasional well-prepared documentaries, that the electronic media have won the confidence of a considerable segment of the public as dispensers of news, and that newspapers cannot be beaten in presenting full texts of public documents, commentaries, and tabular material such as stock market reports, box scores, racing charts, want ads, amusements, and similar detail. In one sense, the better newspapers have actually benefited from the growth of radio and television reporting, for the electronic bulletins and lengthier presentations have made more people turn to the newspapers for details.

A major instance of this dual role was the reporting of the Hollybush "Summit" on June 25, 1967, with President Johnson racing by helicopter and jet to Washington from the site at Glassboro, N. J., to appear on television and radio a scant 20 minutes before the Soviet premier, Alexei Kosygin, held a televised news conference at the United Nations. After the impact of this dramatic firsthand report, a vivid instance of television's usefulness as a news medium, it remained for the newspapers to present the texts, substance, background, and interpretation of the event. And there still was enough left for the news magazines and the Sunday newspapers to feature in their usual roundups.

Yet, such is the nature of journalism today that both the electronic and print media continue to fire away at each other with all manner of devices in the daily struggle for a greater share of the advertisers' dollar. One of the most popular weapons is the sampling of public opinion, carried out by respected analysts whose findings are solemnly presented with the air of a Moses descending from Mount Sinai, Decalogue in hand.

As an instance of such rivalry, the Television Information Office in 1965 put out a brochure by Elmo Roper proclaiming that 58 percent of those polled in a national survey had said they received most of their news from television. What outraged the press even more was the response to another Roper question, in which 41 percent of his respondents said they found television news to be more believable, as contrasted with 23 percent for newspapers, 10 percent for magazines, and 8 percent for radio. Just why 41 percent should believe television and only 8 percent radio never was made very clear, particularly since both frequently use the same news agency bulletins as the basis for their

36   main news announcements.[22] Walter Cronkite commented: "If that's the case, 58 percent of our public is inadequately informed." [23]

Soon, a Gallup Poll was issued covering 1957–1965, showing that 71 percent of its respondents had read a newspaper yesterday, as compared with 58 percent who had listened to news on radio and 55 percent who had viewed television.[24] Gallup also found that adult readership of papers had risen from 78 to 81 percent, that ownership of radios had increased from 94 to 96 percent of all homes, and that ownership of television sets had gone from 83 to 95 percent of all homes.[25]

What Gallup did in stressing the gains newspapers had made among adult readers was followed up by a Louis Harris report in 1967, contending that television viewing was declining among college-educated people earning more than $10,000 a year. The Harris report added that, of those polled, 26 percent said they were viewing more; 21 percent, the same amount, and 53 percent, less than before.

To this, the A. C. Nielsen Company, pillars of the television rating system, responded with figures that were intended to refute the contention that better-educated people are souring on television. For lower-income families, Nielsen contended, the hours of weekly television usage remained at 38.4 as in previous years; for middle-income families, he reported a 24-minute gain to 44.9, but he conceded that there had been a dropping off by upper-income families of 30 minutes a week to 40.2.[26] It just depended on whom you were willing to believe.

Regardless of the virtues or weaknesses of these and other surveys, they have scarcely uncovered any great new truths about the news media and the public that cannot be easily observed in most homes. Nor has Madison Avenue been rocked by the Harris warning that television is less effective with busy people of better education than with younger people of little education. The surveys thus have changed nothing and improved nothing.

THE DIVERSIFIED MEDIA

Actually, the burden for change and improvement rests where it always has—on the proprietors themselves. And their main thrust, particularly among the most successful, continues to be a search for greater diversification of investment. There appear to be two principal reasons for the modern phase of this development—first, the eminently practical one of finding new ways to invest their profits, and second, an entirely praiseworthy effort to improve their services in order to hold current audiences and attract new ones.

This works out in different ways, depending on the companies involved and their philosophy of operation. To give three current examples of resounding successes:

1. The Times-Mirror Company of Los Angeles. Norman Chandler, head of the family that owns the company and the *Los Angeles Times,* characterized its expansion as a "spreading out into the knowledge industry." * It is all of that. With the growth of the *Times* into a national and international newspaper of consequence under the leadership of Norman's son, Otis, the Times-Mirror Company has purchased the New American Library, the World Publishing Company, the map products firm of Jeppeson & Company, the art book publishers, Harry N. Abrams Inc., and made general investments.[27]

2. The Columbia Broadcasting System. Under the leadership of William S. Paley, the television and radio network also has developed and acquired a diversity of interests. These include the book publishing firm of Holt, Rinehart and Winston; Columbia Records, Fender Musical Instruments, the New York Yankees, a toy company, and general investments.[28]

3. The National Broadcasting Company. Guided for much of its history by General David Sarnoff, NBC still is owned by the Radio Corporation of America and in turn owns the book publishing firm of Random House, RCA-Victor Records, the Hertz car rental firm, a drug company, and has a variety of general investments.[29]

There is also a recognizable trend toward the ownership of electronic interests by successful newspapers and magazines, although the reverse is not very widespread. In fact, while Newton N. Minow was the chairman of the Federal Communications Commission, he once argued that there is a relationship between successful newspapers and electronic media owned by the same firm. He cited, for example, an informal study that indicated almost every daily newspaper that died between 1945 and 1947 and 1958 and 1960 did not have a radio or television allied interest. Therefore, he contended that newspapers in

---

* The federal government won an antitrust action in 1967 to force the *Los Angeles Times* to divest itself of the *San Bernardino Sun* newspapers purchased by the Chandler interests.

38   major cities that lack television licenses are "subject to a significant competitive disadvantage." *

Minow's pattern of the interlocking nature of the media, which follows, still has relevance for American journalism today:

In the top 25 market areas of the land, there are 97 television stations. Of these, 15 are owned by one of the three major networks, while 33 are owned by newspapers. Of the 69 newspapers in these markets, 28 own television stations, partly because newspapers jumped into the television business almost as soon as it began to develop.[30] The rivalry between the media, in these instances, is therefore more apparent than real.

There are, of course, notable exceptions to Minow's Law. The fabulously successful *Wall Street Journal* is owned by Dow Jones, also the proprietors of a financial service and the weekly *National Observer* but not previously identified with broadcast journalism. *Newsday* of Garden City, N. Y., a giant of suburban journalism, is controlled by Captain Harry F. Guggenheim as chief stockholder of a publication that also has an interest in the *Chicago Tribune* and *New York Daily News* but owns no television station. Moreover, no one except perhaps an electronic tub thumper would argue that *The New York Times* has been kept afloat by its radio station, WQXR, its interests in Canadian newsprint mills, and various educational devices.

For every exception, however, there are numerous instances of newspapers that are being squeezed by a combination of television, news magazines, and new newspapers springing up in the suburbs. There is little doubt that there is validity to Minow's argument that a dependable electronic anchor to windward is likely to steady a shaky newspaper property. Most sensible newspapermen long since have come to recognize it. Mason Walsh of the *Phoenix* (Ariz.) *Gazette,* for example, addressed his fellow-editors as follows in the mid-1960s:

"Television has been responsible for widened readership for newspapers. It has been a boon to newspaper reader interest in sports and other fields. The necessary bulletinizing of the news by the electronic media serves to stimulate the individual's appetite for news and information, for more detail and

---

* Unfortunately, Minow's argument did not hold good for the *New York Herald Tribune,* which was merged in 1966 and vanished altogether in 1967 when the *New York World Journal Tribune* folded. The *Herald Tribune* had been owned by Whitney Communications, which had electronic interests.

more depth. And readers satisfy that appetite by reading their newspapers. I believe the newspaper and the electronic media each has a widening role in the communications field. Instead of assuming that we are in a free-for-all, struggling for supremacy or survival, we should each utilize our strengths and try to correct our weaknesses." [31]

All this sounds quite sensible and, without doubt, is perfectly defensible on the ground that an organization that offers news to the public in an open society must be financially invulnerable if it is to maintain its independence. Yet, it is worth asking whether the fundamental character of the news is going to be affected by the process of diversification. For, with the exception of the period when political parties ruled the press in the earlier days of the republic, there has never been a time in American history when so many news organizations have accepted obligations to interests that have little or nothing to do with the gathering and dissemination of the news. In some foreign countries, these diverse associations sometimes have proved awkward—even scandalous—to news organizations of high character. The trend in the United States therefore deserves the closest scrutiny.

THE ROLE OF THE FCC

It was for this reason, among others, that the Department of Justice asked the Federal Communications Commission to reopen its inquiry into the merger between the American Broadcasting Companies and the International Telephone and Telegraph Company. For journalists, one of the high points of the investigation was the testimony by Stephen Aug, a reporter for the Associated Press, that while he was writing his story of the FCC decision ordering a temporary stay of the merger, ABC complained to his New York office that his first paragraph was "erroneous." The AP stood on Aug's story. In another instance, Eileen Shanahan of *The New York Times* testified that she had been "badgered" by Edward J. Gerrity, senior ITT vice president, who came to her office and talked in a tone which was "accusatory and certainly nasty."

Although the merger was upheld by a 4–3 majority of the FCC, the majority report did find that in one instance Gerrity's activity with regard to Miss Shanahan's coverage was "improper." This was in connection with the reporter's testimony that Gerrity had asked her if she was aware "that Commissioner

40   Johnson was working with some people in Congress on legisla-
        tion that would forbid any newspaper from owning broadcast
        property." The FCC majority noted that the statement about
        Commissioner Nicholas Johnson, a member of the minority
        group opposed to the merger, was erroneous. It also stressed
        Miss Shanahan's belief that the intent was to show "that since
        the *Times* owns radio stations, it would want to consider its
        economic interests in deciding what to publish in its news medi-
        um." [32] Nothing, of course, would have been further from the
        beliefs of the *Times*'s editors.
                Although the FCC majority took a benevolent view
        otherwise of the activity of Gerrity and his associates in their
        contacts with reporters covering the case, the three-member mi-
        nority group expressed themselves as follows in their dissenting
        opinion: "This conduct, in which at least three ITT officials,
        including a Senior vice president, were involved, demonstrates
        an abrasive self-righteousness in dealing with the press, a shock-
        ing insensitivity to its independence and integrity, a willingness
        to spread false stories in furtherance of self-interest, contempt for
        government officials as well as the press, and an assumption that
        even as prestigious a news medium as *The New York Times*
        would, as a matter of course, want to present the news so as to
        best serve its own economic interests (as well as the economic
        interests of other large business corporations)."
                Thus, in upholding the merger despite the certainty
        that the Department of Justice would continue the fight, the FCC
        was narrowly split between the four members who held there
        was no evidence that ITT would attempt to "influence the jour-
        nalistic functions of ABC," and their three dissenting associates
        who warned: "There is a very significant danger that ITT's other
        interests will be allowed to intrude on the journalistic function-
        ing of ABC and subvert the proper use of this electronic outlet
        for independent information, news opinion and public affairs
        programming." No one can say what the eventual result would
        have been, for in 1968—while the Justice Department still
        awaited a U. S. Appeals Court's verdict—ITT called off its agree-
        ment to merge and ABC had to look elsewhere for help.[33]
                This is not to suggest that all efforts to diversify
        among the news media are bad, or that diversified companies are
        automatically open to suspicion. On the contrary, as any first-rate
        newspaper organization demonstrates, a diversified company can
        do a perfectly good job of news presentation if it sharply separates

the editorial function from business and advertising. As the FCC   41
hearing into the ABC–ITT merger indicates, something more
than the public interest is at stake here. The issue is continued
public acceptance of the news media at their face value.

NEW TIMES FOR

4

NEWSPAPERS

There is nothing in the annals of the world press, controlled or independent, that is comparable to the development of modern American newspapers, daily and particularly on Sunday. In sheer size, with only a few notable exceptions among the elite, they dwarf their foreign contemporaries and swamp their readers under an avalanche of printed matter. Because they generally use more newsprint and pay higher salaries to their employees than the press in any other land, they are in large part the most costly to produce and the most expensive for both advertisers and subscribers.

It may be argued, and it has been most persuasively, 43
that the standard American newspaper, far from being a luxury,
is in reality a great bargain because of its massive content. The
point has some merit if it is applied to the best newspapers, but
this is not at issue here. The fact is that many of the most serious
problems of American newspapers today stem directly from their
size and the expense of production and distribution. And this is
bound to become increasingly true in the future unless there is a
remarkable change in the attitudes of the media managers.

GIANTISM AND THE PRESS

Far from fading or dying on the nation's doorstep, as some have
put it in dramatic overstatement, the typical American newspaper is actually in process of expansion beyond its current 53-
page average size. In the past decade, the press in the United
States has spent more than $1 billion in plant expansion and
modernization, $140 million in 1966 alone.[34] The householder
who picks up five or six pounds of neatly folded printed paper
outside his door of a Sunday morning is therefore unlikely to
mistake it for a ghost in the foreseeable future. It may very well
cross his mind, as he begins discarding the sections he does not
want to read, that there is a point of diminishing returns beyond
which mere size becomes an almost intolerable handicap to consumer, advertiser, and producer alike. But there are precious few
media managers who have had the courage to cry, "Hold!
Enough!"

Giantism, as an operating philosophy, has paid
enormous dividends to American automobile manufacturers but
even they have produced typically American versions of compact
cars under the pressure of foreign competition. With the exception of papers like the *Wall Street Journal*, however, there is no
movement of consequence for the production of newspapers of
more sensible size; whatever the original purpose of the tabloids,
the successful ones are now as thick as telephone books and
almost as difficult to read. In general, newspapers of smaller size
would require higher advertising rates and there are no Pulitzer
Prizes for media managers who buck Madison Avenue.

It is undeniably true that giantism in its present
form, the end product of mass advertising in an affluent society,
has an almost compulsive fascination for the American press.
The benefits of the system are obvious to those it favors—
growth, wealth, influence, and prestige. But the weaknesses are

44   also clearly apparent, for the whole topheavy structure rests on a foundation of somewhat uncertain strength—good times, good management, editorial pragmatism, and public confidence.

Through a combination of circumstances, the newspapers in the small and medium-sized cities of the United States—the backbone of the American press—have come to believe that they can only compete with television, big city newspapers, and news magazines through vastly expanded local news coverage. A typical instance of what is involved may be found in Morgantown, W. Va., population 36,000, the seat of West Virginia University with an enrollment of 11,000. During 1965 and 1966, the local paper, the *Dominion-News & Post,* pushed a new Sunday newspaper, the *Dominion-Post,* in opposition to the Sunday *Pittsburgh Press,* which had been selling 5,400 copies in Morgantown Sundays by trucking them 80 miles. There was lesser opposition from the *Fairmont West Virginian,* 20 miles south, which had been selling nearly 2,000 copies in Morgantown Sundays. What the Morgantown paper did was to provide color comics, a family magazine, a TV program guide for an entire week, a business page, farm and garden page, two special pages for news of nearby counties, *The New York Times* syndicated columnists, and an adequate quota of wire service news. After eight months its Sunday circulation was 15,000, compared with its combined morning–evening daily circulation of 20,000.[35]

Necessarily, the format through which many small city dailies have been able to stave off the heaviest metropolitan competition on Sunday has been slimmed down for daily use as well. Consequently, the little fellows have come to believe for the most part that they must provide their public with all the service and entertainment of their giant rivals, plus much more home town news than their nearby contemporaries can give. By doing so, the successful ones have become converted to the philosophy of giantism to an even greater extent, proportionate to their total resources, than the metropolitan dailies they emulate.[36] The process is thus an almost endless spiral of production and cost increases for those who can keep up the battle and persuade their advertisers and subscribers to support them.

This, of course, is the principal reason for the rapid decline in competitive newspaper operations in the United States. The coming of television has merely speeded up the process with its reduction in the press's advertising revenue. At the end of 1967, in the nation's 50 largest cities, there were only

23 single-ownership newspapers. Even among the remaining
newspapers that maintained a semblance of competition, there
were 21 instances of combined operations. Under the terms of
the so-called "Failing Newspaper Act," as it was introduced in the
Senate, publishers sought to exclude these arrangements from
the antitrust laws.

GROWTH OF THE CHAINS

Should these and other remedies fail, the singly-owned, unaffil-
iated independent newspaper is likely to become something of a
curiosity in the United States. For if weak newspapers are not
diversified, or fitted into a combined operation with a competitor,
they are likely to die or be absorbed by one of the rapidly expand-
ing chains. With the exception of those older groups that have
chronic management and operational problems, most of the existing chains—and even some of the independently owned newspapers—are looking for properties to acquire. Already, seven
large chains control 24 percent of all daily newspapers sold in
the land.* In all, more than 700 dailies are owned by some 160
group operations that may be described as chains; of these, 30
chains with a total of 300 newspapers control some 40 percent of
all daily newspapers sold in the country.[37]
          If an individual newspaper dedicated to expansion
in a single community constitutes giantism on a vertical scale,
then certainly the newspaper chains demonstrate the practice of
giantism on a horizontal scale. There is no real difference in
philosophy between the chains and the individual operations
that seek growth so anxiously; where the chains have the advantage is in the undoubted economies they are able to achieve
through group purchasing and group operations. In news space
and over-all size, the better operated chain newspapers compare
favorably enough with newspapers of single ownership in the
same class. But where an individual proprietor may be indulgent
now and then with his managers, the chain cannot be. Woe
betide the chain manager who does not give the closest scrutiny

* The largest chains, in point of readership, are the *Chicago Tribune* group,
Gannett, Hearst, Knight, Newhouse, Ridder, and Scripps-Howard. Numerically,
with the acquisition of the 12 dailies and four weeklies of the Brush-Moore chain
for $75 million, Canadian-born Baron Thomson of Fleet owns more American
newspapers than anybody else. His world-wide total has reached 160 papers,
52 in the U. S., but all the American papers are in cities of less than 125,000
population and their total circulation is under 2 million.

46   to income and outgo and who does not know to a penny his page production and distribution costs.

Because of the tight economic rein on which they are held, the chain managers sometimes go to extraordinary lengths to demonstrate that this has nothing whatever to do with the editorial independence of their newspapers. It is a difficult equation for some to work out, particularly an extreme right wing group like the Hoiles Newspapers with a record of opposition to the income tax and public education. Among the evidence frequently submitted by some of the more obtuse managers is the practice of permitting some chain members to endorse candidates for public office "in the best interests of their communities." Freely translated, this sometimes means that candidates need not always be endorsed on the basis of principle, but in line with the political orientation of the community. Such things do not add to the public respect for chain operations; nor, for that matter, do they increase the reputation of newspapers as a whole.

Where efficient chain managers have come out of the newsroom, their newspapers more often take positions that are not necessarily in line with the economic interests of the home office. But it is always a struggle. Most editors of conviction engage in running arguments with proprietors of individual newspapers over problems and policies; in chains, the burden on responsible editors is even greater. Under the limiting circumstances of group operations, it is remarkable that so many good ones are able to persevere and carry their managers along with them in support of editorial policies that are initially unpopular.

If there is another saving grace of the better group operations, it is the willingness to experiment with modern production methods. While the bulk of American newspapers are still being produced under processes familiar to Horace Greeley a century ago, the chains are among the principal users of computers for more efficient typesetting operations and offset printing to reduce the soaring costs of production. In 1967, many of the 250-odd newspapers using offset printing were chain-operated, as were most of the 150 computers in service. The uses of cold type, through photographic process, were being tested as never before over the historic method of setting type a line at a time through the casting of molten lead. A respectable number of the 600-odd newspapers that spent $142 million in 1967 for plant improvement were chain-operated.[38]

There is no doubt that the system based on giantism works for the benefit of proprietors and stockholders on small and medium-sized city dailies under current circumstances, whether or not they are chain operated. The average medium-city newspaper in 1965, for example, was shown to have returned a net profit of 23 percent before taxes. Moreover, the paper's total editorial budget including salaries and overhead, totaling $584,000, could have been increased 40 percent and net profit still would have been 17 percent.[39] While it is possible to produce good newspapers on such a basis, most knowledgeable editors have long since come to the conclusion that many managements in a monopoly situation are prone to coast along on their editorial product if they can get away with it. One public-spirited proprietor who went looking for a small-city newspaper property to add to his interests told of one seemingly excellent prospect in a growing community during the latter 1960s. It was making a very large profit with a very small staff but, on closer examination, the prospective buyer learned that it was regarded in the community as little more than a daily shopping throwaway. He called the deal off.[40]

High-mindedness, however, has not been a particular characteristic of growth, and for much of the 1960s the emphasis was on expansion in the newspaper field both individually and collectively despite the very real distress in some of the key metropolitan areas of the nation. Vincent J. Manno, a newspaper broker, had so much business at one time in the decade that he did not mind admitting some of his clients were paying at least 10 percent more than the papers were worth. "But," he said, "it's a sound investment. The publisher just has to wait longer for a return on his capital." He had helped sell, among other properties, the *San Jose* (Calif.) *Mercury-News* to the Ridder group for $4 million and the *Portland Oregonian* to the Newhouse group for $5.6 million.[41]

Another characteristic of the era has been the willingness of media managers, mainly in chains, to start new newspapers in growth areas of the country. The Gannett group, which operates successfully in television as well as in newspapers, broke out of its northeastern stronghold and launched a new newspaper, *Today*, in the heart of the Florida space age complex at Cocoa, in Brevard County. The method is instructive, for Gannett left as little as possible to chance and the whims of readers. The chain bought up the rival *Cocoa Tribune*, the *Titusville*

48   *Star-Advocate* and the weekly *Eau Gallie Courier,* which reduced
the available competition to the *Melbourne Times,* owned by the
John H. Perry group, and the *Orlando Sentinel-Star,* of the
Chicago Tribune group. Having had the way well prepared,
Today began publishing early in 1966 and within two months
had reached its first-year circulation goal, 35,000. A year later, it
was solidly established.

Two big-city print and television group operations,
Marshall Field Enterprises in Chicago and Cowles Communica-
tions in New York, tried the flourishing suburban field with new
publications. Field, branching out from its base properties in
Chicago, the *Sun-Times* and *Daily News,* founded a new suburban newspaper, the *Arlington Day,* in Arlington Heights, Ill.[42]
And Cowles Communications, the publishing empire created by
Gardner (Mike) Cowles following the success of *Look* magazine,
founded its new daily, the *Suffolk Sun,* in fast-growing eastern
Long Island soon after spending $6 million for two Florida news-
papers, the *Gainsville Sun* and the *Lakeland Ledger.* In less
than six months, the *Suffolk Sun* had 50,000 circulation,[43] and
was putting out newspapers of substantial size that compared
respectably with the competing *Newsday,* with 425,000 circulation, and the Newhouse chain's *Long Island Press,* with 320,000.

For sheer acquisitiveness, the greatest success story
of the time of the giants—and the least understood—has been
that of Samuel I. Newhouse, a small and retiring proprietor born
of Russian immigrant parents. During the years when the once
dominant Hearst chain was in process of liquidation, he fought
his way to the top through a process that combined severely
economical operations with an astonishing ability to finance the
acquisition of new properties. With the purchase of the *Cleveland Plain Dealer* for a reported $50 million in 1967, when he was
72 years old, he rounded out a group operation that included 21
daily newspapers, 9 on Sunday, 4 wholly owned television stations and 6 magazines of the Conde Nast Publications. Although
it is the largest of American newspaper chains, comparatively
little is known about its financing, which once caused Newhouse
to comment solemnly, "I know there is a lot of talk about people
who are supposed to be my backers, but I prefer to buy things
with my own money and not go to banks or anyone else." [44]

Newhouse has never had the prestige accorded to
such group rivals as Knight, Gannett, or Scripps-Howard, probably because of his resolute economies. While the conservative

editorial postures of his newspapers have drawn strong criticism   49
from time to time, nobody of consequence has ever quarreled
with his business judgment. It is his stock in trade; because of it,
he has had an impact both on his times and on journalism as an
industry that is significant even if it is little recognized at present.
Whether it was through good luck or good manage-
ment (and probably there was a bit of both in his case), Newhouse based his eventual prosperity on what seemed originally to
be a desperate shoe-string gamble on the growth of the lesser
communities and suburban areas around New York City. His
Long Island Press and *Star-Journal, Staten Island Advocate,
Jersey Journal,* and *Newark Star-Ledger* were shaky, indeed,
during the early 1930s when he fought and won long strikes by
the then infant American Newspaper Guild against his Long
Island and Newark properties. Few gave him much chance then
of becoming one of the overlords of the American press, tagged
as he was with the label of anti-unionism in the most liberal-
minded metropolis in the nation. But with the shifting of population to the suburbs and the growth of shopping centers to accommodate them and advertise for their patronage, the Newhouse
interests in the New York metropolitan area grew in affluence
and size and became the base on which he built his national
expansion. Even today, however, these dailies are not commonly
granted the status of metropolitan newspapers because, with a
parochialism that is peculiar to New York City, they are not published on the island of Manhattan. Queens, Staten Island, Jersey
City, and Newark are beyond the magic circle; in a very real sense,
it has been Newhouse's good fortune that he chose to concentrate
on them rather than invade the inner citadel where so many
newspapers, both good and bad, have died.

THE PROBLEM OF NEW YORK

For if giantism is the prevailing faith in American newspaper
operations, then New York City—and particularly Manhattan—is representative of its best and its worst, its greatest and
its most prestigious publications as well as its most abysmal
failures. It was inevitable that when the great social and technological American revolution gathered headway in the 1960s, its
worst effects would be felt in the nation's communications capital, with shock waves radiating out to some of the other large
cities throughout the land. Those like Newhouse who had prepared to ride out the storm appeared to be safe enough for the

50   time being; however, some of the greatest names in American
journalism went down under the combined impact of insupportable losses, antique management methods, stubborn union
opposition to modernization and changing readership values.

The catastrophe in New York was not something
that burst without warning over the metropolis; it had been
many years in the making. For change is the first law of journalism, but there was not much of it among the newspapers in the
nation's largest city. There had been 15 newspapers in New York
in 1900, a dozen as late as 1930, and by 1950 there were seven.
Of these, the *Times* and the *News* had established a clear superiority over the rest, the former as a class publication and the
latter with the largest daily newspaper circulation in the country.
The advertisers naturally spent most of their money where they
could find the kind of readers to whom they wanted to appeal in
the largest numbers, which made chronic losers out of the remainder of the newspaper opposition in the central city. Thus,
the *Herald Tribune,* a great newspaper with 350,000 circulation,
and the tabloid *Daily Mirror,* with 1 million circulation, plus
all three afternoon papers with a combined circulation of 1.5
million could make no headway against the *Times,* with
700,000, and the 2 million daily readers of the *News.* Worse still,
the drift of the population from the central city to the suburbs
tended to take still more readers away from most of the under-
privileged press.

As a further complication, the peculiarities of the
New York newspaper setup in the labor field acted to the advantage of the strong and the disadvantage of the weak. Ten newspaper unions each insisted on bargaining individually with the
publishers, who initially acted together in one organization. And
as if that were not enough of a problem, the unions themselves
were struggling for primacy, with the printers pitting their century-old union against the American Newspaper Guild's amal-
gam of editorial and commercial employees. With the rising
costs of inflation, the pressure for wage increases and fringe
benefits became so great that the unions began rivaling each
other to see which one could wring the most benefits out of the
employers. It was the end result of the policy of giantism and it
was to produce disastrous results in New York, despite the obvious prosperity of the press in other parts of the nation.

There was a series of newspaper strikes in the

city—10 days in 1953, 19 days in 1958, and a whopping 114-day strike in 1962–63, after which Hearst's *Mirror* gave up without a struggle at a time when its circulation was the second highest in the country. But neither side apparently learned anything. The economic strife continued unabated in the city while the shift of population to the suburbs speeded up, drawing ever more retailers with it. Papers like *Newsday* in Garden City, L. I., the *Record* in Hackensack, N. J., the small dailies in Westchester County and the Newhouse papers all benefited and some began automating their production machinery. But in New York City time stood still. The desperate managements of the losing papers could not even get the unions to agree on minimal automation in the interests of economy. But by that time the costs of operation had grown to such an extent that not even automation could have saved a property like the *Herald Tribune,* which was reputed to have lost between $15 and $20 million during the decade of its ownership by John Hay Whitney.

Although every major party to the long newspaper wrangle in New York could see where it was headed, the fitful drama moved toward its climax with the inevitability of Greek tragedy. There was a 25-day strike in 1965. Then, as a last-ditch effort to stay in business, a merger was announced between Whitney's *Herald Tribune,* Hearst's *Journal-American,* and Scripps-Howard's *World-Telegram and Sun,* with the former as the morning paper and the latter two as a combined evening publication in a 24-hour one-plant operation. The scheme never had a chance; on April 25, 1966, the day when publication was to begin, a 10-union tieup started that did not end for 140 days. On August 15, Whitney suspended publication of the *Herald Tribune* and entered into a three-sided agreement with his partners to put out a single evening publication, the *World Journal Tribune,* or "Widget" as it became known. The unions hung on, each grimly insistent on saving a few jobs or getting a little more money, so that the "Widget" did not have much substance behind it when it finally appeared on September 12. From its first robust day of 900,000 sales of an 80-page paper, it soon relapsed into a rather anemic-looking publication of about 700,000 circulation. While its three ill-assorted partners hoped for the best, they quickly found that their losses were continuing on a rising scale. At length, after they had lost an additional $10 million, the "Widget" abruptly suspended publication on May 5, 1967. Thus

52 the *Times, News,* and the surprisingly tenacious *Post* were left alone on Manhattan—the survivors in the long and acrimonious struggle.[45]

It is probably accurate to say that the unions were the immediate cause of the death of both the *Herald Tribune* and its successor, the "Widget," but that is not the whole story. Some have argued that their respective managements should have had the gumption long before the end to insist on more efficient ways of doing business. Others, the inevitable players of tax angles as answers to all problems, have pointed out that the corporate setup of the *World Journal Tribune* had denied to each owner the advantage of obtaining a tax writeoff for newspaper losses that could be applied against the profits each derived from other well-diversified ventures. But singly or together, these explanations do not take into account the basic truths that the losers never did have the faintest idea of how they could compete successfully with the *Times* and the *News,* that their combined publication stood for nothing of consequence, and that even its giant size did not attract the public and the advertisers to it in sufficient numbers to keep it going.

There is one other lesson that may be derived from the New York experience. Despite the gains of the *Times* and *Post* after the demise of the "Widget," it was clear that almost 500,000 daily and almost 1 million Sunday newspaper readers deserted the New York metropolitan press in the aftermath of the merger. Just where they went, if anywhere, is debatable, because all suburban publications combined did not show very spectacular gains. The inevitable conclusion was that literally hundreds of thousands of New Yorkers quit buying newspapers.* Very possibly, with the slow rise in the circulations of newspapers in the New York metropolitan area over a period of years, the apparent loss of readership will become less drastic; however, it is a demonstrable truth that if newspaper publication is interrupted consistently over a period of years, a certain number of readers learn to do without newspapers.

As *The Times*'s knowledgeable A. H. Raskin wrote after the death of the *Herald Tribune:*

"The contrasts between the community indifference

* After five months of study, the *Times* announced it would not enter the New York evening field because the financial risk was unacceptable. Those familiar with the field estimated it would cost up to $60 million to start a New York paper and it would take ten years or more to break even.

that attended the passing of the *Trib* and the sense of personal   53
loss, even grief, that gripped millions when the old *World* died is
a dismaying indication of how far newspapers have slipped in
public esteem in the last three decades in this communications
capital. Part of the answer, of course, lies in the senseless cycle
of strikes that have blacked out large sections of the metropolitan press for long periods in the last four years. The surest way
to become convinced that you can do without newspapers is to
have to do it over and over again for weeks or months on end.

"But in this case, too, it is much too easy to point to
labor strife as the culprit. The problems of New York's newspapers extend far beyond primordial labor-management relations;
they are problems of function and meaning in a society that is
changing faster than our capacity to comprehend or interpret
it." [46]

Despite the New York experience, no lasting cure
has been found for the persisting ills of giantism in metropolitan
journalism in the United States. In a number of cities outside
New York, similar problems have cropped up without any promise of lasting settlements. To name only two, the *Detroit Free
Press* and the *Detroit News* were shut down by a 134-day strike
in 1964* and the *Toledo Blade* was put out of business for 148
days in 1966–67 by another walkout. Such tieups have also
affected Boston and smaller cities, but not for as long a time.[47]
The conclusion is inescapable that more metropolitan newspapers will have to suspend publication if this kind of pressure
keeps up without any recourse to automation and other labor-
saving methods.

While strikes thus become one way of eliminating
the weaker economic units in the metropolitan newspaper field,
they are not the only method. Sales, mergers, and suspensions by
agreement have been used in various cities without incurring
any punitive action to date from the Department of Justice. In
Los Angeles, for example, the Chandler family dropped the *Mirror* and the Hearst interests abandoned the *Herald Express*, thus
leaving the morning field to Chandler's *Los Angeles Times* and
the afternoon field to the merged Hearst *Herald-Examiner*. In
San Francisco, Hearst and Scripps-Howard cut their losses by
successive sales and mergers that left the *Examiner* alone in the
afternoon, with the independent *Chronicle* surviving in the morn-

* The same papers were closed down again in 1967 and 1968.

54   ing and both merging into the *Sunday Examiner & Chronicle*. In Chicago, through much the same process, the Field and McCormick interests divided the field between them with the *Sun-Times* facing the *Tribune* in the morning and the *Daily News* competing with the *American* in the afternoon. Albany, Pittsburgh, Cincinnati, Miami and other metropolitan centers have gone through somewhat similar experiences, and others are likely to do so in the future. For although the greatest of the giants are pushing ahead to new gains, as witness the record of *The New York Times, Washington Post, Chicago Sun-Times, St. Louis Post-Dispatch,* and *Los Angeles Times* among others, there are still a number of unhealthy spots in metropolitan newspaper journalism where further adjustment or contraction is inevitable.

The prosperity of the majority of newspapers can neither obscure nor minimize the ills of the metropolitan press. Nor can it conceal the hard truth that giantism, as a way of life, is not the ultimate in American journalism. It has not been able to save a number of good newspapers and it has prematurely forced many an indifferent one to the wall, forestalling all efforts at rescue operations. Some better way to run newspapers in the United States will have to be found.

NEW KINDS OF NEWSPAPERS

There are, of course, exceptions to the practice of giantism among American newspapers, the most notable being the *Wall Street Journal* and its little brother, the weekly *National Observer*. It is true that both are specialized publications which do not depend for their existence on a vast bulk of retail advertising, a basic reason for big newspapers. However, despite a formidable standing content of stock market tables and other economic data that is published daily, the *Wall Street Journal* has demonstrated that a sturdy independence, editorial innovation, superior writing, and a lot of good, hardheaded investigative reporting can be far more important than mere size to a large and discerning public.

On this basis, while retaining its stylish slimness, the *Journal* has gone from 35,000 to more than one million circulation in 30 years at 15 cents a copy. It has unceremoniously dumped a century of newspaper tradition, beginning with the fetish that breaking news must be told three times—in the headlines, the beginning of the story, and finally in detail. It is experimenting today with high speed tape news transmission, cold typesetting, offset printing, and facsimile publication. Its managers have found that there is greater efficiency in maintaining a central composing room at Chicopee Falls, Mass., than next to the main editorial offices at 30 Broad Street, in the heart of New York's financial district. As a result, they have not hesitated to decentralize their operations to the eight plants throughout the nation from which publication and distribution are conducted.

By following the same basic disregard for most of the accumulated beliefs of how an American newspaper should be run, *The National Observer* within a few years has won more than 500,000 circulation. At the beginning, the old-time professionals scoffed at it as a hopelessly provincial sheet, thin and emaciated in appearance, which would soon fade out of existence. But *The Observer* has gained consistently while some of its giant daily contemporaries have had to give up the struggle for constant expansion. Nor has it proved to be as dull and provincial as its detractors thought it would be; some of its editorial innovations have the quality of first-rate magazine work. By 1968, however, it still was not a profitable operation.

Except for the small dailies and weeklies that have made a virtue out of necessity and specialized publications in the field, the two Dow Jones papers are almost alone in abandoning the concept of outsize newspapers as a way of journalistic life in the United States. There are any number of predictions that the technological revolution will create a new kind of newspaper, even one that is transmitted directly into the home,[48] but the media managers do not seem to be worried about it at present. They go on in the same old way, piling Macy's on Gimbel's, on the assumption that they will continue indefinitely to be able to maintain their current profit margins. There is no business like the newspaper business for such sweet and sour dreaming.

Some of the basic principles of making newspapers in the United States probably will have to change before there is any considerable difference in the appearance, substance, and financial base of the press. With few exceptions, the way the system operates today, the advertising department in effect determines the size of the paper when it prepares the dummied pages showing the placement of the day's quota of advertising. If the editorial managers have a heavy run of news, or expect a big news break, there may be grudging agreement from the business office to go up two pages to provide more news space. But other

56 than that, the size of the newspaper is basically determined more often than not by the amount of advertising at hand. On *The New York Times* and the *Wall Street Journal*, the editors have the right to toss advertising out of the newspaper in favor of news whenever they believe it necessary, and it happens with a fair amount of regularity on the *Journal*. But other editors generally do not exercise that amount of power.

Once a determination is made that editorial content and not advertising is to be the major factor in the size of a newspaper, then the system may possibly change. Of course, the media managers are bound to look upon such a philosophy as unbusinesslike and otherwise impossible, just as they laughed at *The National Observer;* nevertheless, it is the only hope for reversing a process that has caused so much damage to the American newspaper and is likely to take an additional toll, particularly in the metropolitan field. Necessarily, a limitation on advertising rather than the news is dependent in large part on a newspaper monopoly situation that would permit a proprietor to charge a more realistic price for his advertising. This situation already exists in most American urban communities, since a very large amount of local retail advertising does not lend itself to electronic reproduction.

It may be argued that "shoppers"—the generic term for the free shopping guides that are issued at small cost by enterprising operators—will threaten any small or medium-sized daily that raises its advertising costs. Foy McNaughton, a publisher of small newspapers, dealt with this threat by issuing an opposition "shopper" at cut rates that quickly put his competition out of business. A more conventional way of handling such situations is to build more reader values into the newspaper itself.

However, if there is continued emphasis on the publication of news that is already known to the public through radio or television instead of a better presentation of the main stories in some depth, then not even a change in size is going to help the marginal newspaper very much. It merely begs the question for full-size newspapers to cut their column format from eight to six or five, a source of some experimentation today. In the first place, a change in appearance without more substance is in effect an attempt to fool the reader and it will not work; in the second, most of the five- and six-column newspapers

have been and still are successful and do not have to play with   57
type to create a good opinion of their work.

The point has been made repeatedly and deserves to be made again. In the United States, with its vast communications network, there is room for a limited number of great dailies of the character of *The New York Times, Washington Post,* and *Los Angeles Times.* But for the average daily, the *Wall Street Journal*'s calm acceptance of a position as a supplemental newspaper is probably more realistic than insistence on trying to be a little *New York Times.* The very expression is a contradiction in terms. In many small and medium-sized cities, it is still possible for a newspaper to be first with local news in many cases; but, with the development of local radio and television news staffs, even this is bound to change.

The average American newspaper, in short, is going to have to find a new identity, something beyond sheer size, if it is to retain whatever power it still exercises over public opinion. In many cases, particularly those of marginal newspapers, the change may have to be drastic; there is too much competition from other news media today to insure the maintenance of current profit margins indefinitely for even successful newspapers. Consequently, if the American daily continues to follow the mounting spiral of giantism with its attendant ever rising costs, it will invite far more casualties in its ranks than are either desirable or necessary if the press is to continue to serve the public interest in the future as it has in the past.

MAGAZINES

5

AND THE NEWS

W̶hile *Look* magazine was publishing excerpts from William Manchester's *The Death of a President*, the editor of one of the nation's greatest newspapers somewhat pensively asked some of his colleagues: "Is it right for us to let the magazines have these newsworthy books for exclusive publication without making a real effort to get them for ourselves?" The question was not answered satisfactorily then, nor has it been since.

Basically, there are two reasons for the continued leadership of the magazines in carrying off exclusive rights to

many newsworthy books, memoirs, and articles by the famous   59
and infamous. The first is that the "real effort" posed in the
editor's question generally means putting up a great deal more
money than most newspapers care to spend for this type of
material. The second, which actually grows out of the first, is
grounded in the conviction of most newspaper proprietors that
they cannot add much circulation through the serialization of
the average newsbook, certainly not enough to justify a major
expenditure.

Both beliefs are worth examination. In the case of
the Churchill history of World War II and the memoirs of Stalin's daughter, Svetlana Alliluyeva, *Life* magazine and *The New
York Times* shared the publication rights with benefit for both.
The judicious sale of syndication rights cut down the high initial
investment in both books; furthermore, the *Times* attributed a
small circulation increase to both the Churchill history and the
Alliluyeva memoirs.[49] But the disgraceful disregard of *Look*'s em-
bargoes of advance material from the Manchester book more
than anything else made the public skeptical of newspaper pre-
tensions of disinterest in newsbook serialization. To many, it
seemed as if the bulk of the newspapers wanted something for
nothing and were willing to cut corners to get it.[50] Of course,
Look benefited enormously because of the uproar, with circulation gains that dwarfed any comparable publication of book
excerpts in recent times.* There is also no indication that any
newspaper made a serious effort to obtain Svetlana Alliluyeva's
first article, which Editor Robert Manning of *The Atlantic* carried off—much to his own surprise—because he went after it
with thoroughness and persistence.

It is puzzling that all save a handful of major newspapers are apparently willing to abdicate their responsibility for
publishing this kind of news until some magazine sends them an
advance publicity handout. Moreover, when there is competition
for important news photographs (such as the celebrated Zapruder color pictures of the Kennedy assassination published by
Life), a magazine usually is able to outbid its daily competitors.

Many papers, it is true, have a historic aversion to
paying for articles, interviews, pictures, and other material from
free lances on the theory that their own staffs should be able to
cover the news without additional expense. The ingrate who asks

* However, the book itself sold only moderately well.

60   payment for setting forth his views at some length, when the newspaper is perfectly willing to give him free space, has been roundly condemned in newsrooms throughout the land. But the more competitive magazines that base themselves on the news have no such compunctions, except in the obvious cases of public officials and similar common news sources, even though their staffs on the whole are better paid than those of most newspapers. Nor do television officials balk at legitimate compensation for effort by someone not associated with their generally well-paid staffs.

Thus, with the exception of the leading newspapers and the Sunday supplements, the press in most instances is lagging in the quest for "name" writers and the serialization of books of demonstrable appeal. Occasionally, a syndicate of newspapers may come up with a feature of some importance or a single newspaper may be able to divulge important background or documentary source material through the enterprise of its staff. But the serialized book and its derivatives in large part remain in the magazine field, although Charles Dickens more than a century ago demonstrated the journalistic importance of such works by serializing some of his most famous novels in his paper, *Household Words*.

It is entirely possible, as many newspaper editors contend, that the time has passed when the serialized book or similar feature may be counted on to add significantly to daily circulation figures, regardless of what the effect may be on the magazines. But for a serious newspaper, which takes its public responsibilities to heart, the central purpose for publishing such material is seldom based on potential circulation gains. Certainly, *The New York Times* did not enter into its agreements with *Life* on the Churchill or Stalin works to put on circulation; the gains, on a percentage basis, were comparatively small as far as the newspaper was concerned. The *Times*'s purpose, basically, was to provide significant material of consequence to its existing readership; if new readers were added, that was considered a by-product. And this, in essence, is what should motivate a superior magazine or newspaper in obtaining publication rights to books and derivative data. Self-interest is not the prime yardstick that should be applied.

MAGAZINES: QUANTITY AND QUALITY

The enterprise of a few large and powerful magazines is, without doubt, the most distinguishing feature of news presentation in the periodical field. Unfortunately, it is not characteristic of magazines in general, which is probably not an entirely fair statement because magazines are so numerous in the United States and they have such diffuse aims, many of them strictly commercial. Actually, nobody really knows how many magazines there are in the land. Excluding nearly 10,000 house magazines (publications put out by companies for their employees, customers, or stockholders), there is an enormous range of periodicals estimated at more than 4,000 by the Department of Commerce with an aggregate circulation of 400 million weekly, semimonthly, monthly, and quarterly.[51] *Ayer's Directory,* which includes trade publications and weekly magazines distributed by newspapers, runs the total to 8,000.

No more than a few hundred magazines, even by the most generous estimate, have particular importance either because of their size, specialized field, prestige, or broad influence on important groups. They run the gamut from *The Reader's Digest,* with 15 million readers, and *TV Guide,* with 10 million, to *The New Yorker,* with 475,000, and the *Saturday Review,* with 380,000; from *McCall's,* the women's leader, with 8.3 million to *Scientific American,* with 390,000; from *Time,* with 3,000,000, to *Motion Picture,* with 500,000.[52]

Before the advent of television it was a prosperous field in almost every respect. For some it still is. But with the coming of keen competition from the electronic media, primarily in the area of diversion and entertainment, almost 35 of the 250 largest magazines vanished and more are likely to go as costs and publication problems increase. No less than in the newspaper field, giantism has had its failures as well as its successes among magazines. *Coronet* and *Collier's,* each with more than 4 million circulation, were forced out of business and *The Saturday Evening Post* had a bad time of it for a considerable period.

Just as has been the case with newspapers, the woes of the failing magazines have tended to obscure the general prosperity of a number of the leaders. Magazines such as *Cosmopolitan,* once given up for dead, have boosted revenues by 50 percent. The century-old *Harper's Bazaar,* co-leader with *Vogue* in the fashion world, has taken in $8 million a year in advertising alone on a circulation of 425,000 and in a single month sold 100 pages of ads to a single organization, Celanese Corporation, for $500,000. *Playboy,* which based its success on the national preoccupation with sex, has been paying good dividends on its investment. McGraw-Hill, Inc., with its specialized magazines in

62 business, industry, and science, has rolled up a net annual income of $8 million. But the earnings champion is Time, Inc., which has compiled a record net income of almost $18 million a year.[53]

Such success has something to do with the angry buzz of social criticism that has afflicted American magazines throughout their history, much of it justified. If anything magazines are even more sensitive to criticism than newspapers and most of them are less able to profit from it. The standard magazine response to critics of all shades of opinion is either an ostrichlike attitude or an indignant citation of the latest circulation figures, as if this kind of success amply justifies the most dubious means of achieving it.

Outside the pornographic magazines, the most frequent target of attack among the periodicals has been the largest of all, *The Reader's Digest*. The *Digest* has also been the most impervious to criticism; having first accepted advertising in 1955, it soon began running more than $4 million worth of ads in each issue and obviously considers self-examination unnecessary. In the *Digest*'s dour lexicon, it is cricket to advance some of the far right causes that have the support of its publisher, De-Witt Wallace, in bite-sized articles that are intended to persuade the reader. It is equally righteous, the *Digest* believes, to shut off the opposition from a hearing except in the most specialized cases. Just what effect the long-time conversion to conservatism by anecdote has had on the American mass mind is difficult to determine. However, there is no doubt that the *Digest*, at one time or another, has attacked some of the most beneficial legislation ever enacted by Congress.

After a particularly lively clash with the *Digest* for an assault on various urban renewal policies, Professor Reo M. Christenson of Miami University, Ohio, wrote: "The *Digest*'s public relations book, *Of Lasting Interest*, notes that the *Digest* prefers to set forth its opinions in an unqualified manner and 'in black and white clarity.' Black and white makes for dramatic reading, but there's something to be said for reporting all sides of the truth, too." [54]

Next to the *Digest*, the fashion magazines are most often held up for critical examination in the United States although, curiously enough, they have been and still are extravagantly admired abroad for their imagery and their originality. It is a matter of satisfaction to the fashion books that they can sell

anything—from stacked heels to miniskirts and from bikinis to   63
prance suits and zebra-striped mink coats. They are, as one
headline put it, "kicky, kooky, ginchy, zilchy," and then some.[55]
They promote their message with brass bands, but exercise their
critical function with piccolos.

 To their credit, they have never pretended to be
anything they are not. Of all the types of magazines on the
newsstands of America, an unexampled display of high quality,
showmanship, and downright vulgarity, the fashion books are
the handsomest commercial ventures. Their highest purpose is
to merchandise the output of the garment trades. They pay
monthly obeisance to the trivial in the grand manner. In publicizing the leotard, *Vogue* published a photograph of the nether
half of a woman's body in tights with the caption: "Thigh—The
Newest Bone in Fashion." And *Harper's Bazaar* paid tribute to a
new perfume as follows: "Since even a whiff of Emilio Pucci's
non-cliche Vivara Perfume is heavenly, a whole new galaxy of
products in this free-as-the-wind fragrance sends dedicated Vi-
varaites into a happy flutter." [56]

 If the fashion books have any concern whatever for
the public interest in their field, they have disguised it behind
rows of awkward-looking far-out mannequins. Sometimes, fashion designers wail that their new clothes are unrecognizable in
the kind of advanced pop, semipop, and ultrapop art found in
many of the big fashion magazine photographs. But the books
sell, despite that; even more important, they sell clothes. And
that makes them a vital necessity to the American garment and
allied industries where their approval means much and their
silence can be deadly.

 Although the magazines of more general interest for
women do not have the undisguised arrogance of the best fashion books, there is no doubt that they are equally devoted to the
advancement of commercial interests. In many of the issues of
McCall's, Ladies' Home Journal, Good Housekeeping, and the
rest of the handsome and healthy breed, there seldom appears to
be much effort to differentiate between their own fine color
layouts and the adjacent advertising. The women's world of
fashions, food, beauty, homemaking, and odd bits of inspiration
fits nicely into the philosophy of the leading women's periodicals,
and their advertising format as well.

 But, despite a certain number of serious articles and
thoughtful editorial discussions, few women's magazines seem

64   to give any space to the kind of criticism that could be unsettling to large advertisers. From time to time, it is true that the leaders do make substantial efforts in the public interest by discussing controversial subjects ranging in importance from "the pill" to alcoholism and dope addiction. But too many others set up a false front of public service, singling out some amorphous and impersonal subject for attack when they are reasonably sure there will be no danger of a kickback. This kind of pseudo-crusade is scarcely to be confused with a serious and consistent intent to serve the public interest.

Unlike the old magazine muckrakers of an earlier and far more important time in the history of American periodicals, today's mass circulation magazines for the most part merchandise sex, sympathy, and dreams. Helen Gurley Brown, author of *Sex and the Single Girl*, showed how the recipe worked when she took over the hard-pressed *Cosmopolitan* magazine and made both circulation and advertising jump within a year. The faded old Hearst publication began perking up with such articles as, "How To Get a Divorce," "How To Make Good at the Beach," and "How To Find Men in a Big Rich Country." For good measure, there was "Cosmopolitan's Husband-Hunting Wardrobe" and some exercises that were billed as suitable for the development of more "kissable lips." [57] To promote the publication, a series of advertisements was placed in newspapers featuring "Cosmopolitan Girls" and sounding the theme: "Did you know there are millions more unmarried girls than single men?" As far as the public interest was concerned, this kind of thing adds up to precisely zero.

But whatever the sins of the women's magazines in their drive for success, they can scarcely compete for sheer unadulterated commercialism with the most persistent of the sex merchants, *Playboy*. In a relatively few years, it has soared to the top of the men's magazine field with more than 3 million circulation—ahead of *True*, *Argosy*, and the old champion, *Esquire*, now in the bald-headed row. *Playboy* promotes Playboy clubs, jewelry, books, garments, an occasional serious article or editorial, and girls-girls-girls. The revealing covers and photographs are the come-ons, the pulpy text is the filler. There are a few "name" writers, purchased to lend respectability to the operation, but what is really being sold is entertainment for lonely men. The advertiser in large part gets what he pays for, which includes a large number of descendants of H. L. Mencken's "Booboisie" among the audience.

Playboy's occasional attention to sermons, disarmament, the nation's water resources, and similar serious magazine
fare is scarcely a sign of coming reform, although there is always
hope that success will bring with it a greater sense of public
responsibility. Before *Playboy*'s drive to the top, *Esquire* turned
itself into a magazine of some substance, an interesting experiment in reversing the Gresham's Law that applies to American
periodicals in general. While few are likely to confuse the reformed *Esquire* with *The Economist* or the *New Statesman,* the
serious intent of its editorial policy can scarcely be mistaken and
it is entitled to both consideration and respect.

There is, however, little possibility of any similar
transformation that will bring a modicum of concern for the
public interest into the lush pages of many of the mass circulation magazines. The so-called service area for periodicals—
where some worthy publications still manage to survive—is in-
undated with meretricious sheets. Like the girlie magazines,
service publications generally appear to have been less affected
than others by the competition of television, on the one hand,
and newspapers, on the other. Consequently, large-scale magazine operators think nothing of starting a magazine one month
and killing it a few months later if it does not "go." Anything
from pet care to hairdos may become a fit subject for a service
magazine; one hairdo book, indeed, became such an instant
success that its delighted owner had it put out in translation in
other parts of the world. Thus, it became an exhibit of the
cultural influence which the United States exerts abroad.

Among the "shelter" magazines, still another large
and popular class of periodicals, there is a kind of split personality that leads some to publish a good deal of material of benefit to
homeowners, although their editors at the same time seldom do
anything to disturb the equanimity of their advertisers. Consequently, the giant *Better Homes and Gardens* and its principal
rivals, *The American Home* and *House & Garden,* are as mild in
their way as the women's magazines. The "shelter" group in
consequence is an attractive advertising medium. In many an
individual issue, it may be noted that advertised products also
are editorially supported; the reader, in fact, is often stimulated
to buy as much as he can.

ADVERTISERS AND MAGAZINES

A critic who looked over some of the "shelter" books once observed, "For journalists, perhaps the most discomfiting aspect of

66 the magazines is the amount of space, produced as editorial matter, that is either advertising, tie-in, or promotion. The mail-order and new-product sections are the most obtrusive." [58] The "shelter" periodicals are not alone. In fashions, women's, sex, and other magazines aimed primarily at the mass purchaser, the issues of the day are seldom permitted to intrude on the dreamy buy-buy mood, which is created for the average reader. There is, in consequence, a separation between the real world and the world as advertised that sometimes amounts to a delusion on the part of the mass audience. Such notions of advertiser accommodation began in the journalistic nether regions even before the abysmal years of the Great Depression but they have now spread to some of the highest and most principled organizations in the land. Nor can it be said that this is confined to the periodical field; it may be observed in newspapers, particularly special sections, to as great an extent. The corrupting influence on the news columns, in short, is painfully obvious to any thoughtful reader.

It is a relief to be able to go behind the polished array of glossy printing jobs and find a substantial number of important magazines that still refuse to turn themselves into publications whose interests are swayed more by the advertiser than by the reading public. They exist primarily in the quality field, ranging from weekly to quarterly publication, and are headed by one of the handsomest and most prosperous of all, *The New Yorker*. In its advancing years, *The New Yorker* may be accused of many things but not generally of truckling to advertisers or interfering with the independence of its writers. This is also true of such other magazines as the *Saturday Review, The Reporter, The Atlantic, Harper's*, and a few others in the prestige area. The leading publications devoted to business and industry, science, agriculture, health, and education try within their own limitations to represent the public interest over the advertising interest. To an even greater extent, this is true of such publications on religion as *The Commonweal, America*, the *Christian Century*, and *Commentary*.

Sadly enough, the so-called magazines of dissent, typified by *The Nation* and *New Republic*, are more afflicted by hardening of the intellectual arteries than any sins of commercialism; most of them have perpetual financial problems and comparatively little influence.[59] As for the unimpressive cavalcade of little magazines and underground sheets, few contribute anything substantial to public enlightenment except for the established cultural publications that are respected in their own areas. Of the magazines that formerly thrived on tax breaks, the *National Geographic* does very well.* And as for scholarly quarterlies, of which there seems to be no end, *Foreign Affairs* is at the top in both prestige and influence.

The news and picture magazines are, of course, in a class by themselves because they constitute so important a part of the American system of mass communication. Of all the periodical groupings, they are probably less subject to advertiser influence and pressure than magazines as a whole even though instances of both crop up now and then. But as a whole, the news and picture books have built up such wealth and power of their own that it would take a very brave advertiser, indeed, to try to twist them to his own purposes. The extent to which they favor their advertisers is not generally determined on an individual basis, therefore, but as a matter of over-all policy. The breaking news and the exigencies of putting out the book under deadline pressures make it impossible to guarantee any advertiser that the text facing his appeal will tie in with it, or at least not detract from it. The most that could be guaranteed is, say, a place for an advertiser facing a particular department such as entertainment, books, or the like, or a special section type of understanding regarding complementary editorial space, but this kind of thing is done far more in the newspaper field than it is in the news and picture magazines. Even so, an unholy alliance between advertisers and editors is very difficult to maintain under the pressures of developing news. This is not the principal fault of the news weeklies and the picture books by any means.

To give credit where credit is due, *Look* and *Life* both have conducted superior campaigns in the public interest and have exerted wide influence in the dissemination of pictorial news of importance to the nation. The news weeklies, in part, have helped fill an indefensible gap in the reporting of national and international affairs by the less qualified daily newspapers of the nation and the bulletin-type coverage of radio and television. This is the main strength of the news weekly operation and its principal reason for existence; to a lesser extent, the exploitation of "back of the book" departments ranging from business and finance to science and cultural affairs has also helped them to achieve a deserved popularity.

* From December 12, 1967, the profits of such "nonprofit" organization magazines were taxed at the corporate rate of 48 percent. About 700 were affected.

68   Where the news and picture magazines are open to serious criticism, in the main, is in the circuslike performance they often give on the most important issues of the day. Often, through flamboyant word pictures and catchy illustrations and layouts, they seem determined above all else to amuse first and to instruct last. The old newspaper fault for snatching at the irrelevant fact and the quote out of context is often seen in exaggerated form in some of the news weeklies; moreover, it is scarcely a coincidence that a very large body of news magazine interpretation appears to coincide with the known prejudices of some of the proprietors.

True, the policy slants that are to be found in every issue of *Time* and, to a lesser extent, in *Newsweek* and *U. S. News and World Report*, constitute a hazard that now is also being encountered with increasing frequency in newspapers under the label of analysis or interpretation. But it is one thing to leap at a likely interpretation and make an honest mistake in the process; it is quite another to try to make the facts fit into a neat but smelly bouquet as an offering to the proprietor and his preconceived notions.

Often, even for the knowledgeable journalist, it is difficult to say where the honest effort to interpret the news begins and the hatchet work of the editorial policy man ends on a number of news publications, daily and weekly. The burden of proof in all cases of doubt inevitably rests with the interpreter and his medium. And this is where a reputation for integrity counts so heavily—a public recognition that the publication of news, comment, and criticism is independent of both advertiser interest and editorial policy pressure. Such repute is dearly earned—and it can be quickly lost. It is unfortunate that *Time*, which has the most to offer in the news weekly field, also has the worst reputation for permitting office policy to slant both its news and its interpretation. There is nothing new in this. It is a state of mind that has bedeviled *Time* from its beginnings and not even the inauguration of a rather dull weekly essay has served to distract attention from the very serious policy flaws in a publication that would gain in stature by playing the news straight. Not everything needs an angle to make it interesting.

THE MAGAZINE AS LITERATURE

Finally, magazine journalism at its best has made some outstanding contributions to American literature and this is, by all

odds, its strongest claim for public recognition. It is, however, an
elementary observation that the magazine writers' general reputation for excellence is based to a very large degree on the work
of such graceful stylists as E. B. White, John Hersey, Robert
Shaplen, Lillian Ross, Marya Mannes, Russell Lynes, John Bart-
low Martin, and others who operate almost exclusively in the
quality field. Because much of the unsolicited or specially assigned material in the leading magazines is based on the work of
150 to 200 professionals who know how to write to an editor's
specifications, the notion has been assiduously spread that there
is something mysterious about superior magazine writing. Not
so. By comparison with the dull stuff in much of the daily
American press, the better magazine work naturally shines. It is
obviously better than most of the trashy writing in the litter of
nonfiction that cascades from the presses of book publishers. But
this scarcely means that the magazines of the United States,
always allowing for exceptional articles, can stand comparison
with the kind of writing that is consistently published by *The
Economist, The London Observer, The Guardian,* or the *London
Sunday Times.*

The superiority of American magazine writing over
much of the work produced in other areas of American journalism, consequently, is scarcely something to warrant celebration.
It does not mean that the magazine writers of the upper echelons
are masters of English prose; rather, it shows how comparatively
impoverished American journalism is today for writers of capa-
bility, influence, and standing. The bulk of magazine writing in
the United States is often depressingly routine. It shows no more
sparkle, on the whole, than a very large volume of material that
is in newspaper or book form or read over the air.

What is wrong? Many things, basically, beginning
with a lack of attention in the American school system to the
fundamentals of clear, understandable English prose. A writer
requires time to mature, but in American journalism he is seldom given time to think, much less to grow. The habit of reflection is not encouraged. The pressure for production at all costs is
made well-nigh overwhelming. Small wonder, then, that all except the truly superior writers in the United States suffer from
the fatal habit of compressing substance into a set of predeter-
mined editorial forms instead of permitting substance to determine the form.

The factors of time and space and editorial misdi-

70   rection have been combined in much American writing to pro-
      duce a structured news story, a structured magazine article, a
      structured radio or television program, a structured nonfiction
      book. The British, with a fine contempt for such structured
      thought, continue to lead in originality of expression because
      they rightly emphasize grace and wit and, above all, style. It is
      for such reasons that the best of the British magazines and
      Sunday newspapers have a decided impact on British public
      opinion—an impact that does not generally exist in American
      periodical journalism. Obviously, it takes more than courage,
      effort, and fidelity to the public interest to develop qualities of
      public leadership in the mass media in a democratic society; to
      be truly effective, the journalist must have something to say and
      he must know how to say it in such a way as to capture public
      attention. Despite the considerable progress that serious maga-
      zines and their staffs have made in the past two decades, such
      writers are still comparatively rare in the United States.

TRENDS IN

6

TELEVISION

The American television networks, which can sell everything from soap to automobiles to a complacent public in large quantities, have had their troubles in establishing equal acceptance for news and public affairs. A fairly convincing case can be made out against some of the elements in top management for not having tried very hard, but the same accusation can scarcely be documented against the zealots of broadcast journalism. They *have* tried, sometimes at excessive cost to themselves. But on the whole they have not been too successful. The Federal Communications Commission, which is

72   supposed to worry about such things, has scarcely been noted in its history for taking bold and forthright positions in support of the need for stronger, larger, and more independent broadcast journalism services. "Public service programming, particularly in the entertainment and news fields, is often the most expensive and the least profitable," the FCC said in its final decision on the American Broadcasting Companies' request to merge with the International Telephone and Telegraph Company.[60] It is not much of an excuse, particularly when it is put forward by a federal regulatory agency. Since when has public service been supposed to show a profit?

It is not lack of talent or ideas in broadcast journalism, but an almost continual carnival atmosphere on television that has caused a substantial proportion of local stations to reject some well-intentioned network news specials on major topics. There should be no surprise, consequently, over the decline during much of the 1960s in the network offerings of scheduled public affairs material. Thus, particularly in foreign affairs, the same kind of a news blackout that has existed for years in areas serviced by the purely local-minded daily press has spread to a large section of the local electronic media. Under such circumstances, a mass audience does not often have an alternative between show business and the news except for all but most of the compelling events. When it does happen, as in the case of the $500,000 Theodore H. White documentary, "China: The Roots of Madness," produced by David Wolper for the Xerox Corporation and shown on 102 local television stations, the ratings can be surprisingly good.[61] But in the current atmosphere of television, it takes very real journalistic statesmanship to embark on such ventures.

THE SCOPE OF TELEVISION NEWS

True, the all-sponsored major network Monday–Friday news programs have had wide acceptance on local stations, primarily because the early evening news has no fixed commercial competitors in most areas. NBC's "Huntley-Brinkley Report" and the CBS "Evening News," with Walter Cronkite, both have been shown consistently on nearly all the approximately 200 affiliates of each network, with ABC in third place and admitting to losses of $19 million on news and public affairs in 1966.[62] However, the principal network commentators have generally been the first to concede that they are obliged to deal with bulletin-type news, supplemented by filmed reports when available, and can neither explain

nor interpret for more than a minute or two at a time on a sched- **73**
uled program.

Thus, news coverage in depth is seldom possible during one of the regularly scheduled network programs of news. For this, there is no substitute today except a good newspaper but these, too, are in short supply. Confronted with what amounts to a considerable local radio, television, and newspaper censorship of world and even national news in some parts of the nation, the serious-minded citizen who wants to keep informed has no alternative but to wait for the news magazines, a responsible Sunday newspaper, or specialized publications. And this in a nation that so often boasts it is the best-informed in the world.

It is a dangerous illusion, moreover, that the networks, for all their vast expenditures and claims of large editorial staffs, originate a great deal of their own news. Even at the time of the escalation of the Vietnam War in early 1966, when American bombers were ordered to blast North Vietnam for the first time, the indifference of the irresponsible part of the local electronic media was matched only by the supine performance of an important segment of the strongly local daily press. A study showed that network news specials on the Vietnam War, much of it superb footage put out February 12, 1966 by CBS and NBC, were carried by only 30 percent of NBC–TV affiliates and 42 percent of CBS–TV affiliates.* Six days later, the use of another Vietnam War news special was only a little better. In other words, approximately half of the network affiliates of each chain refused to break into the evening's routine entertainment (and advertising) to show the American public a vitally necessary program. These were superior jobs by television correspondents and cameramen, covering their first war, and merited full-scale public attention instead of a selfish and self-serving local censorship.

Just as is the case with the daily press, television has its stalwarts in the area of public affairs who make up in part for the negligence of the majority. All the network news and public affairs programs in the 1966 survey were carried by 20 NBC–TV affiliates, 21 for ABC–TV and 14 for CBS–TV. But 34 CBS–TV affiliates, 19 for NBC–TV, and 14 for ABC–TV showed fewer than half such programs that were being offered. It is clear that advertising on sponsored programs counts for far more with

---

* NBC has 206 primary TV affiliates, CBS 192, and ABC 137.

74   many local stations, regardless of merit, than public interest on unsponsored programs.[63]

This was the background for the widely publicized internal argument in CBS that led to the resignation of Fred W. Friendly as president of CBS News. No mere local station was the issue here, but a great national network with a major responsibility to the public that transcended considerations of advertising and entertainment. Both NBC and CBS had been covering the Senate Foreign Relations Committee hearings on the Vietnam War with meticulous thoroughness until 10 A.M. on February 10, 1966. At that time, NBC initiated live coverage of the testimony of George F. Kennan, former American ambassador in Moscow, and CBS put on a fifth rerun of the comedy series, "I Love Lucy."

The new president of CBS Television, who also had been made responsible for news policy, was John A. Schneider, who had previously been a local station manager and was schooled in the value of dollars and cents. He had been interposed between the CBS top management, William S. Paley and Frank Stanton, and the volatile and dedicated Friendly. To newspaper reporters, Schneider made various explanations for curtailing the marathon coverage of the Senate hearings. "We just didn't feel it was the kind of thing to carry," he told one newspaperwoman. "Nobody's looking at it, not even housewives." Another reporter quoted Schneider as saying that the CBS–TV audience had fallen 50 percent on two previous days, although NBC for the same programs reported an audience of 27 million. In effect, what Schneider had decided to do was condense the whole business for showing in compact form later in the day, or in the evening.

Five days later, Friendly resigned as president of CBS News with a public letter to CBS that said: "I am resigning because CBS News did not carry the Senate Foreign Relations Committee hearings last Thursday, when former Ambassador George Kennan testified on Vietnam. It was the considered news judgment of every executive in CND (CBS News Division) that we carry these Vietnam hearings as we had those of other witnesses. I am convinced that the decision not to carry them was a business, and not a news, judgment." [64]

After the uproar had quieted, the immediate result was that CBS missed one day's live network coverage of that particular series of the Fulbright hearings on the Vietnam War.

ABC, which had given up covering the live hearings, resumed
full reports for the finish; as for NBC, its reputation for public
service was substantially increased for staying with what was, in
retrospect, an inconclusive performance. When CBS went back
to capsule summaries on additional Fulbright hearings that
spring, the criticism was minimal.

It was undoubtedly a source of dour satisfaction to
Friendly that the three networks canceled all regular entertainment programs and commercial announcements for more than
four hours of prime time on the night of June 6, 1967 to carry
the United Nations Security Council debate on the six-day Middle East war.[65] If it cost television millions of dollars in revenue,
it also did much to make up for the instances of negligence that
have cost the electronic media dearly in public confidence in the
past. For this is what television public service is really all about
and this is television's job; no other medium can bring national
and world issues before a mass public with such immediacy and
impact.

PUBLIC TELEVISION
The nationwide discussion of public television, which Friendly
among others has helped to stimulate, undoubtedly has played a
part in the willingness of network television as a whole to pay
more attention to its responsibilities to the nation. It would, of
course, be both uncharitable and unfair, and very probably
untrue, to ascribe the motivation for the pooled United Nations
coverage to such pressures on commercial television. However, it
cannot help but play a part in the thinking of the principal
television proprietors as they contemplate the situation in which
they find themselves today.

They have control of what is without doubt the most
powerful of all instruments of mass communications, properly
used, and a source of income of consistently high potential because it is 'a business with a limited possibility for competitive
entry. Unlike published material, which in theory anybody with
the means and the desire can issue in the United States, the
number of usable broadcasting signals that can be transmitted
in any given area at a particular time is now limited; moreover,
there are competing uses for the radio spectrum. Thus, while
Congress under the Bill of Rights may make no law restricting
the freedom of the press, it has in effect subscribed to some sharp
limitations on the electronic media that have been imposed by the

76 Federal Communications Commission. In many populous areas of the country, the number of television signals that may be decently received is restricted to as few as two or three, and sometimes only one; in other places, such as the Los Angeles area, for example, a dozen television stations are authorized.

"Although this same physical limitation and governmental restraint does not make networking . . . necessarily oligopolistic," the FCC has pointed out, "the economies of scale in program distribution have conspired with the restraints on numbers of stations to produce only three national television networks and four national radio networks. While the importance of networking to radio has declined greatly since the rise of television, the networks have continued to dominate television production and distribution. This has meant that three large corporations are responsible for the bulk of the television programming which goes into American homes." [66]

It was inevitable that such power in private hands would be challenged, particularly after a period of rising complaints against inadequate public service programming. A number of ingenious ideas were put forward, the first being the McGeorge Bundy–Fred Friendly proposal for the Ford Foundation which would have financed noncommercial television out of the partial proceeds of a system of domestic satellites to cut the costs of commercial television. Friendly also provided the inspiration, and the Ford Foundation put up the money, for an experimental series of Sunday night programs over National Educational Television, the Public Broadcast Laboratory, which got off to an indifferent start late in 1967. But it remained for the Carnegie Commission on Educational Television to take the big leap away from private television and propose to put the government behind what it called public television. This has since become the generic term for educational and all other forms of noncommercial television.

The Carnegie Commission headed by Dr. James R. Killian Jr., chairman of the Massachusetts Institute of Technology, may not have done a definitive job but it enormously stimulated public discussion of the alternatives to the continued dominance of television by private corporations with advertiser support. It was Killian who put forward the notion that there should be a federally chartered, nonprofit, nongovernmental Corporation for Public Television which would be run in large part by

a manufacturer's excise tax on new television sets. While it was   77
debatable from the very outset whether government influence
could be avoided in such an operation, despite all the high-flown
declarations of independence, nobody could brush aside the im-
plications of the Carnegie report. What it meant, in sum, was
that public television had found acceptance in influential quarters as a possible rival to the private television networks in the
fields of news, public service, and educational and cultural affairs. It led directly to the passage by Congress of the Public
Broadcasting Act of 1967, which President Johnson signed into
law.[67]

Conceivably, both commercial and public television
may be radically altered in the foreseeable future by the swift
pace of technological innovation. The growth of cable television
(CATV), and the enormous power that it places in the hands of
private operators to offer or shut out whatever programs they
wish regardless of the desires of subscribers, is one facet of
television that requires constant surveillance. Another is the
increase in satellite transmission with its promise of greater
efficiency and scope for television as well as the prospect that it
will reduce operating costs eventually. Just what the broadening
of ultrahigh frequency transmission and reception will do to
television can only be guesswork at this stage in its development.
Beyond that lies the imponderable influence of the laser (light
beam) and other techniques that are now in the laboratory stage.
Certainly, the electronic media are poised on the threshold of an
age of monumental change that will add immeasurably to their
opportunities as well as their problems.

TOWARD A BETTER OPERATING STANDARD
What the public therefore has a right to expect from commercial
as well as public television is a manifest of good intentions, not
merely in the form of a single program of public service or even
a group of programs, but an operating philosophy that puts the
public interest ahead of every other consideration. It is easy to
take the pledge, particularly for public television which has nothing to lose, but to carry it out faithfully is something else again.
Consequently, it is heartening to find individual television stations scattered throughout the country that do not have to be
prodded into the practice of public service journalism. While
they are still comparatively few in number, they are creating a

78   new standard for the electronic media—one that approaches and sometimes matches the work of a superior public service newspaper.

It is worth noting that the leaders in local television are trying to move into the area so long pre-empted by the press. Moreover, they are doing it for the most part with skill, spirit, and courage. One of the better stations, WDSU–TV, New Orleans, became the terror of slum landlords in its area with its probing investigative reporting. Another, KUTV, Salt Lake City, did an investigation of local vice conditions that brought results. KING–TV, Seattle, sent a reporting team aboard one of a fleet of Russian trawlers off the northwest Pacific coast to reassure local opinion as to their peaceful intentions. In Chicago, St. Louis, Jacksonville, Boston, New York, and other cities, similar efforts have produced noteworthy results.[68] But just as the laggards in the daily press trade on the reputations of their public-spirited leaders, the even larger number of commercially minded electronic managers merely cheer the pace-setters but do as little as possible themselves.

The responsible ones of television, conscious of the increasingly critical attitude of the better educated segment of the population, know perfectly well what is wrong. Dick Pinkham, of the Ted Bates Advertising Agency, argues that the direction and thrust of television programs—including news and public affairs—have been outside the mainstream of American society for a considerable time. "We are, after all, an increasingly educated nation," he said. "And yet, television—in the direction it is going now with programs like 'Batman'—is exactly counter to this." An even more obvious ailment has been diagnosed as follows by Howard K. Smith, the ABC news commentator: "Balancing each thought or statement with its opposite is the order of the day. If you find a man who says the world is round, you'd better find a man who says the world is flat." [69] There is no hope for television in a sterile objectivity; long ago, the better newspapers decided that a basic honesty and a devotion to the "on the other hand" objectivity are not necessarily synonymous.

Television's problem with the top level of its audience was summed up as follows by Senator Robert F. Kennedy of New York in a taped interview with David Susskind:

Q. Do you watch television very much? A. No, I don't.

Q. That's discouraging. The evening programs aside from news and public affairs—do you have any appetite for that at all? A. No, not really. I don't watch it. I don't think I really watch it hardly at all.

Q. Well, is that because you find it not worth to watch? A. Well, the times I've watched it, I thought it was awfully boring, so I didn't watch it any more.

Q. Do your children watch it very much? A. I think the ones that are getting older watch it less. They started to watch it and then I think they're getting bored with it, too.

Susskind had the dubious satisfaction of prying loose an admission from Senator Kennedy that neither he nor his brother, John F. Kennedy, could have been elected to high office in 1964 and 1960, respectively, without the power of television.[70] But the political uses of television, like its undoubted power as an advertising medium, can scarcely excuse the generally lack-luster quality of many of its programs and its failings in the general area of news and public service. Of course, there are first-rate institutional sponsors like Hallmark cards, Xerox, American Telephone and Telegraph Company, and others who insist on quality when they can get it, as do the networks themselves. But years after Newton N. Minow's devastating criticism of much of television as a "vast wasteland," the term is still generally applicable.

"You will see," Minow said in 1961 as chairman of the FCC, "a procession of game shows, violence, audience participation shows, formula comedies about totally unbelievable families, blood and thunder, mayhem, violence, sadism, murder, Western badmen, Western goodmen, private eyes, gangsters, more violence, and cartoons. And endlessly, commercials— many screaming, cajoling, and offending. And most of all, bore-dom. True, you will see a few things you will enjoy. But they will be very, very few. And if you think I exaggerate, try it." [71]

Few among the proprietors of television have paid much attention to Minow and their other critics. One of the latest trends is a tendency to increase the number of advertising spots in nighttime television in order to boost revenues. With the cost of network television programs estimated at a low of about $100,000 an hour for production alone, the supposed justification is obvious. For example, NBC has increased the number of spot commercial announcements in its feature-length films from 14 to 16. It may not seem like much until a little elementary

80   calculation shows that the cost of each spot to advertisers is $57,000, which means an increase in gross revenue of $228,000 a week or more than $11.8 million a year for a single network.[72] And the end is not yet. Station breaks may be extended, second by second, and still other ingenious ways may be found to crowd in additional advertising. Rising expenses, of course, add to the pressure for more revenue, but the increasing investment of the television companies in diversified interests creates the impression that cost is neither the only reason nor even the main reason for expanded advertising content.

CONFLICTS OF INTEREST

No sensible person will argue that television companies should not diversify; nor can it be contended that newspapers or news magazines should have no outside financial interests whatever. That is flying in the face of reality. What does matter very much, however, is that any proprietor who deals in news and opinion must realize his outside investments will be carefully scrutinized by a discerning public to determine if they are influencing the quality or presentation of his news. The big objection to government operation of, or substantial power over, the news media is precisely the fear that it will slant, twist, or directly change the quality of news reporting to suit its own ends. The danger is no less grave in the privately operated news media when proprietors, either innocently or willfully, let their financial interests sway their responsibilities to the public.

In the diversification process in television, some very large questions have been raised over the sponsorship within the electronic media of various amateur and professional sports, particularly big money football. The effect of offers of as much as $600,000 to a college fullback to play professional football, a by-product of television sponsorship, has created concern among the universities of the land where such things are countenanced. The practice of having sports announcers paid by sponsoring television interests has also led to considerable criticism, as has the television "time out" to permit the insertion of commercials in a rapidly moving game. If the refusal by a CBS official to permit his network television cameras to show vast empty spaces in Yankee Stadium during a CBS-owned Yankee game had been an isolated incident, it would have been laughable. But it is part of a pattern that has scarcely added to the stature of television.[73]

As Jack Gould pointed out: "The leverage exerted by
most sports, professional and collegiate, derives from the whopping total of millions of dollars that are involved in TV coverage.
The club owners and their commissioners look upon their ventures as precious properties to be guarded in every way. But what
this does to TV's reportorial standards is something else again.
Throughout the country, there are hosts of sports announcers
who also appear as newscasters theoretically committed to fearless objectivity in their fields of expertise; yet, in reality, they are
beholden to sports promoters, either directly as paid employees,
or as certified selections." [74]

If public suspicions of journalistic probity are thus
confirmed in so seemingly innocent a field as sports, the work of
television in the far more complicated areas of labor relations,
civil rights, national affairs, and foreign policy is also likely to be
questioned from time to time. It is no answer to point to polls
that show the particular respondents are impressed by the basic
fairness of television in covering the news; presumably, they are
a part of the audience that can also be sold cigarettes in ever
larger quantities despite the federally imposed warnings that are
stamped on each package. Moreover, it should never be forgotten
that the pressures for regulating news that arise within journalism are very small compared to the tremendous influence that is
so often brought to bear from outside the profession.

There is still another source of difficulty in television's handling of the news that is somewhat more common to
the news media as a whole. These are the cases of conflict of
interest, which very often differ in intent from the rather pitiable
efforts to promote rather than report sports. A Wolper production entitled "Wall Street: Where The Money Is" shows the embarrassment that can result in television, even when those involved are people of unquestioned integrity.

Just before the presentation of the documentary,
CBS made this candid announcement: "Portions of the following
broadcast were submitted by Wolper Productions to participants
for their approval." What it meant was that Gerald Tsai, Jr.,
president of the Manhattan Fund, and other interested Wall
Streeters, had been given an advance showing. CBS had become
involved as something more than a viewing medium because one
of its staff, Harry Reasoner, had been assigned to read what a
responsible critic called "one of the longest free commercials in
TV history." After advance assurance of what the program con-

82   tained, the reaction of the financial community was predictable. Two brokerage houses—Bache & Co. and Merrill, Lynch, Pierce, Fenner & Smith—published advertisements on the day of the program, calling attention to its merits. Other brokers bought commercials close to the presentation.

Richard S. Salant, the president of CBS News, conceded in retrospect that the business had made him uncomfortable. He told how he had tried to resolve the problem of an outside narrator for the film, but all efforts at agreement had failed. "In desperation," he said, "I finally had to supply somebody, so I told them to use Harry Reasoner. But I goofed. I won't do it again. I wasn't happy about it and the whole thing leaves me with discomfort." [75]

Salant's frank disclosure was just about the only action he could have taken under the circumstances, short of canceling the program at the last minute, which would have been quite expensive. While it averted at least part of the unpleasantness over the incident, it did serve to focus attention on another weakness of television—relations with sponsors. In some cases, the networks have been entirely too casual in their work with sponsors and the making of documentaries that happen to coincide with a particular sponsor's interests. An NBC show called "The Anatomy of Defense," for example, featured middle commercials exploiting General Electric's performance as a prime defense contractor. The Hughes Aircraft Company, which had a dominant role in the production of the Surveyor 1 satellite, sponsored a CBS documentary about it.

In defense of the networks, it may be said in such cases that they are doing no more—and probably not really as much—as the newspaper that puts out a special section for an advertiser and stuffs it with editorial matter about the company's interests. However, the ills that newspapers have developed over two centuries can scarcely justify the practices that have been adapted to television in a little more than two decades. Both the special puff section and the puff documentary are commercial ventures, undertaken primarily to benefit an advertiser, and are morally indefensible as journalism.

TV AND EDITORIAL OPINION

The electronic media, however, have done something more than merely pick up bad habits from their older contemporaries. As a primary force in the development of public service, the slow

and careful evolution of editorialization in broadcast journalism
provides the basis for hope and promise of better things to come.
For example, the editorial leadership of WMCA Radio in New
York as a champion of such causes as better housing and legislative reapportionment has been outstanding. Stimson Bullitt, operator of several Pacific Northwest television stations, did not
hesitate to broadcast editorial criticism of the conduct of the
Vietnam War when he thought it justified. And in scattered
places throughout the land, both radio and television stations
since 1960 have endorsed candidates for political office.

This is still just a trend and not a movement, for the
broadcast editorialist has many built-in handicaps that do not
affect his associates in print. While the FCC encourages the
broadcast of opinion in theory, it actually inhibits such work in
practice under the equal opportunities provision of Section 315
of the Communications Act. What this means, in effect, is that
time must be given to opposing opinions if a station takes an
editorial position that arouses controversy. Consequently, at regular intervals, any station with strong editorial opinions has no
choice but to provide time for rebuttal, whether the opposition is
qualified or not.

In recognition of this troublesome situation, Congress partially suspended Section 315 in the 1960 Presidential
campaign but only 62 stations broadcast editorials for or against
candidates. In the next national election, in 1962, the total rose
to 148 and it has been slowly increasing since despite the continual threat that someone will have to be granted equal time for
response. The FCC in effect has held to its position "that licen-
sees devote a reasonable percentage of their broadcasting time to
the discussion of public issues of interest in the community . . .
and that such programs be designed so that the public has a
reasonable opportunity to hear different opposing positions on
the public issues of interest and importance to the community." [76]

Without doubt there is wisdom in the continued
insistence on time for rebuttal in the electronic media, where the
power to influence public opinion may be more easily abused
than in the press. But what constitutes a "reasonable opportunity" is something that defies precise definition. This is the heart
of the controversy over Section 315 and it is not likely to be
settled very quickly. It does not excuse the sanctimonious TV
editorial, picked up from a spineless section of the press, that
comes out four-square against dope addicts, prostitution, and

84   crime, and celebrates the virtues of home, mother, and the flag. But it also scarcely justifies a position of neutrality in broadcast journalism toward the issues of the day. The licensing authority of the FCC is, of course, a constant threat to the freedom of expression of the electronic media in cases involving the interest of the government, but it should not be permitted to cow the broadcast journalist into abject silence when the public interest is involved.

Radio, which exerted a tremendous influence on American public opinion during the campaign for intervention preceding World War II, may well do as much as television—and perhaps even more—in developing the potential of the electronic media for broadcasting news and opinion. The FCC rule, which requires commonly owned AM and FM stations in large cities to offer different programs at least 50 percent of the broadcast day, places more pressure on radio to delve into public service journalism on both the fact-finding and opinion levels. In addition, despite the boredom of the "grind" all-day news programs of some of the pioneering radio stations, it has proved a ready source for the dissemination of news in capsule form. The steady training of radio news staffs and the efforts of editors to diversify the news "grind" have yielded some improvements, though not many. For as long as proprietors and advertisers are willing to support the "all news" station experiment, it is bound to be a laboratory for the trial of all manner of electronic innovations in public service journalism. The pity is that so few of the "all news" stations are trying to grasp the opportunity.

Neither radio nor television is consigned indefinitely to a diet of news and entertainment geared for the most part to the lowest intelligence. The strength of broadcast journalism is growing in the United States. The need for it is demonstrable. What remains to be supplied is the determination to broaden and deepen current practice, particularly among local stations in television, and provide the public at all times with the news, opinion, and relevant background it must have if self-government is to be anything more than a carefully nurtured delusion in the United States.

PART 2

OF MANNERS

AND MORALS:

TRUTH

OR

CONSEQUENCES

THE MEANING

7

OF THE NEWS

In two centuries of independent journalism, the art of divining the meaning of the news has been at once the most challenging and the most frustrating to seasoned professionals. William Bolitho once compared the process to "seeing through a brick wall," which has nothing whatever to do with the relatively easy business of differentiating between events and pseudo-events. It is, in essence, the separation of the truth from the news.

This is, by all odds, the least likely of all the journalist's practices to win him the admiration of a mass public in

88   these dangerous times, although it is one of the most essential. If he is right, he is, as the saying goes, only doing his job, and what is so remarkable about that? Yet, when he is wrong, his detractors take pains to point out for his benefit that scholars are still worrying about the meaning of events in the seventeenth century, with perhaps a bit of apprehension over what happened in ancient Greece, so why all the rush? As for those timid souls who invariably do not know or cannot say, and have access to no one who might be able to help them, they are not journalists. This may seem utterly unreasonable, but it is a recognized way of journalistic life and some actually enjoy doing it.

In those shrinking areas of primarily Western civilization where the journalist still is permitted reasonable liberty of movement and expression, his work necessarily involves him in difficulties that are almost unavoidable. The gathering and distribution of the news in a reasonably impartial and accurate manner are in themselves complicated processes, as a rule. It takes somewhat more than good will and academic honors, including the Ph.D., to cope with the basic reporting of the ordinary processes of life and self-government in an open society and the administration of justice, let alone such extraordinary events as civil disturbances, panics, disasters, national emergencies, and wars. When the journalist in addition is called upon to disseminate instant wisdom while great events are unfolding, he knows that he is often laying himself open to furious challenge, primarily from his own kind. Therefore, unless he is a syndicated columnist or another imposing personality who commands the unique trust of his proprietor and editor, the system under which he operates requires him to qualify, to hedge, and to dredge up un-persons as his sources.

There is, unfortunately, no way of hedging gracefully. Taking refuge in the cliches of American journalism, many back into the interpretation of events with an apologetic, "It is believed . . ." or, "It is said . . ." Others, seeking support from threadbare mystery, adopt the time-worn formula of crediting or blaming the un-person with such expressions as, "Sources here indicate . . ." or "In authoritative circles it is felt . . ." Finally, a few will take a bolder line by forthrightly stating the opinion of impartial observers, generally meaning themselves. Only a handful can be read with the admiring exclamation of a Ralph Waldo Emerson, upon perusing *The Times* of London in the mid-nineteenth century: "It is *so!*"

The ailment is endemic to the journalism of the

THE MEANING OF THE NEWS

space age, when the generalist may be rendered helpless by

space age, when the generalist may be rendered helpless by events he does not understand and the specialist may be too muscle-bound to move quickly enough to service the news media. In one sense, the American journalist superbly fulfills his function by quickly organizing and presenting the factual developments surrounding great events, from space shots to war, and from national elections to the civil rights crisis. As long as the news is hard and hot (shop talk terminology that makes sense to the journalist if no one else), he usually does his work with consummate professional skill. But where the news is based on rival propaganda claims, exaggeration for striking effect, or deliberate untruths put forward by eminent persons, groups, or nations, then the press is at a disadvantage because it has as yet devised no machinery for consistently dealing with such matters. Occasionally, a newspaper simply will refuse to publish mendacious material, regardless of the prestige of the source. In one instance, celebrated within the profession, a determined reporter crumpled a statement handed out by a distinguished American ambassador and told his colleagues in cold fury, "This is a goddam lie and I refuse to send it to my paper." But generally the rule that is followed, as stated in various forms by authorities from John Milton to John Knight, requires publication of truth and falsehood alike on the hopeful assumption that the public will recognize the former and turn its back on the latter.

 Aside from these ethical considerations, the news itself is often difficult for the average citizen to comprehend (and that sometimes includes the average editor). It is not unknown for sources to add to the complications by deliberately putting a construction on the news that is favorable to some particular interest, public or private. Moreover, the journalist himself may add to the process of distortion quite innocently with his selection of a fact to be featured and headlined in a complicated article. Or, he may omit comparatively dull material that is important but requires too much space or time to explain. The two-line quote, the brief angled description, the loaded word or phrase, and misplaced emphasis all can be dangerous. But the journalist who sins the most against the public interest is the one who writes or speaks to appease his superiors' set notions of what is going on or to conform to the policies of his organization.

WHEN THE ANGLE IS THE MESSAGE
There is no question that experienced journalists are generally able to handle these difficulties in their daily routine, but even

90   they cannot hope for perfection. As for the television newscasters, the demands of the clock and the lack of picture possibilities restrict their interpretive reporting in regular news programs. A minute or two is not sufficient to explain the meaning of such things as the struggle in China, the decline of NATO, the meaning of "black power," or the "death of God," and the machinery of Medicare. But it is in the news magazines, which generally do not receive sufficient credit for their good work, that the temptation is greatest to make the angle the message.

Sometimes the angling is harmless and even amusing. *Newsweek's* cover story on Pop Art, a passing fad of the mid-sixties, began with a breathless glorification of the trivial in this manner:

"It's a fad, it's a trend, it's a way of life. It's pop. It's a $5,000 Roy Lichtenstein painting of an underwater kiss . . . It's a $1 poster of Mandrake the Magician. . . . It's 30,000,000 viewers dialing 'Batman' on ABC every week. It's 'Superman' zooming around on the Broadway stage. . . . It's a Pow! Bam! commercial on TV. . . ." [1]

The historic cure for this kind of writing is to force the culprit to read it out loud before an audience of fellow-journalists and take the consequences. It has no dubious intent, nor can intelligent people take it very seriously. Usually, it can safely be ignored or, once read, forgotten.

But the same exaggerated technique, applied to a serious subject, can have a quite different result. As Great Britain was wrestling with a grave economic crisis, *Time* gaily head-lined a cover story: "London: The Swinging City." In glib and colorful language, the account reported as follows on the state of affairs in the capital of the United Kingdom:

"In a decade dominated by youth, London has burst into bloom. It swings; it is the scene . . . London is switched on. Ancient elegance and new opulence are all tangled up in a dazzling blur of op and pop. The city is alive with birds (girls) and beatles, buzzing with minicars and telly stars, pulsing with half a dozen separate veins of excitement. . . ." [2]

It was one thing for one of Britain's angry men, John Osborne, to equate the highest British values with down-and-out vaudeville in his play, "The Entertainer." It was quite another for *Time* to present the image of Britannia in a miniskirt, an aging and hefty grand dame miscast in the role of a go-go girl. The British were not pleased by the effusive, schoolgirl prose in the leading American news magazine.

Henry Fairlie, a British journalist who attracted an admiring following of American editors because of his talent for insult, responded with measured invective: "If I were given to conspiracy theories, I would believe that there is a plot to denigrate Britain by praising everything in it which is mindless and nasty, which is senseless and corrupting, which is meaningless and deadly." It was perfectly true, he agreed, that a small section of highly publicized British life was giving the impression that "Britain seems destined to sink giggling into the sea." [3] But he argued that it was a distorted picture. The headlines announcing the Wilson government's devaluation of the pound soon confirmed his astringent analysis. It was just about as accurate for *Time* and others to cast all Britain in the Beatle mold in the late 1960s as it had been for the Hearst newspapers and others in the 1930s to welcome John Bull into the Cliveden Set as an appeaser of Hitler.

When Prime Minister Wilson clapped on a wage–price freeze, it became difficult if not impossible for any responsible publication to sustain the happy and carefree image of a swinging Britain. American tourists, curtailing their own spending, found the British people anything but switched on. The fact was that the British were deeply concerned over the chronic economic problems of their great and ancient land; with money tight, and little hope of relief in sight, the average Britisher was as far from "the scene" as his quiet neighborhood pub. Of course, extreme fashions were being vended with promotional skill on Carnaby Street and a thin, bony teen-ager dubbed Twiggy caused American fashion houses to fall all over themselves to engage her services as a model. There were prostitutes in Soho and effeminate, long-haired boys in Piccadilly. Strip clubs were operating and most Britishers continued to be enthusiastic smalltime gamblers. But none of this was really news. As Herbert L. Matthews observed, those who knew Britain and the British could scarcely conclude that their national character had changed.[4]

The daily newspapers, of course, have their own troubles with both the glorification of trivia and the dangers of distortion in dealing with the news. While no one can know all the faults and virtues of 1,750 newspapers at any particular time, it is readily apparent from the most sketchy and unscientific examination that not all editors are bemused by great events and even fewer are patient with seemingly insoluble issues of overwhelming importance. In considering the future of disarmament negotiations, for example, some editors published a column by Holmes Alexander on the subject which began: "Geno-

92   cide is a horrid crime but sometimes it is tempting. What a better
       world we would have if we could put a merciful quietus on our
       Utopians, those persons who look for perfectability in man." [5]
       The *New York Daily News* could become apoplectic over the hurt
       feelings of girls who received obscene telephone calls from
       strange men, devoting a whole tabloid page of advice to the
       ladies (Point 1: "Hang up!") while summarizing the passage of
       Britain's drastic wage–price freeze law in one paragraph buried
       on Page 8. [6]

       Even in the prestige newspapers there can be awk-
       ward moments, such as Ambassador Edwin O. Reischauer's fare-
       well interview in Japan which the *Washington Post* headed,
       "Reischauer Backs U. S. Viet Policy," while *The New York Times*
       headline was, "Reischauer Critical of Viet Policy." The ambiva-
       lence of editorial thought, as evidenced in New York and Wash-
       ington, produced a certain amount of grim humor in a Senate
       Foreign Relations Committee hearing room when it was publicly
       displayed by Leonard Marks, director of USIA. [7]

       The hard-working wire services, always compara-
       tively easy targets because of the tremendous volume of news
       they handle under great pressure and tough competitive condi-
       tions, also have made their share of errors for various reasons.
       When James H. Meredith was shot by a roadside sniper in 1966
       outside Hernando, Miss., United Press International correctly
       reported he had been slightly wounded and taken to a hospital
       while the Associated Press through a reportorial misunderstand-
       ing filed a bulletin that he was dead. The erroneous information
       was retracted after a half-hour. [8]

       The failure of both American wire services and Reu-
       ters, the British agency, to file prompt reports on the death of
       United Nations' Secretary General Dag Hammarskjold in 1961
       was an even more striking instance of reportorial error. Newsmen
       at the airport at Ndola, Northern Rhodesia, (now Zambia) had
       mistaken a visiting British official, Lord Lansdowne, for Ham-
       marskjold and had bulletined his arrival on a Congo cease-fire
       mission at a time when he already was dead. As the agencies
       discovered to their chagrin hours later, the Hammarskjold plane
       had crashed before he had ever reached Ndola. It was sadly
       recorded in the AP Log thereafter that AP men should "never
       assume to be a fact what they did not know to be a fact." [9]

       Although the Hammarskjold case emphasizes the
       vulnerability of the independent news media to wire service

errors, this has given rise to few signs of concern either among journalists or the public at large. The disposition is to accept the occasional factual error as "just one of those things." Actually, it would be a mistake to assume that the relatively rare instances of bad factual reporting on major stories has hurt the credibility of the American news media. The evidence is all to the contrary. As those who were around at the time will recall, there was much more hue and cry over the "false armistice" report spread by Roy W. Howard of the UP at the end of World I, the premature and erroneous AP report of a life sentence for Bruno Richard Hauptmann in the Lindbergh baby murder in 1935, and the premature but accurate AP bulletin on the German surrender in 1945. The celebrated nature of each of these cases, and the controversy that surrounded them, points up the comparatively isolated nature of factual errors that mar the reporting of big news in the United States.

These are generally not the things that bother the journalist about his news organizations and their performance. Nor do many knowledgeable persons inside or outside the profession take stock any longer in the outdated criticism in Upton Sinclair's *Brass Check*. As Walter Lippmann once stated the position: "If the press is not so universally wicked, nor so deeply conspiring, as Mr. Sinclair would have us believe, it is very much more frail than the democratic theory has yet admitted. It is too frail to carry the whole burden of popular sovereignty, to supply spontaneously the truth which democrats hoped was inborn." [10]

There are several ways in which this frailty of the press manifests itself, one of the most important being the treatment of the substance of a controversial issue in the news columns. A. T. Steele, a distinguished correspondent in the Far East for many years and scarcely a devotee of the *Brass Check* school of criticism, has singled out the coverage of Communist China for close examination. He believes that the editorial orientation of a newspaper is a "factor of importance" in the handling of news about China. "Indeed," he contends, "it can be argued that the generally conservative attitude of the American public on China is more attributable to this influence than to any other. Newspapers of conservative outlook—and they are predominant in the smaller cities and towns—tend to give prominence to news and to background stories that favor their point of view. They also tend to use columnists of a predominantly conservative viewpoint. The total impression of China conveyed week

94   after week to the readers of such a newspaper is likely to be different from that conveyed by a militantly liberal or independent newspaper." [11]

The difficulty with such observations, scarcely a new theme in the discordant symphony of American journalism, is that there is no way of determining which interpretation is right except by awaiting the course of events. Nevertheless, the very wide disagreement in the press on the position of Red China, the Vietnam War, the turmoil in the Middle East and Africa, and some of the more controversial domestic policies of the Kennedy and Johnson administrations has caused many more questions to be raised about the handling of the news than mere factual accuracy, important though it may be. For editors may pledge at meetings of the American Society of Newspaper Editors to keep a complete separation between the news and editorial columns, but it takes a lot of doing. In any event, the public remains skeptical on the basis of the daily evidence. True, the good newspapers do try to keep their basic interests from affecting what they publish in the news columns on controversial topics. But their numbers are limited, and the less scrupulous keep on doing what comes naturally.

As for television, there is so little of substance that appears on the networks outside the regular news programs and their hasty expansion for big stories that every innovation is greeted with somewhat muted applause. Thus, a documentary on China, the Middle East, the Congo, Harlem, Watts, or Appalachia becomes a matter for enthusiastic comment. A long and perhaps wearisome documentary on foreign policy may be regarded as just short of a triumph. Where so skimpy a diet is generally available, a small addition makes the regular fare seem like a banquet—and perhaps sometimes it actually is. Yet, few can doubt that the burden of presenting the substance of the news, fairly or not, is still the job of the press.

THE "BACKGROUND" SYSTEM

Because this is so, what thoughtful journalists do and say about their own situation becomes something more than mere shop talk to a discerning public. It is a matter of record, documented at professional meetings and other public occasions too numerous to mention, that those not under compulsion to remain silent are becoming increasingly concerned, not only over slanted interpretations of the news but also over the manner in which such material is obtained. The "background" system, under which officials and others freely offer their views of the news in return for a pledge of anonymity, has proliferated beyond anything imagined by its founder, Ernest K. Lindley. The Lindley rule, which was supposed to produce nonattributable news, now is yielding almost everything else. The "background" session, originally intended to be a quiet private talk between an official and a reporter or small group of reporters at most, has become a weekly event in which large numbers of correspondents hear the Secretary of State or the Secretary of Defense state opinions, but not for attribution to them.

New terminology has been invented that makes for even greater confusion than the usual exercise in nonattributable obfuscation. President Johnson, for example, once talked to reporters on what he called an "off the record" basis, which even to a neophyte means the material is not for publication in any form. When someone expressed regret because the material was off the record, the President exclaimed in surprise, "But I didn't mean you couldn't print it!" Under the code propagated by Lindley, when he worked for *Newsweek,* the President had changed the rules from "off the record" to "use for background," but the reporters were surprised by the whole business.

In a similar manner, Secretary of State Dean Rusk invented a term called *deep background.* Instead of the regular background, which could be attributed to an informed source or some other unperson, he held his "deep background" conferences only for an elite list of "trusties," the British term for correspondents who are particularly in the government's confidence. In such sessions, the Secretary of State would cover extremely sensitive situations but only in return for the correspondents' pledge to use the material without any attribution whatever. This was, in its purest form, what James Reston once called "compulsory plagiarism"—the acceptance of an official view as one's own.

Such abuses of what was once recognized as a perfectly reasonable reportorial device have had serious consequences in Washington and elsewhere. Respected public figures of the stature of McGeorge Bundy and Bill Moyers have called for a more principled stand by both journalists and public officials in their dealings with each other. Some of the major correspondents for the better newspapers have refused publicly to use, for attribution to unnamed sources, the kind of material that should be labeled with the name and position of the official

96   issuing it. As Max Frankel of *The New York Times* once told a
State Department briefer at a White House background conference, "There's no reason why most of this can't be on the record.
The *Times* will not print this story unless it's on the record." It
went on the record.[12]

Alan L. Otten of the *Wall Street Journal* called reporters who attended background conferences the "prisoners of
the system." He pointed out that once they committed themselves, they were well-nigh obliged in most cases to rush into
print with the government's unattributed material because of
competitive pressures. Like so many others, he also ridiculed the
supposition that any source in Washington could be kept secret
for very long after putting out news or views that made major
headlines. Nor could it be successfully argued that the device in
all cases divested the government of responsibility for what was
said and done under the fragile seal of journalistic confidence.
Too often, such confidences proved to be a contradiction in
terms.[13]

Benjamin Bradlee, managing editor of the *Washington Post,* put it this way: "Take Secretary Rusk's Friday afternoon backgrounders. Who doesn't know that the stories in the
papers the next day came from Rusk? Every embassy in town
knows, and so does every government official and every
reporter—everybody except the reader." [14]

Despite the somewhat mild rebellion, it should not
be imagined that backgrounders are out of style or that the
practice is on the point of being abandoned. For both professional and personal reasons, some understanding must be maintained between the journalist and his sources that will make it
possible for them to talk together, even to argue, without guard-
ing the utterance of every word. Long before Lindley dreamed up
his World War II system of journalistic protocol, the better reporters and editors of the nation maintained such confidential
relationships with some of the most important figures in public
and private life. They still do. A negligible part of the many
private conversations between reporters and their sources
reaches print or the broadcast media in attributable form; under
a kind of unspoken gentleman's agreement, which varies from
source to source, the reporter generally knows what he can use
and what he must pass up for the time being. If all background
conferences were abandoned, it would not hurt the skilled

professional one bit because he has gained the trust of his
sources and they are scarcely likely to abandon a beneficial
two-way relationship. Under today's mass background conference routine, therefore, the only ones who really benefit are the
junior reporters without sources, the lazybones who would rather
pick an official's brains than use their own and do some independent work, and the numbskulls who worry more about the
exact form of a quotation than the meaning behind it.

There is no law in the land that requires any source
in government or out of it to trust all reporters; in fact, sheer
prudence would rule against it. True, formal announcements or
other news developments must be given to all the media representatives on a fair and equitable basis; however, when it comes
to discussing the meaning of the news, every source is going to
pick the reporters he trusts and who are likely to be of most
benefit to his interests. Those who are shut out will not like it. On
occasion, they may kick up such a fuss that they will break their
way into the circle of journalistic "trusties" on their own terms.
That kind of rivalry always has existed, regardless of the growth
of the system of handing out background information and opinion, and it is bound to continue.

Despite the abuses of the backgrounder, all available
evidence indicates that the use of material derived from it is
increasing steadily in the American news media and abroad. The
wire services and the newspaper syndicates are making available
a great deal more explanatory material today than they did a
decade or two ago and many more newspapers are using it. Such
interpretation may on occasion be faulty, windy, or difficult to
understand, but editors need not run it if they do not approve of
it. The imperfections of the system, in short, are not sufficient
reason for abandoning the effort to explain the news.

Of course, editors still exist in the United States who
conceive it to be their duty to play Horatius at the Bridge and
keep out of the paper all notions that run contrary to their own
pure beliefs. They are a hardy breed; although their numbers are
dwindling in the space age, they still have a considerable influence in the far right wing of American journalism. If there were
a far left with more than token access to print, undoubtedly the
situation would be the same but there have been no far left
publications of significance in the nation for many years. In
consequence, the "play it safe" school of journalism flourishes

98   primarily in places where editors either do not care about the
meaning of the news or do not dare arouse local opposition by
presenting views contrary to prevailing sentiment.

No one should underrate the extent of this kind of
neutralism in the American press. Mark Ethridge, one of the
most respected of American journalists, once observed, "I think
the responsibility of the newspapers . . . is to explain what the
issues in the world are. And yet . . . there seems to be a trend
for the newspapers to become only commercial enterprises.
There are exceptions, of course. But I think some publishers
think it doesn't make much difference what a paper says as long
as the balance sheet is right." [15] Much the same verdict has come
from reporters who have had the time to think about their
profession and its responsibilities. Gladwyn Hill of *The New
York Times,* for example, believes that too many newspapers pay
only "lip service" to the idea of depth and explanation and analysis. "Too much of what we print still has the starkness of radio
bulletins and the earmarks of shovel makeup. Editors have become more and more just railroaders of copy instead of people
able to exercise fine editorial judgment and gumption." [16] For
those who invariably demand exact documentation of such
charges, let them make their own examination of the average
American daily instead of holding up the leaders as examples.
They will find more evidence that Hill is right than wrong,
although they will also note that a certain amount of progress is
being made against the journalistic know-nothings.

INTERPRETING THE NEWS

It is extraordinary, on balance, for so many inside the profession
to adopt so critical an attitude on the problem of interpreting the
news. In view of the long and undistinguished record of the
American press in stubbornly facing down its critics, the movement toward greater realism in dealing with both the news and
its sources is healthy and heartening. The mere acceptance of
interpretation as a proper function of journalism, achieved after
so many years of argument, is not enough. The methods of
achieving it cannot be exactly defined; nor, for that matter, can
they ever be expected to attain perfection. No computer is ever
going to be invented that will emit acceptable explanations of the
news at the touch of a button. No magic formula can be devised
by science for clarifying, in one blind flash of revelation, the
meaning of the convulsive upheaval of peoples and values in

the world of the declining years of the twentieth century. Like the companion arts of exposition and illustration, interpretation has to be worked over, developed, and guarded against abuse and excess. Nor can it be assumed that everybody in journalism automatically inherits the right to interpret the news by the mere declaration that he is a journalist.

Conscientious editors rightly attempt to restrict the interpretation of events to those who have the ability, the background, and the experience to attempt it. Even so, there are many pitfalls before the qualified interpreter. What is true one day in a rapidly developing situation is not necessarily so the next, but often only the passage of time will cause the difference to be revealed. It took two years for the Communist hierarchy in Moscow to dump Nikita S. Khrushchev as premier after his failure to keep Russian rockets in Cuba aimed at the United States. It was even longer before the average American editor realized that there really was a split between the Soviet Union and Communist China. On September 30, 1965, the Western correspondent who flew into Djakarta could assume with reason that Indonesia was becoming allied with Peking; next day, with the failure of a Communist uprising, the opposite was the case although it was some time before the new position was clarified.

Writing of an equally difficult stage of the Vietnam War, Vermont Royster pointed out in the *Wall Street Journal:* "The deficiency is inherent in the situation. Therefore, there is probably no way to remedy it." [17] This is so often true that it is pointless to try to define precisely the position of interpretation between the function of reporting, on the one side, and editorializing, on the other. Many editors have tried to do it; some even believe the process can be compartmentalized. However, no set of compartments or definitions can dispose of difficulties that are, as Royster has said, inherent in the situation. For as all able journalists know, interpretation uses both the techniques of reporting and editorial writing without finally being either a report or an editorial. It is, by and large, an honest judgment of the meaning of events, suitably documented by whatever evidence of fact or opinion that can be marshaled to support it.

The identity of the writer or commentator, and the integrity of his organization, are the only guarantees that can be provided to the public of the good faith behind the interpretation. Usually, it is sufficient. The notion that the public will be satisfied if an analysis is labeled as such really means very little, for

100   the news columns are replete with unlabeled interpretation in the prestige press. More to be desired is the absence of any sign in the work of an analyst that he is an advocate of one cause or another, or that he has any special interest to advance. The same is true of his organization. There should be only one advocate—the editorialist. It is not seemly for the interpreter to try to persuade or to exhort; once he does, he sheds his assumption of disinterest which is all that separates him from the editorialist. The line between the two may be fuzzy, but few things in journalism can be laid out like a military table of organization. It is not a profession that uses either calipers, slide rules, or Geiger counters—and fundamentally that is the prime reason why it seldom makes much sense to those who do.

     Those who have their doubts about the press have been quick to seize on the confusion over this area which has been, particularly since World War II, a source of increasing strength for the better newspapers and continuing weakness for many of average and less than average competence. Within the government, one of the most formidable critics was Chester Bowles, a successful advertising executive who had by turn become Governor of Connecticut and twice Ambassador to India. While he was a special adviser to President Kennedy, he lamented the public's lack of knowledge on many basic issues, a deficiency for which he blamed the mass media most.

     "There are," he wrote, "many responsible communications outlets working passionately to give people a true picture of the world today. Yet, the inability of many of our newspapers, radio and television stations and magazines to communicate the true depth of today's problems is clearly apparent. The current tendency to dramatize non-essentials, to oversimplify complex questions, and to imply U. S. impotence one day and omnipotence the next has helped foster a national mood of confusion and frustration." [18]

     Such attitudes naturally encouraged some of the rivals of the daily newspaper, particularly the journals that aspired to give a more acceptable meaning to the news than the press. As a group, they had long since adopted an adversary philosophy. Marya Mannes, a critic for *The Reporter* magazine, spoke for example of the "tragedy" of the "decline of public confidence in the daily press" and warned that the public would turn to television for something better. However, despite Miss Mannes's prophecy, there has been no perceptible mass move-

ment to follow the intellectual leadership offered by either television or the magazines in the United States.

THE TEST: CIVIL RIGHTS

The truth is that no element of the news media in the United
States has any ground for complacency today. All are under
critical scrutiny by informed public opinion as never before—
some more than others. If there is a single continuing issue that
tests the public's belief in its news and communications system,
it is by all odds the handling of the civil rights crisis. While there
have been instances of superb work by all sections of the news
media on this story in every part of the nation, the record on the
whole is not one that satisfies most thoughtful journalists. More
heat may be generated by the lively debate over free press and
fair trial, but bench and bar are well able to fend for themselves
in the rough and tumble of the democratic arena. This is not
necessarily so as far as the protagonists in the turbulence over
civil rights are concerned. Their leaders, by and large, do not
command the kind of respectful attention from the news media
that is invariably accorded the American Bar Association and its
distinguished spokesmen. The fair reporting of the civil rights
story, in all its confusing aspects, depends in effect on the good
faith of the news media as a whole.

Ralph McGill, the publisher of the *Atlanta Constitution*, posed one of the most disturbing aspects of the problem
when he described the failure of the South to adjust to the
realities of desegregation after the 1954 school decision by the
United States Supreme Court. "I must enter a *mea culpa* plea for
my own profession of journalism and that of local television and
radio," he wrote. "Some of the failures of our regional press and
other media to offer truthful, honest leadership have been tragic
and contemptible in spirit and in the encouragement of extremists to violent defiance of the law. The fact that the business
communities, the chambers of commerce and the professions
also share in this guilt does not reduce journalism's accusing
conscience." [19]

Some of the editors and publishers in the South
have refused to let anything prevent them from telling the truth
about noncompliance with the law in all its unlovely aspects.
Some reporters, photographers, and newscasters of impeccable
Southern lineage have repeatedly exposed themselves to mob
violence in order to cover the news of their own and neighboring

102 communities. Yet, there is no doubt that in the beginning—and to some extent even today—many Southern newspapers have quailed before the rebellious majorities in their communities and the threat of terrorism. They have not reported violence against Negroes and white integrationists, including burnings of Negro churches, or deliberately played them down. Their editorial pages have condoned resistance to the law, even when it meant the endorsement of crimes up to and including murder. The lawlessness and violence of Negro gangs in the metropolitan centers of the land, particularly the North, has been big news to them. But what has happened at home has been something else again.

Except where a Southern newspaper has been strong enough to withstand violence and boycotts of advertising and circulation, the journalists of principle and courage have often had to face difficult times. The losses of the *Arkansas Gazette*, which gave such strong support to federal intervention in the 1957 Little Rock school integration crisis, ran into the millions in the years thereafter. Its Pulitzer Prize-winning editor, Harry S. Ashmore, deliberately decided to leave the paper in order to help it to recover. Long afterward, he wrote:

"I think I can say that I enjoyed the best of the old tradition of journalism. This required that the hazards and the rewards be rooted in a deep sense of responsibility shared by those who made policy. A considerable degree of financial risk and personal discomfort was inherent in the assumption that the newspaper could survive its readers' wrath if it maintained the community's respect. Circulation (and advertising) were important, but they were regarded as a by-product of sound policy, not a determinant. I can't say that we always lived up to the ideal; I can say that on the *Gazette* it was never abandoned.

"I do not believe this tradition has effectively survived the corporate trend among newspapers, with its inevitable diffusion of responsibility. I do not think it ever existed in broadcast journalism which, despite its showcase display, is no more than a secondary adjunct to a lucrative business dominated by the mores of advertising and show business." [20]

Despite Ashmore's gloomy conclusion, there are still resolute journalists in the South who uphold the tradition of personal responsibility—Ralph McGill and Eugene Patterson on the *Atlanta Constitution*, Barry Bingham and Norman Isaacs on the *Louisville Times* and *Courier-Journal*, Hodding Carter on the

Greenville (Miss.) *Delta Democrat-Times,* J. O. Emmerich on
the *McComb* (Miss.) *Enterprise-Journal,* and others in a number
of trouble centers. By their example, they have caused a substantial part of the press in the South to lift its standards in handling
the news of America's great social crisis.

   It is true that there is still little encouragement that
can be given to the smaller and weaker papers in segregationist
centers. Ira B. Harkey, Jr., a symbol of defiance in Mississippi,
had to sell his *Pascagoula Chronicle* and turn to teaching journalism. Hazel Brannon Smith, who made her weekly *Lexington
Advertiser* respected everywhere except in Mississippi, led a precarious existence for years. Consequently, relatively few cared to
follow her forthright example.

   Although a segregation-minded populace continues
to buy complying newspapers in the deep South and patronizes
their advertisers, this scarcely implies respect for the press. In a
Germany where might made right, Bismarck also was able to
force newspapers to do his bidding but he referred to them
contemptuously as the "reptile press," crawling on its belly before him. Naturally, the average Southern editor and publisher
would consider such terminology a mortal insult, especially in
the deep South where segregation remains an article of personal
faith for the majority. But even a community of the most violent
segregationists can measure the stature of a newspaper that
prints only what its readers want to see and voices only editorial
sentiments that can be applauded by the crudest and most vi-
cious elements. It is not an image that registers on the poll-
taker's pad, but it is there, nevertheless, for all to see.

   It is difficult to determine how much the prevailing
attitude of the segregationist Southern press has had to do with
the almost instinctive mistrust of the news media in the Northern and Western ghettos where Negroes periodically have broken
into savage rioting. Certainly, any reporter or photographer assigned to a ghetto by a Northern newspaper has learned very
quickly at firsthand of the mistrust, sometimes even the hate, of
the populace. And this sometimes is true even of staff members
of newspapers that have, on the whole, taken a sympathetic
attitude toward the civil rights movement and given it thorough
coverage. The Negro bent on violence in the ghetto does not
differentiate between a friendly press and segregationist newspapers; his suspicions, unfortunately, cover both the best and the
worst.

104   The feeling apparently is much the same as that inspired in the deep South by "outsiders" from the Northern press, the networks, and the national magazines.[21] Some Northern editors have hired Negro reporters to cover the turmoil in the ghetto on the not unreasonable assumption that they would be safer from harm than their white colleagues. But the scheme has not worked too well. For one reason, the ghetto often has been just as cruel to Negro reporters as to white ones. For another, no Negro reporter of standing will consent for very long to cover only events affecting Negroes. And finally, even today, there are very few Negro reporters in an overwhelmingly white profession.

Rightly or wrongly, with the rise of civil rights violence across the land, the news media have often been as unwelcome in the ghetto as the police and other elements of the Establishment. This was particularly true in the Newark and Detroit riots of 1967. Reporters never know when they are likely to be jumped upon. Photographers with still or television cameras cannot be sure of their own safety, let alone their equipment's. The relatively good record of most of the news media in covering disturbances does not seem to count for much. Nor have the excellent and often sympathetic documentaries about the civil rights movement on television made any significant impression on the militancy of the Negro masses. In effect, the lack of belief attached to the segregationist press in the deep South has also encompassed a considerable part of the press elsewhere among the ghetto-dwellers of the land. The difference in the motivation of the more liberal elements of the press has not loosened the growth of a belief among the extremists, white and Negro, that the news media constitute a symbol against which an effective protest may be registered.

As might be expected, the stormy young advocates of "Black Power," H. Rap Brown and Stokely Carmichael, have been in the forefront of those who attack every generous effort of the liberal press, as well as the backlash of the segregationist papers. Carmichael did not differentiate between friend and foe, saying: "It sees to me that Black Power would not cause this disturbance unless the white press wanted it to . . . They're the ones who have maliciously distorted it."[22] The attitude of the more conservative Henry Lee Moon, public relations director of the National Association for the Advancement of Colored People, has been even more disturbing. He argued that the Negro can expect commitment only from the Negro press—something the Negro "cannot expect to get from even the most sympathetic and

liberal white media." [23] No journalist of consequence is likely to
agree with Moon, but that is not the point; the willingness of
responsible Negro conservatives to believe such nonsense is what
makes the problem so difficult. For the Negro press by itself can
scarcely shoulder the whole burden of communicating with more
than 22 million Negroes in the United States. And if communication cannot be maintained between the powerful forces that have
been called "two nations" existing in the same place, then a deep
and lasting turmoil can scarcely be averted.

Thus, the frailty of the press that so concerned Walter Lippmann is very much in evidence in the civil rights issue. It
is, in fact, no exaggeration to say that the press has been made a
part of the issue. While accepting some of the failures in the
South and the neglect of dangerous conditions in a number of
cities elsewhere until they exploded into rioting, most working
journalists do feel that they have done a decent and considerate
job on the whole in telling the civil rights story. Outside the deep
South, the record generally sustains them. But no one can persuade the militant Negro that this is so. He does not believe it. To
him, the news means something entirely different than it does to
the press he calls "white" because he will not acknowledge it as
his own.

This state of mind, and the civil disorder it breeds,
has shaken some of the complacency out of the news media and,
to some extent, forced its more progressive elements to re-
examine their methods. What mob coverage does to inflame
rioters to even greater acts of looting and sabotage will be examined later in this book, together with the general problem of
controlling herd journalism.[24] But that is far from being the
whole problem. As Ben Gilbert of the *Washington Post* put it,
"Government officials, Riot Commission members and private do-
good organizations think the media are doing a lousy job." [24]

NEEDED: A NEW APPROACH

Historically, journalism is not a profession that is founded on
starry-eyed optimism. It glorifies its Cassandras and ridicules its
Pollyannas. It scorns the uplifter as much as it suspects the
reformer, having had grievous experience with both in the course
of its daily dealings with human affairs. As an echo to events, it
cries woe, knowing full well that such an automatic reflex action
has a better chance of being right than wrong. The journalist
who predicted 19 times at the opening of League of Nations
meetings that this one would be its last had the dubious satisfac-

106   tion of seeing events bear him out at the 20th session. Such a philosophy glorifies the prophet of doom as he and his followers are being consumed by the flames they themselves have kindled.

Clearly, the journalist needs a different approach to the reporting of a controversy such as civil rights that goes to the very roots of national existence. As the position was stated by George Hunt, managing editor of *Life,* it is no longer sufficient to practice "blind adherence to news for news's sake, and playing it for all it's worth." Such laissez-faire philosophy is out of date. Nor can it be propped up by some new gimmick in presenting the news, or a tricky method of writing interpretation to get more people to read it. What is required is a greater degree of editorial commitment—the decision, for example, of editors in Rochester, N. Y., to go out and look for signs of progress in civil rights as well as the daily yield of bad news; the publication, as a further example, of an enormous volume of material on crisis areas by editors in Los Angeles, Philadelphia, Kansas City, St. Louis, Hartford, and other cities. The telling of the Story of the City is the No. 1 assignment in American journalism today.

What this means, in short, is that the more progressive journalists at length have realized that there are both civic and national responsibilities that come ahead of their normal professional duties. Merely telling and printing the news is not enough; nor is it sufficient to keep chanting a litany about interpreting the news without finding better people, better ways, more space, and more time to do it before a crisis makes it imperative. The journalist is no longer justified in wrapping himself in the guise of a philosophical anarchist and pretending that he is someone set apart with a mission beyond that of ordinary men. For the fact is that he no longer is a mere news gatherer; often, in the act of gathering news, he makes it and even influences the course of events. Surely, the time has come for him to recognize it. He is not part of a gigantic shadow play; he is one of the principal actors, and what he says and does can have a substantial influence on its outcome. He must face up to his responsibilities as a good citizen first, a good journalist second.

Whether the journalist likes it or not, this is the standard by which the public is judging him and will continue to judge him and his works. His are the responsibilities of the innovator and leader, not merely of the critic, and he must exercise all of them if he is to continue to exert his right to give meaning to the news.

THE

8

CREDIBILITY GAP

W ashington takes itself very seriously, as befits a great world capital. It does not yet rank with the Athens of Pericles or the Rome of the Caesars, the London of Elizabeth (the *other* Elizabeth, of course), or Napoleonic Paris, but its aspirations and its hopes are high. Moreover, nobody could possibly mistake it for Fun City. This being so, nothing annoys Washington more than the cloud of doubt that swirls so often over its weightiest pronouncements.

To those in authority, ruling over the mightiest concentration of wealth and power yet assembled on earth, it is

108   often annoying to be submitted to a daily test of their good
intentions, common to most practicing democratic states, and
downright galling when they are not believed. Such resentment
is only human. But it does nothing to settle the equally human
doubt on the other side, which is exploited with blunderbuss
profundity by the news media.

Not since the unhappy depression era, when Herbert Hoover solemnly assured the nation from the White House
that prosperity was just around the corner and the Wall Street
apple sellers jeered, has there been quite as poisonous an atmosphere in the nation's capital. The charge of news management,
which was common during the Eisenhower and Kennedy administrations, has been amplified by the credibility gap attributed
to the Johnson administration. And perfectly serious government officials and correspondents feel they have good reason to
discuss whether an official lie is permissible or impermissible.
When the innocent bystander brings up the alternative of telling
the truth, he is likely to be withered by the scorn of his sophisticated associates who invariably ask the age-old question: "What
is truth?"

RATIONING THE TRUTH
From Machiavelli to John Foster Dulles and from Metternich to
Dean Rusk, truth by whatever definition has cropped up at unexpected times to serve as an embarrassment to policies of national
and international importance. In this area, tension between a
free press and a freely elected government has always been the
greatest, and rightfully so. Here, too, such factors as national
morality, a strong consideration among American statesmen,
inevitably have clashed with the hard facts of national security.
No one has ever been able to devise a system under which truth
can be accommodated at all times without peril to the nation.
But it is also evident that no one has ever been able to perfect a
guarantee that truth will not be withheld, distorted, or entirely
suppressed as a convenience to the government. Nor can the
possibility for human error be overlooked in this highly sensitive
field.

The manner in which a tragic collision of military
aircraft in 1966 was made public illustrates some of the risks for
both government and the news media. Two test pilots were killed
in the accident on June 8 when a $500 million experimental

bomber, the XB70, and an F-104 fighter crashed and burned on the Mojave Desert near Barstow, California.

"Joe Walker and Major Cross gave their lives in advancing science and technology," President Johnson said in a statement that was prepared for him. "Their deaths remind us how dependent we are on men of exceptional ability in the development of new vehicles in flight. They died while training for demanding assignments in a new field of major national interest—research and supersonic transport flight."

Two days later, after questioning Air Force officials behind closed doors, Representative George H. Mahon of Texas, chairman of the House Appropriations Committee, told a different story. "The formation was formed," he said, "in order that photographs could be taken for the use of the General Electric Company, which manufactured the engines of the five aircraft (that participated in the flight). The loss of these men, and an aircraft in which more than $500 million has been invested by the taxpayers, while accommodating the public relations department of a private company, is indefensible." [25]

Despite Representative Mahon's indignation, little more was heard of that particular incident in Washington. Seemingly, the news media had grown accustomed to the use of the high office of the Presidency, as well as other leading government offices, for statements that could not always be taken at face value. It was, as one leading correspondent remarked wearily, a "part of the business." As he explained it, "We know that the government is always trying to put its best foot forward. It's just that a little more of it is being done in this particular administration." [26]

Not long afterward it became known that President Johnson had secretly authorized high priority assignment of materials for the manufacture of a new superjet. This was the controversial 300-passenger, 300-foot-long aircraft that was expected to travel 1,800 miles an hour and compete with similar planes under construction in the Soviet Union and, jointly, in Britain and France. As in the case of the Mojave Desert air crash, no security was involved in the superjet affair. The published explanations of the Presidential decision were that he wanted to avoid debate over the superjet and what was likely to be the diversion of perhaps as much as $5 billion from the nation's more pressing needs. [27]

110   There were other nonsecurity incidents that helped establish the basic pattern for the news media in Washington during the Johnson regime. The President was particularly sensitive to advance announcements of his appointments and his plans; accordingly, he sometimes would deliberately change them after a leak. Once, when he had read of published reports of a speech he intended to deliver before the 20th anniversary celebration of the United Nations at San Francisco, he called in the Secretary of State and had him eliminate the key passage—a plan to solve the United Nations financial crisis of that era.[28]

When the President was hospitalized in the fall of 1965, he announced that his "only trouble" was a diseased gall bladder, which was to be removed; however, it later turned out that a kidney stone was also removed and another remained in his left kidney. On July 27, 1965, the President assured the press that he had not begun to consider a replacement for Justice Arthur J. Goldberg, who had been named to the United Nations after the death of Ambassador Adlai E. Stevenson; next day, he announced the appointment of Abe Fortas to the Supreme Court. It is no wonder, in view of these and other incidents, that Ambassador Goldberg unguardedly spoke of a "crisis of confidence" a few months later when he sought to explain why Washington had disclosed what it called a "peace feeler" from Hanoi. While he argued that the feeling was justified, he conceded, "We have a great problem maintaining our credibility with our own people." [29]

Thus, the expression, "credibility gap," like its forerunner, "news management," became a part of the American idiom. The public impression was that some new and devious device had been added to the twists and turns of Washington life. That was not the case. All Presidents and most Secretaries of State have managed the news, some skillfully and others poorly, from the time that President Washington handed his undelivered Farewell Address to Claypool's *Daily American Advertiser*. More often than not, their credibility has been bitterly challenged, justifiably or not.

Within the last four generations alone, there are numerous instances that demonstrate the nature of the problem and its growth on the body politic. In the cases of three Presidents—Cleveland, Wilson, and Franklin D. Roosevelt—serious illnesses were deliberately concealed from the public. President Theodore Roosevelt consigned correspondents who offended him

to his mythical "Ananias Club" and once threatened to jail an
editor, Joseph Pulitzer, for opposing the acquisition of the Pan-
ama Canal.[30] The saintly Woodrow Wilson, who preached the
cause of "open covenants openly arrived at," never did anything
of substance to carry it out. After the death of Warren Gamaliel
Harding, the first (and until now the last) editor-President, the
press helped expose the Teapot Dome oil lease scandal, as a
result of which his Secretary of the Interior, Albert B. Fall, was
convicted of accepting a $100,000 bribe and sent to prison.

Franklin D. Roosevelt, who liked to humble nagging
reporters with ridicule, had no luck in keeping political secrets.
One of the most sensational, the agreement to give the Soviet
Union three votes at the United Nations in order to insure its
adherence, was revealed by Bert Andrews of the *New York Herald Tribune*. However, FDR's great personal secret was not disclosed until many years after his death. Then, Jonathan Daniels,
his last press secretary, wrote of the President's friendship for
more than four decades for a one-time secretary of Mrs. Roosevelt, Lucy Page Mercer, later Mrs. Winthrop Rutherford. It was
Daniels who disclosed that Mrs. Rutherford had been with FDR
at Warm Springs, Ga., on April 12, 1945, the day he died, something that had not been publicly acknowledged at the time nor
for nearly a generation thereafter.[31]

THE SECURITY ISSUE

The use of the security issue to keep the press from disclosing
military secrets, a by-product of every war, was intensified under
Presidents Wilson and Franklin D. Roosevelt during two World
Wars. However, the Creel Committee's propaganda machine in
World War I aroused the justifiable suspicion even then that not
all military information was held secret for security purposes.
Later, at the Versailles Peace Conference, such reporters as Herbert Bayard Swope of the *New York World* and Fred Ferguson of
UP had a field day with exclusive publications of official texts
and other critical material that had been considered secret. However, in World War II, Byron Price's voluntary press censorship
office did a much better job. It was tragic that the masterful work
of keeping the secret of the atomic bomb from the American and
allied publics could not prevent spies from passing it on to the
Soviet Union.[32]

Under the Atomic Energy Act, for the first time in
the history of the nation during an era that was technically

112   peaceful, the news media came under a legal system that involved both advance censorship and prior restraint of publication or broadcast. Thus, despite the specification of the First Amendment that Congress shall make no law affecting the freedom of the press, the most stringent regulations took effect to impose atomic secrecy. Anything of a sensitive nature bearing on nuclear science had to be cleared for publication by the Atomic Energy Commission, and still does. Undoubtedly, the law helps to preserve a necessary amount of atomic secrecy, but it also increases the difficulty of detecting the difference between the safeguarding of genuine security information and the suppression of nonsecurity material that would embarrass the government if published.

In many critical cases, it is the fixed purpose and even the duty of the government to conceal information in the national interest, which is often diametrically opposed to the purpose of the news media. The trouble is, as always, to define what constitutes national security, and on this no agreement appears possible. It is, by common consent, left to the good sense of those involved, which really satisfies nobody.

After all, there are many in government who neither understand the function of the news media nor care to risk talking with correspondents even when they are authorized to do so. Moreover, there are journalists around who are unqualified to deal with sensitive and intricate matters involving the national interest. For example, a general, exasperated by a small daily that insisted on sending a blundering 21-year-old reporter to an air base at odd times, once demanded of a nationally syndicated columnist, "What do you expect me to do with a fellow like that?" The columnist replied laconically, "Shoot him."

Thus the issue between the government and the news media boils down to a rough understanding among the more knowledgeable and sophisticated reporters and those in government who can fathom their point of view. Basically, the government's right to classify information bearing on national security cannot be challenged successfully. Nor can the news media be denied the right to disclose errors in classification if reporters can find out about them. However deplorable it may seem to some in this connection, news management is a legitimate and often a necessary part of the orderly processes of government. The belief that news springs from some mysteriously pure and undefiled source, and can be caught in its pristine

state by a knightly journalist, is a myth right out of a journalistic
Camelot.

Representative John Moss, the California Democrat who devoted much of his career to a campaign for greater freedom of information, made the point in this manner: "I don't regard 'news management' as any great problem. News management exists in government at all levels; it exists in every private business. Any newsworthy personality attempts to manage news by either timing releases or by playing up the activities which reflect most favorably on him or on his organization. The problem is not management of the news—it's the availability of the facts regarding the activities of government and of those who are charged with the responsibilities of running the government." [33]

Regardless of what the system is called, its intent is to channel the news in Washington when it is possible to do so. While there is no Ministry for Information and Propaganda as such in the United States (and there would be an uproar if an attempt were made to create one), the function has always existed. By the inexorable political law that power gravitates to the President and the White House, the loose organization of government information policies generally rests in the White House Press Secretary's office. When there are good ones who have the unquestioned support of the President and the ability to speak and act for him in an emergency, few complaints are generally heard about news management because the job is done so well. This was particularly true of James C. Hagerty, President Eisenhower's press spokesman, who exercised far more authority than any other occupant of the office in recent times. While Hagerty may not have handled or cleared every major announcement of the government, he was always the one man whose judgment in the field was indispensable—and the reporters knew it and trusted him.

In the Kennedy administration, the situation was different. President Kennedy was his own information officer, in the broadest sense, and had more success at it than any President of this century with the exception of Franklin D. Roosevelt. While Pierre Salinger ran the White House press office and held weekly meetings of the information chiefs in other leading government offices, he did not have the same access to his chief as Hagerty did in the Eisenhower administration. It would have been unthinkable for Kennedy to permit his press secretary to exercise even a minuscule part of the Presidential power.

114 President Johnson played it both ways. With such press secretaries as George Reedy and George Christian, the President decided what could be said and how it would be said in considerable detail. But during the relatively brief time when the mercurial Bill D. Moyers ran the White House press office before becoming the publisher of *Newsday*, the President let him work in the free-wheeling Hagerty manner. Finally, because the President never was comfortable with the news media and disliked the formal news conference, he let a lot of the essential backgrounding for the correspondents come out of the Thursday afternoon background soirees at the Pentagon with Secretary McNamara until his departure and the Friday afternoon backgrounders at the State Department with Secretary Rusk. But for as long as the sessions lasted, the President knew what was going on; at the White House, some suspected that he even listened in at the regular twice-a-day press secretary's routine briefings. His extreme sensitivity to the handling of the news about himself, his family, and his office was often a major problem for the correspondents—and for the administration.

But regardless of differences between Presidents and press officers, the news channels of government in Washington have become reasonably well defined over the years. When the White House press secretary is given sufficient authority by the President, all chief information officers of major government departments—and sometimes their superiors as well—check at the No. 1 press office if they are in doubt on either procedure or substance. But they do not have to consult on every point any more than a correspondent has to ask about his newspaper's policy if he is a diligent reader of the editorial page. Government departmental officials have their guidelines. They also are well aware that all major announcements come from the White House, unless there are political reasons for letting them originate elsewhere. This is the way the system is supposed to operate; but, like all systems, it is only as good as the people who run it.

Ever since World War II, the trend toward the centralization of information has been characteristic of the policies of the federal government under both Democratic and Republican administrations. With the coming of the atomic age, and the threat of widespread destruction through misunderstanding or miscalculation in the Cold War, every President has been deeply concerned with information policy. In the peculiar language of

Washington, the objective has been to have the American gov-   115
ernment "speak with one voice," an impossible dream in a diverse democratic society.

NEWS AND THE PENTAGON

Nevertheless, beginning with President Truman, a series of White
House executive orders sought in effect to regulate what the news
media could publish in sensitive areas. The Truman Executive
Order No. 10290 laid down strict standards for handling security
data, taking what amounted to a censorious attitude toward a
restless and dissatisfied press. It authorized heads of agencies to
appoint classification officers to label documents "Top Secret,"
"Secret," "Confidential," or "Restricted." When editors set up an
outcry, President Truman sternly told them, "This is your country,
too." [34]

Coincidentally, the National Security Act of 1947
set up a new governmental intelligence system dominated by the
Central Intelligence Agency which soon would be spending several billion dollars a year and employing 200,000 persons. Its
first director, Allen W. Dulles, announced that it had "a more
influential position in our government than Intelligence enjoys
in any other government of the world." [35] Journalists soon labeled it the "Invisible Government" and took some satisfaction in
exposing its frailties, whatever the cost.[36]

When the Truman directive was modified by President Eisenhower's Executive Order No. 10501, the restraining
intent on the news media remained as an irritant. It was not an
effective deterrent, as became evident in due course. At one time,
Defense Secretary Charles E. Wilson ordered Pentagon officials
to give information only on work that would make a "construc-
tive contribution" to the mission of the Armed Forces.[37] The rule
was impractical and was never obeyed.

Curiously, one of the factors that slowed the drift
toward a centralized information system was the resistance of
competing elements within the government itself to a limitation
on their ability to publicize themselves, particularly at budget-
making time. This was illustrated in dramatic fashion at the
Pentagon, where the separate military services quickly realized
that they could lose their identity and much of their bargaining
power in the great military-industrial complex if they could not
impress their accomplishments on informed public opinion and
on Congress.

116   The famous "Revolt of the Admirals" in 1948 was a
last-ditch Navy operation against the Air Force's overblown
claims for the B-36 bomber. At a later stage, General Maxwell D.
Taylor's retirement from the Army gave him a chance to write
"The Uncertain Trumpet," a warning against all-out reliance on
air power and a plea for the buildup of the Army for limited
war.[38]

          There was so much of this interservice warfare,
carried on openly through Congressional and other nonmilitary
sources as well as covertly, that Defense Secretary Forrestal
finally took drastic action. On March 17, 1949 he abolished the
separate information offices of the military services. Each was
ordered instead to supply 25 officers for a single Defense Department information service. But, as it turned out, officers who had
given their lives in the service of the Army, Navy, Marines, and
Air Force could not shift their loyalties overnight and most of
them merely sat out their time in the Defense Department's
news operation. When the Korean War began a little more than a
year later, the unification of information was abandoned for the
time being.

          Toward the end of the Truman administration,
Thomas K. Finletter, Secretary of the Air Force, revived the offensive against the military information machine under his jurisdic-
tion. Reacting angrily to Congressional criticism of "Pentagon
press agentry," he abolished the Air Force Public Information
Office. Only 15 officers were retained at headquarters to do what
little they could to service the news media; none, theoretically, remained at wing and base level in the field. However, what actually happened was that the whole operation went underground,
with PIOs popping up in strange guises—even as a Chaplain in
one instance.

          With a change in administration, Air Force informa-
tion was quickly revived in a different form—a combined external, internal, community relations and historical program. The
Army copied it, but the Navy stayed with its own PIO system.
Together, the services maintained a total of several thousand
military and civilian operatives around the globe as information
specialists of various kinds. As the Defense Department budget
soared past $70 billion a year during the Vietnam War, it was
evident enough to official Washington that the services were
scarcely likely to give up their independent efforts to impress
Congress and the public.[39]

Whenever the Defense Department tried to curb the   **117**
information output at the Pentagon, the services protested vi-
olently. In 1958, for example, they made such an impression on
the House Government Operations Committee that it reported as
follows on the efforts of the Defense Department to limit their
publicity: "It has become apparent that tighter controls are being
used for greater manipulation of information—for the management of news—on the Defense Department level. Under the
President's new orders for still further centralization and control, it appears that information officers of the various services
may be relegated to the status of a ventriloquist's dummy on the
knee of a Defense Department publicity man. The vast military
establishment, thus, would speak with one voice—and that the
voice of a politically appointed propaganda expert."

The House committee might have spared itself the
expression of concern over "those press agents at the Pentagon,"
as they often were called, Murray Snyder, who then was serving
as Assistant Secretary of Defense for Public Affairs, had his
troubles trying to keep the information offices of the separate
services in line. Each actively continued to push its own interests, with the Defense Department information office becoming
almost an appendage. Compared with the dozen or so officials
assigned to information work at the State Department and even
fewer in other major departments of government, the military
propaganda machine was staggering in size, diversity, and
power.

When there was a military crisis or an investigation,
the Defense Department press room on the second floor of the
Pentagon attracted several score reporters from the principal
news media represented in Washington. But on routine days, no
more than a score of regulars, sometimes fewer, covered the very
heart of the American military-industrial complex with its
30,000 people, larger than a half-dozen state capitals. Consequently, the Pentagon's version of its own news—except in a
state of crisis—often had a pretty good chance of acceptance in
the bulk of the news media.

The form that the military publicity machine took
under Eisenhower has not changed substantially since. In the
Defense Department and each of the three separate military
services, there are public information offices to handle spot news
or inquiries that develop daily from the news media. In addition,
there are special television departments to service networks and

118 local stations, departments for the promotion of movies, books, and magazine articles about the military, speakers' bureaus with access to a wide range of talent and scheduling organizations, a well-defined but not always effective troop indoctrination program, and well-staffed bureaus for maintaining persuasive liaison with Congress.

The public has heard little of these activities, and probably could care less, the military being the powerful influence that it is in the nation's life today. But to those who are familiar with the structure of authority in Washington, the strength of military public relations is a factor worth the closest scrutiny in the operations of government. In these quarters, it is not forgotten that President Eisenhower, in his farewell to public office, drew attention to the influence of the military in the information and legislative liaison fields with this warning:

"In the councils of government we must guard against the acquisition of unwarranted influence . . . by the military-industrial complex. The potential for the disastrous rise of misplaced power exists and will persist. We must never let the weight of this combination endanger our liberties or our democratic processes." [40]

TRIAL AND ERROR

During the Eisenhower years, both the virtues and the well-nigh tragic drawbacks of the government's information network and its relationship with the news media were illustrated in two important instances in which national security was directly involved. In one case, the news media cooperated wholeheartedly with resultant national benefit; in the other, the system was severely shaken by the hammer blows of suspicion and the superior tactical position of the Soviet Union, which combined to create a national diplomatic disaster.

General Eisenhower's six-day trip to the Korean battlefront in the late fall of 1952, as President-elect, was the basis for the felicitous cooperation of the news media with the government. The voluntary self-censorship that had worked so well in World War II was again invoked so that the General would be able to take the first long step toward bringing peace to Korea, as he had pledged in his campaign. Hundreds of journalists of many nationalities could not help but know of the visit, for Seoul was decked with banners in honor of the President-elect. Yet, not a word was published or broadcast in the American news media,

and those of the other United Nations members with troops in
Korea, until General Eisenhower's departure. The burden of coverage fell to three wire service correspondents who accompanied
him on his mission. One of them, Don Whitehead, then of the
AP, won a Pulitzer Prize for his 4,400-word account of what he
called "The Great Deception." [41]

There were no Pulitzer Prizes, or honors of any kind,
for those who participated in the imbroglio over the destruction
of Francis Gary Powers's U-2 spy plane over the Soviet Union in
1960—the real beginning of the "credibility gap" between the
words and deeds of government in the United States. In the
welter of recrimination that followed, it turned out that the chief
Washington correspondent of *The New York Times*, James Reston, knew more of what was going on than Lincoln White, the
able spokesman for the State Department. "I knew for a year,"
Reston wrote, "that the United States was flying high-altitude
planes (the U-2) over the Soviet Union from a base in Pakistan
to photograph military and particularly missile activities and
bases, but *The New York Times* did not publish this fact until
one of the planes was shot down in 1960." [42]

By contrast it was White who in all innocence issued
the CIA cover story that the missing U-2 had been a weather
plane that had wandered off-course from a Turkish base and that
"no-NO-no-deliberate attempt" had been made to infringe on Soviet air space.[43] Then, six days after Powers had been shot down
near Sverdlovsk on May 1, 1960, Premier Nikita S. Khrushchev
sprang his trap before the cheering delegates of the Supreme
Soviet. He provided documented proof that the U-2 had indeed
been a spy plane, flying at 70,000 feet across the Soviet Union
from the Pamirs toward its destination in Norway to photograph
military and industrial objectives. The only course remaining for
the United States was to admit the truth. Because President
Eisenhower insisted on taking the responsibility for ordering the
flights, the high office of the Presidency for the first time in the
Cold War became directly involved in the devious game of au-
thorizing half truths and untruths to try to trick the enemy.

The kickback in the U-2 case was a blow to national
pride as well as national honor. Adlai E. Stevenson said in Chicago, "One could say with the cynical diplomat, 'Sir, it was worse
than a lie. It was a blunder.' " Walter Lippmann charged the
Administration had "stumbled into an untenable policy which is
entirely unprecedented in international affairs." Senator Richard

OF MANNERS AND MORALS

120   B. Russell of Georgia, chairman of the Senate Armed Services Committee, called the whole business "almost incredibly stupid." It was, he added, "just like a boy getting caught with his hand in the cookie jar." The world was not particularly surprised when Khrushchev subsequently torpedoed the Paris summit conference.[44]

Once the commitment was made to such a policy, on which the CIA exerted so strong an influence, it became difficult for official Washington to abandon the notion that it could trick the Cold War foe with words and slaughter him with headlines. Despite a change in administration, the White House soon was involved in an even worse mess of untruth, haphazard planning, and defeat within less than a year—only this time the result was a military disaster in Cuba. It was scant comfort that President Kennedy said afterward to Turner Catledge, then the managing editor of *The New York Times*, "If you had printed more about the operation you would have saved us from a colossal mistake." To which Arthur M. Schlesinger, Jr., the historian who was a White House aide at the time, added the post-mortem: "I have wondered whether, if the press had behaved irresponsibly, it would not have spared the country a disaster."

Actually, within the limits of their responsibilities, the news media did what they could to alert the nation to what was going on. As early as November 19, 1960, before the Kennedy administration took office, *The Nation* published a detailed account of how the CIA was training a band of Cuban exiles in Guatemala for an eventual invasion of Castro's Cuba. The author was a responsible scholar, Dr. Ronald Hilton, then the director of the Institute of Hispanic-American Studies at Stanford University. Previously, the invasion preparations had scarcely been a secret in Guatemala, either. *The New York Times* published a piece to the same effect on January 10, 1961 by a Latin-American correspondent, Paul P. Kennedy. At the end of March, the *New Republic* prepared a pseudonymous piece (written by Karl Meyer) about the CIA's invasion preparations in Florida, but President Kennedy persuaded the magazine not to run it.

The Kennedy administration now became extremely edgy about the whole business. Tad Szulc, one of the most knowledgeable and responsible of Latin-American correspondents, filed a story to *The New York Times* early in April, reporting that the invasion was imminent and the CIA was in charge. It was more than two columns long and began bluntly:

"For nearly nine months Cuban exile military forces dedicated to the overthrow of Premier Fidel Castro have been in training in the United States as well as in Central America.

"An army of 5,000 to 6,000 men constitutes the external fighting arm of the anti-Castro Revolutionary Council, which was formed in the United States last month. Its purpose is the liberation of Cuba from what it describes as the Communist rule of the Castro regime. . . ."

The story was dummied to lead the paper on April 7, 1961 under a four-column head. Because of its position of leadership in the American press, such a display in the *Times* would have been tantamount to full acknowledgment of everything the government was trying, without success, to keep secret. Consequently, Orvil Dryfoos, then the publisher of the *Times*, became worried that his newspaper might be blamed for a "bloody fiasco" and asked Catledge what Reston thought about it. "I told them not to run it," Reston said later. In the heated discussion that followed in the *Times* office, the Szulc story was sharply edited. The role of the CIA was eliminated. The imminence of the invasion also was taken out of the story. And the whole thing was played down.

It did no good. At the end of the Szulc piece, a summary was printed of a CBS newscast announcing the invasion was imminent and planes were at their stations in Florida. The sheer diversity and independence of the news media, in this case, did operate in the public interest, had the government realized it at the time.

President Kennedy, however, scarcely recognized this when the enormity of defeat in Cuba swept the United States. While he accepted full responsibility for the catastrophe that overtook the Bay of Pigs invasion on April 17, 1961, he was furious over the role of the news media. When he appeared before the American Newspaper Publishers Association in New York at the end of April, he called for voluntary self-censorship to avert future danger to the national interest. "Every newspaper now asks itself with respect to every story, 'Is it news?' " he went on. "All I suggest is that you add the question, 'Is it in the interest of national security?' "

Although nothing came of the self-censorship proposal as far as the broad range of the news media was concerned, it did have important consequences during the atomic confrontation between the United States and the Soviet Union in

122   1962 over the installation of offensive-type missiles in Cuba. A
great deal of information had been published and broadcast in
the United States, well in advance of the showdown, that the
Russians were building missile bases in Cuba. Some accounts,
notably one in the *Miami News*, had even specified that these
were offensive missiles. But the American government lacked
proof until late in October when overflights provided photographic evidence. Once again, *The New York Times* had the
story and another paper, the *Washington Post*, suspected something was up.

This time, though, a plan for advance consultation
already had been arranged between the White House and the
Times. President Kennedy therefore telephoned directly to Dryfoos in New York to ask him "to refrain from printing on October
21 the news, which only the *Times* possessed, on the presence of
Russian missiles in Cuba." Dryfoos agreed without hesitation.
After Dryfoos's untimely death, the President wrote to his widow
on May 28, 1963, "This decision of his made far more effective
our later actions and thereby contributed greatly to our national
safety." While the *Washington Post* published a speculative story
on the crisis, the virtual ultimatum to the Soviet Union delivered
by the President in a national telecast on October 22, 1962 came
as a stunning shock to Moscow. The Soviet government backed
down and its Cuban bases subsequently were rendered harmless
to the United States. Thereafter, both Khrushchev and his supporters repeatedly claimed, in the face of routine American denials, that the United States had pledged itself in return not to
invade Castro's Cuba.

Four years after the "eyeball to eyeball" confrontation, Clifton Daniel, who became managing editor of the *Times*
when Catledge moved up to executive editor, had this post-
mortem on the press's role in the affair: "Information is essential
to people who propose to govern themselves. It is the responsibility of serious journalists to supply that information . . . Still,
the primary responsibility for safeguarding our national interest
must rest always with our government, as it did with President
Kennedy in the two Cuban crises." [45]

CENTRALIZING INFORMATION
The high drama of Cuba I and II necessarily overshadowed the
struggle for primacy over the military that Secretary McNamara
was waging in the Pentagon, but for the long term the effect of

this test of the strength of civilian control was no less important   123
in determining government information policy. At the very outset, McNamara ran into the same kind of interservice rivalry
that had bedeviled his predecessors. The Air Force, fearing that
the Kennedy administration was about to shift its strategy to the
detriment of prevailing air power doctrine, grew extremely nerv-
ous over a private memorandum from Secretary Rusk to McNamara. Actually, in retrospect, it was a rather mild and inoffen-
sive document that sought to discuss ways in which a European
war—if it came—could be limited in order to avert an atomic
disaster. But the very term, "limited war," was an offense to Air
Force zealots who were wedded to all-out atomic strategy. One of
them risked his career by leaking a twisted version of the Rusk
memorandum to the Washington press, a familiar military strat-
agem. In it, the State Department was reported to be demanding
a commitment from the Defense Department against the use of
atomic weapons as a "first strike" strategy. The culprit was never
officially identified.[46]

Soon afterward, following a background briefing for
a dozen correspondents at the Pentagon, the press reported that
McNamara had found, contrary to Democratic charges during
the Presidential campaign of 1960, that no "missile gap" existed
in American weaponry. Translating the headlines of the day, this
meant that fears of Russian superiority over the United States in
number and quality of missiles had been proved groundless. A
White House spokesman denied the accounts, which had actually been issued by McNamara on a background basis; later,
however, President Kennedy merely complained of the hazards
of backgrounders and contended the Pentagon had not yet completed its studies and made a final judgment. McNamara, of
course, had been right in the first place.[47]

The Defense Secretary did not let such things bother
him. Soon, he was complaining that the press seemed to be
publishing too much material about reports of American military
weakness in one field or another. "Why should we tell Russia
that the Zeus (antimissile) developments may not be satisfac-
tory?" he once asked. "What we ought to be saying is that we
have the most perfect ICBM system that the human mind will
ever devise."[48] The Secretary, at that stage, took little stock in
Abraham Lincoln's familiar warning against the perils of trying
to fool all the people all the time. He had to learn the hard way.
Whatever flaws there were in McNamara's charac-

124   ter, lack of courage was not one of them. With swiftness and audacity, he took on the top brass at the Pentagon and at the same time authorized his pugnacious Assistant Secretary for Public Affairs, Arthur Sylvester, to channel all vital Pentagon news through the Defense Department press office. Within a short time, the military information services found they had a tough new master—and so did the chiefs of staff. McNamara's concept of cost efficiency in military programming took such firm hold that he was accused of downgrading traditional military methods. Hanson Baldwin wrote of the "McNamara monarchy." The *New York Daily News* called the Secretary a "civilian on horseback." The *Baltimore Sun* complained of a trend toward depreciation of the military "as essential advisers . . . on strictly military issues." [49]

But neither the military nor their supporters among the correspondents, usually a strong alliance, were able to overcome the superior political power and determination of the Kennedy-McNamara combination. President Kennedy, in fact, had so many ardent supporters in the Washington correspondents' corps that he was bound to make a stronger impression on the public than the military figures who could not afford to be caught in the spotlight. Just how great the Kennedy influence was could be gauged by the enormous amount of time he spent with the correspondents, singly and in small groups, and in the large attendance at his news conferences. For this was a President with style and grace and daring, who somehow contrived to make the correspondents feel as if they were part of a pageant. He was the first and the last to strip away the final vestige of protection at his news conferences by letting his televised remarks go out live. In the Eisenhower years, when television was first admitted to the Presidential news meetings, the tape had been held up for scrutiny before being released, but Kennedy would have none of that. He had superb self-confidence in his ability to say the right thing at the right time, and generally he was correct.

It was this trait, more than any other, which made it possible for President Kennedy to operate with such precision in the Cuban missile crisis, the high point of his administration. The regard in which both he and McNamara were held at the time also blunted the criticism that arose when the Defense and State Departments instituted a rule requiring all conversations by officials with reporters to be monitored and later recorded with the Public Affairs Office. The State Department dropped the objectionable rule, but at the Pentagon McNamara made it stick until 1967, when it was finally dropped. *The New York Times* called it a "Kremlin-like restriction . . . a requirement that seems more derogatory of the trust responsible officials deserve than it is obstructive to the interviewer." [50]

While the Pentagon monitoring system did not really restrict the correspondents who knew their way around, it did have the effect for a time of crippling the efforts of most of the military camarilla in feeding information to their favorites in the press. For all except would-be martyrs, the danger became too great. And so, McNamara at length made himself the real boss in the Pentagon; accordingly, the military, for a comparatively long time, did "speak as one voice." It became exceedingly difficult for the news media to hear any other.

The drive for security and centralized information had still another major effect on the journalist, perhaps the most unpleasant and obnoxious of all. This was the rise of an unacknowledged policy of surveillance. From time to time, reporters who were usually active in affairs of either a sensitive or controversial nature found that they were being investigated by various government agencies. Frequently, the FBI carried out this chore although the CIA was far from inactive among the correspondents. The main effort of the investigators was to inquire into the reporters' sources, but it seldom did the government much good.

A stronger and more dangerous tactic was the technique used by various administrators to issue private warnings to investigative reporters from a variety of news organizations that they were likely to do great harm to their country. In some cases, when such admonitions had no effect, editors and publishers would be summoned to Washington for personal treatment or reached by telephone with warnings or pleas for greater cooperation with the government. Both Presidents Kennedy and Johnson were extremely active in such matters, either in person or through emissaries.

Whatever justification there might have been for such intervention, there was none whatever for the "brass knuckles" policies that were attributed to the Johnson administration by Anthony Howard, Washington correspondent for the *London Observer*. Soon after arriving in Washington, he wrote that Administration spokesmen were saying that Walter Lippmann was "senile," which was absurd, and the reputation of James Reston

126   was "in a decline," which was laughable. Howard concluded: "It
is hard not to recognize in all this part of a concerted plan of
professional demolition of the President's press critics." [51] A lot
more of this was published in the American press, with various
degrees of indignation, when Walter Lippmann finally concluded at the age of 77 that he would give up his regular column,
leave Washington and settle down in a villa outside Paris.

Regardless of the circumstantial evidence against
the Johnson administration, the charges of Howard and others
would have been difficult to prove. It was evident, however, that
President Johnson, like his predecessors, was loyal to his friends
and merciless to his foes among the journalists. He did not have
the Kennedy charisma, nor could he charm the press corps; but
he did have zeal and tenacity of purpose that aroused grudging
admiration even among his critics and he was by all odds the
most accomplished politician to occupy the White House since
Franklin D. Roosevelt.

It was no accident when the White House press
secretary's office took the unusual line of attacking the correspondents at a particularly low point in the Johnson administration's political fortunes. The Washington Press Corps was taxed
with "too much poor reporting"—a sweeping generality that hit
almost everybody. Such things had been said *sotto voce* during
the Kennedy administration by his information people during
their weekly grousing sessions; under President Johnson, they
went on the record as a kind of backfire to the comparatively
poor press he usually received.

Shortly before Bill D. Moyers himself became a
newspaperman of sorts, if publishers can be so identified, he told
correspondents they sometimes had "limited knowledge" and
were "snared by irrelevancies." He added, for whatever effect it
may have had, "You often see things through a keyhole. You see
only a small portion of what we in the government see. Yours are
the errors of incompleteness.

"You are unable to accept motivation in quite the
same way we believe we in government are motivated. We often
do things out of the purest of motives. The heart of the tension is
that it is difficult for you to understand that our motives have
been as pure as they are." He conceded that there were many
honest journalists, "just as there are honest politicians." But he
added the cynical quip, "When bought, they stay bought." [52]

Robert H. Fleming, the deputy press secretary and

former Washington news director of the American Broadcasting Companies, was even rougher on his former associates, saying: "They want comfort; they want reliable lids (an agreement that no more news will be released for the night); they want transcripts; they want advance travel plans; they want jet-speed airplanes to jet-age hotels where they hope to have a leisurely horse-and-buggy schedule." [53]

Joseph Kraft, one of the more detached correspondents, analyzed the President's problem with the press in terms of "flack," a Hollywood expression for press agents. The press, in the correspondent's view, was "unable to see the President as just another flack." To which another critic, Ben H. Bagdikian, retorted, "What happens if the press has to view the President of the United States as 'just another flack'? The problem is not the existence of public relations in the White House, which has to consider its 'image' if for no other reason than to know whether it is being understood. But there is flackery and flackery and the White House has pushed the technique to the point of negative returns." [54]

The bitterness of the critics was a symptom of the abnormal tensions in Washington. The correspondents blamed many things—the formidable pressures of the Presidency, the "carrot and stick" treatment of the press, abrasive personal relationships between a wide assortment of government officials and the leaders of the news media, the constant efforts to channel the news and the many miscalculations in Vietnam. Perhaps as important as anything else—but not mentioned very often—was the President's Texas manner, which affronted the more snobbish correspondents in Washington. The President, on his own part, heartily damned their arrogance but he never did learn to cut them down with the immense gusto of the plain little man from Independence, Missouri, Harry S Truman.

THE LESSON OF SANTO DOMINGO

Just as President Eisenhower was hurt by the U-2 and President Kennedy by the lying over Cuba I, President Johnson had to contend with a lot of government bumbling over the American intervention in the Dominican crisis of 1965. Like his predecessors, he found that when the showdown came he had to take the responsibility and place the prestige of the White House behind a shaky American propaganda position. It was a dangerous thing to do, as all three Presidents eventually learned to their cost in

128   handling their share of responsibility for the Vietnam War, but it was their only recourse. The evasions and blatant untruths issued on behalf of the American government during the Dominican crisis constituted a case history of how White House influence could be invoked, rightly or wrongly, to bolster a poor case.

When the revolt against the Reid Cabral government began on April 24, 1965, the Johnson administration was concerned for two reasons: 1) The safety of United States nationals in Santo Domingo, which was openly stated, and 2) the possibility that the movement might actually be a Communist takeover in the Castro manner, which was hinted at because there was no immediate evidence to prove it. The declared position of the Dominican rebels was the restoration to power of the exiled President Juan Bosch, which President Johnson privately observed would be "like turning the country over to Arthur Schlesinger, Jr." The American government from the outset was extremely wary of the rebels.

However, for publication, the basis of American intervention at the outset was the safety of American citizens. On April 27, the United States Navy began evacuating 1,100 United States nationals from the Dominican Republic. On the following day, without consulting the Council of the Organization of American States, the President authorized the landing of 556 Marines for the announced purpose of protecting the remaining United States citizens in the country.

A steady stream of private warning messages came to the White House and the CIA meanwhile on the possibility of a Communist takeover in Santo Domingo. But the first mention of it was by a State Department spokesman on April 29 in this highly qualified manner: "It is too early for us to assess or evaluate it, based on available information . . . I am only prepared to say that they [the Communists] are participating. I could not say they are leading and I could not speculate on the eventualities."

That same day, however, while the OAS Council was meeting in Washington, the United States Embassy began issuing unattributed information to newly arrived American correspondents about "Communist street fighting methods" and "Castro-style" massacres. While the correspondents had no way of checking this data, many of them filed stories about it—some cautiously, some without qualification. Next day, apparently emboldened by its success, the Embassy leaked a list of 53 alleged

Communists, later raised to 58, who were said to be leading the revolt; upon checking, the correspondents found the list riddled with inaccuracies.

President Johnson in Washington was reported to have been angered by the issuance of the list without his authorization, but it was too late by that time to do anything about it. The good faith of the government of the United States had been risked on a document of dubious worth. The President's anger was fully justified when he learned later that day from the CIA that there were eight hard-core Communists, not 53 or 58, in positions of leadership in the revolt. When he authorized the airlifting of 2,500 paratroops of the 82d Airborne Division from Fort Bragg, N. C., to Santo Domingo, he did not say anything about the government's fears of a Communist takeover, but put the case in this manner: "We are not going in there to support anybody or to fight anybody. We're going in there to try to keep them from killing our people and themselves."

Yet, on April 30, the background briefers in Washington told correspondents that there was "significant participation" in the revolt by "extreme leftist elements." The President, in his second TV appearance during the crisis, also permitted himself that day his first reference to the signs of Communist activities —"signs that people trained outside the Dominican Republic are seeking to gain control." Accordingly, he pledged resistance to "international conspiracy from any quarter," but he still had no evidence except the distorted list that had been circulated without his authority.

When the President went on TV for the third time on May 2, he finally had to admit the real basis for American intervention despite the lack of enough evidence to justify it. "What began as a popular democratic revolution committed to democracy and social justice," he said, "very shortly moved and was taken over and really seized and placed in the hands of a band of Communist conspirators."

From then on, the American military buildup in the Dominican Republic proceeded until 21,500 troops were on duty, about 20 times the number of United States citizens whose lives they were assigned to safeguard. And in the rising demand from Hemisphere governments of proof of the President's contention, the actual basis for American intervention was cast in doubt. The position of leading newsmen, stated bluntly at the time, shows how the news media in the United States and elsewhere

130 spread that doubt to the discredit of the American government. "If anything was clear here," wrote Roger Tatarian, the editor of United Press International, "it is that nothing was completely clear to American officials in charge of policy and intelligence. In the end the President had to choose between one assessment and the other; and it is no secret that the official assessment is still not unanimously accepted. If the public has been left somewhat puzzled by it all, it is no great wonder."

A more sympathetic newsman, Charles Roberts of *Newsweek,* wrote long afterward: "Why he [the President] took so long in spelling out the threat to the American people has never been adequately explained." A Canadian journalist with graduate school training in the United States and long experience in Washington, Martin Goodman of the *Toronto Star,* pointed out that the errors in the list of alleged Communists "badly damaged its credibility" and were the basis for charges that the United States had intervened on the basis of unverified information.

"Without question," he wrote, "the difficulties in communication, both with the troops in the field and with the policy makers in Washington, made full knowledge difficult for U. S. spokesmen. But too many times it seemed that U. S. spokesmen, from the highest level down, were mistaken or misleading deliberately rather than accidentally. Too many times there seemed to be a determined, even aggressive, effort to give reporters incorrect, exaggerated, or half-true information. The cover story and the cover-up became standard weapons. It is this cavalier attitude toward the truth that is most worrisome in the long run relationship between the government and its public. Once truth becomes a casualty, one can only wonder how and when it will recover." [55]

The United States won no friends in Latin America with its first military intervention in hemisphere affairs in 30 years. However, in retrospect, President Johnson did not add to the enemies he had already made. The forces that had opposed him in Vietnam were also his critics in the Dominican Republic, and by and large they constituted the body of American opinion that irrationally demanded United States intervention to open the Straits of Tiran in 1967 before the Israelis in six days proved that they could take care of themselves militarily. Such critics were not always scrupulous, nor were they fair-minded; they used almost any stick with which to beat a President they mis-

trusted and heartily disliked. Politically, as far as President Johnson was concerned, their opposition could be taken for granted
and he therefore did not appear to worry too much about the
protests over the Dominican intervention. The American people,
after all, did accept his position with relative calm. Many appeared to believe, with the President, that it was better to intervene, even on a shaky basis, than to take a chance on permitting
another Castro to rise in the hemisphere. The summons to fight
Communism, always a potent appeal in the United States, apparently carried the day with American public opinion.

Yet, it is folly to ignore the moral position in which a
government finds itself when it must cast the prestige of its
greatest institutions and its leadership into the balance to preserve its credibility with its people. This kind of thing cannot be
done indefinitely without the greatest damage. As J. Russell
Wiggins, editor of the *Washington Post,* once stated the case as a
general matter:

"If a government repeatedly resorts to lies in crises
where lies seem to serve its interest best, it will one day be
unable to employ the truth effectively when truth would serve its
interests best. A government that too readily rationalizes its right
to lie in a crisis will never lack for either lies or crises." [56]

In the Vietnam War, the United States government
reaped the bitter harvest of such practices. It learned that there
is a limit even to the credibility of the high office of the Presidency—the "bully pulpit," as Theodore Roosevelt called it. Faith
and belief can survive persecution by their foes easier than mis-
treatment by their friends.

WAR, TRUTH,

9

AND VIETNAM

The United States has seldom fought a quick war or won an easy peace. Nor have the American people been conditioned by either history or experience to expect miracles, once their armed forces have been committed to battle. By and large, they have generally given majority support to their Presidents in wartime despite substantial opposition by groups ranging in importance from Tories and Copperheads to Beatniks and Doves. As for the American press, now augmented by radio and television, the principal problem throughout has been to resurrect the truth, inevitably the first casualty of all war.

Even though there has been no foreign invasion of 133
the continental United States since 1812, leaving aside Pancho
Villa's picturesque raids, the strains of war have often made a
deep impression on American life. Except for the Mexican and
Spanish wars, every acknowledged war in which the United
States has been involved, from the Revolution on, began with
grievous setbacks that were overcome with the greatest difficulty
and, with few variations, at an enormous cost in blood and
treasure. It is not an accident therefore that American history is
generally taught in the United States with equal emphasis on
Valley Forge and Yorktown, the burning of Washington and the
battle of New Orleans, the battles of Bull Run and Appomattox,
the two battles of the Marne, Chateau Thierry and Belleau Wood,
and Pearl Harbor, the Normandy landings and Hiroshima.

If the pattern changed in Korea and Vietnam, it was
not because these wars began any differently; in both, the United
States and its allies were on the verge of ignominious defeat at
the outset. But because each was a limited war, fought for limited objectives, the frustrations of the beginning necessarily
could not be wiped out with the announcement of an inflexible
American policy that the conflict would go on until the Communist foe surrendered unconditionally. Thus, while neither became a popular war in the United States, only the far right
insistently criticized what it called a "no win" policy. And although General Eisenhower was elected in part on his promise to
end the Korean War in 1952, it cannot be successfully contended
that this was the only reason or even the main reason why he
was able to break 20 years of Democratic rule. As the election
figures clearly demonstrated, he would have beaten any Democrat who ran against him. Moreover, by 1952, the Communist
North Korean and Chinese forces long since had been obliged to
abandon their hoped for military conquest of South Korea and
the actual negotiations at Panmunjom only served to confirm an
existing military stalemate that still continues.

Nevertheless, much of the stubbornness of the
enemy in the Vietnam War may be attributed to the persistent
hope in Hanoi that the American public would be overcome by
war weariness as was France and that a political overturn in the
United States would make possible a victory that could not be
won in Vietnam itself. Quite the opposite occurred after the 1964
election, when President Johnson escalated the war following his
victory over Barry Goldwater; nor were the Democrats inclined

134 to blame their losses in the 1966 Congressional elections on the reaction to the Vietnam War, for the bombing of the Hanoi–Haiphong area followed. Yet, Hanoi still hung on grimly, hoping for a reversal of American sentiment in the 1968 election, with a consequent increase in the propaganda content of the news from all sides. The war, in fact, was fought almost as vigorously with words in the United States as it was on many an unmarked battlefield in Vietnam.

Under these circumstances, clearly, the United States would have profited much more by a policy of truthful government reporting wherever possible, in the pattern of World War II, than by the long series of evasions, half truths, and untruths that marred the record of the Eisenhower, Kennedy, and Johnson administrations in Vietnam. If it was in the interest of Hanoi to obscure the issue and confuse the American public, it was obviously in the interest of the United States to make sure that the public at home knew the truth and realized that the fight would be a long and bitter one. Edward W. Barrett's summation of World War II policy, *Truth Is Our Best Weapon*,* quite literally could have been applied to Vietnam in spite of the differing nature of the two conflicts and the varying public reactions they aroused. But it was never given a serious and sustained test at a time when it would have helped the most.

FAILURE OF A POLICY

In retrospect, the manner in which the United States entered the Vietnam War set the tone for subsequent appeals to American public opinion. Beginning with Vice President Richard M. Nixon's background talk before American editors in 1954, when he set off a war scare by calling for American armed intervention to save the French at Dienbienphu, Vietnam became the source of countless intrigues to sway the American public. Although Nixon failed, just as so many others did later in ill-conceived public relations campaigns, it did not prevent the rise of propaganda appeals both for and against greater intervention in Vietnam.

President Kennedy at one time feared to authorize Purple Heart decorations for American troops wounded in Viet-

---

* Barrett, who later became Assistant Secretary of State for Public Affairs, never contended the whole truth could always be told, or even hinted at; however, he made the point that the United States could and did conceal military matters without using the "Big Lie."

nam because he did not want to be accused of an arms buildup beyond the authorized quotas at the 1954 Geneva settlement. The North Vietnamese, with Chinese support, long since had violated the Geneva agreement by giving massive aid to the Vietcong insurrection in South Vietnam. Consequently, they were in a position to know very well what the level of American troop strength was and how American military advisers were being used. The only possible effect of concealment under these circumstances would have been to delude the American people, but the correspondents for American (and some British and French) news organizations usually operated in such a manner that this did not happen.

The same sensitivity to world Communist opinion has often been in evidence since. When announcements of attacks by American aircraft on Soviet-supplied missile bases in North Vietnam were suspended for a time, well-intentioned State Department spokesmen explained it was necessary to avoid giving needless provocation to Moscow. Cases of "straying" American aircraft over Chinese territory received the same subdued treatment for fear of offending Peking. When a Soviet supply ship was hit by American aircraft during a raid in the Haiphong area, the United States at first issued an indignant denial (Form A response to all charges during the Vietnam War), then acknowledged 18 days later that "it could have accidentally happened." [57]

If it took the American government three weeks to find out what had happened during that particular Haiphong raid, then something was wrong with its system of gathering information. But if Washington knew in the first place that the Soviet ship had been accidentally hit, certainly nothing was gained by trying to pretend it was all a great mystery, to blame the North Vietnamese or perhaps even the Russians themselves. Both in Cuba II and in the Middle East War of 1967, the Soviet Union amply demonstrated that it would not go to war with the United States in the interests of a small client power. As for China, torn by internal dissension over Mao Tse-tung's so-called cultural revolution, it was scarcely in a position then to intervene. Finally, there was little likelihood that either Moscow or Peking would base an eventual commitment to battle on the zigs or zags of the American propaganda line.

The lying about Vietnam was just as unnecessary for the home front as it was for the effect it had on Communist

136   policy. If it was in fact intended to boost national morale, the actual effect was often exactly the opposite. For a lie, to be acceptable to the public, must be so clearly in the national interest (such as the suppression of the damage to the fleet after the Japanese attack on Pearl Harbor) that its disclosure would cause no disturbance in the United States. In view of the almost continuous cannonading in the news media about the "credibility gap" in Vietnam, American propaganda also failed on this count. The psychological warfare carried on by American experts often created more havoc in the United States than it did either among the Vietcong or the North Vietnamese.

It is worth noting that at a particularly crucial period in the escalation of the American war effort in Vietnam, a poll of American opinion on the truthfulness of official United States announcements about Vietnam showed 67 percent thought they were "sometimes truthful," 15 percent "always truthful," and 13 percent "almost never truthful." Soon afterward, another American opinion survey showed that the public had considerably more confidence in the coverage of the war by part of the news media, with 75 percent expressing confidence in television reporting against 17 percent who found it unsatisfactory, a 71 to 21 percent ratio for newspapers, 62 to 14 percent for magazines and 62 to 20 percent for radio.[58]

This is not to suggest that there is any easy way to handle the fundamental problem of maintaining a relevant balance between the demands of national security in a war situation and keeping the American people informed. In such a situation, the position of the President is infinitely more difficult than that of an editor or a correspondent, to put it mildly, and the possibility of error also is greater for the White House than for the newsroom.

The problem in all its unlovely complications was illustrated by what appeared to be a routine news conference at the White House on Saturday, June 18, 1966, which President Johnson had arranged with his customary lack of extended notice. Nothing of particular importance happened until the President touched on the Vietnam War. "We must continue to raise the cost of aggression at its source," he said with an enigmatic expression.

The correspondents recognized that the President was giving them a signal. One of them asked, "Does the statement imply or mean that there may be a step-up in the air strikes in North Vietnam?" The President made no direct retort, saying he didn't want to be "boxed in," that he didn't care to make a "commitment." But it would have been a dull-witted reporter, indeed, who would not have been able to conclude that the long-expected escalation of the air war to Hanoi and Haiphong was very near. It had been rumored for months, and now here was the President himself saying that the cost of aggression had to be raised "at its source."

A free press has few inhibitions about handling such matters in the United States; unlike the British press, the Americans have never consented to suppress news in the national interest whenever the government requests it.* Consequently, no one was surprised when the Dow Jones News Service reported from the nation's capital on Friday, June 24, that a decision had been made the day before to bomb the oil depots at Haiphong within a few days. It was published briefly in the *Wall Street Journal*, the leading Dow Jones newspaper. The White House issued a routine denial although, as it later became known, the raid actually had been scheduled for that day and postponed because of weather conditions in the target area. It was set for the following day, Saturday, June 25.

That morning, the Columbia Broadcasting System used a report from Saigon that the big raid was scheduled for later that day. For understandable reasons, the attack was canceled. On Tuesday, June 28, Murray Fromsen, a CBS correspondent, reported that the attack had been put off due to what he called "flagrant security leaks in Washington." It was finally carried out on Wednesday, June 29, and declared by the Navy and Air Force to have been an unqualified success. Navy jets from two carriers in the Gulf of Tonkin and Air Force bombers from two technically secret bases in Thailand wiped out what they estimated as 75 to 80 percent of the two biggest oil storage depots in the Hanoi–Haiphong industrial complex. "It's incredible," the President said as he learned of the claims, "it's really incredible that this could happen with the loss of only one plane." [59]

The truly incredible part of the operation, however, was that it could succeed after the world had been alerted to it beforehand. When the President chose to prepare public opinion

* In Britain, this request is called a D (for Defense) Note and breaches of such security have troubled several governments, including the Wilson regime.

138   ten days before the raid, he must have realized that he was risking the chance of further disclosures by the highly competitive news media. Just before the raid, administration officials let it be known that both they and the President were angry about the leaks. But by that time, the damage had been done. As Arthur Krock put it, "In this instance, the normally useful competition of public communications media to be first with the news overcame the higher obligation of the press to the public interest that, in the particular circumstances, involved the lives of United States airmen and the essential element of enemy surprise." [60]

PRESSURES AND THE NEWS

In a general discussion of the responsibilities of government for maintaining security, Allen Dulles once presented the issue in these terms: "Free peoples everywhere abhor government secrecy. There is something sinister and dangerous, they feel, when governments 'shroud' their activities. It may be an entering wedge for the establishment of an autocratic form of rule, a cover-up for their mistakes. Hence, it is difficult to persuade free peoples that it may be in the national interest, at times, to keep certain matters confidential, that their freedoms may eventually be endangered by too much talk about national defense measures and delicate diplomatic negotiations." [61]

All this is very true, but it does not take into account the numerous instances in which governments find it in their own interest to do more talking about security matters than seems either prudent or necessary to the public. The most compelling motive for such conduct is the Cold War practice of "signaling" the enemy through the news media. The publicizing of military capabilities in terms of nuclear power and rocketry as a deterrent to war has been a familiar—and so far an effective—propaganda device in both Washington and Moscow. It has been assiduously copied in Paris and Peking, with less believable results, while London has remained the most restrained center of nuclear activity. Below the atomic level, "signaling" has scarcely added to the credibility of those who have used it, as was made evident in the three-week Kashmir War, the six-day Middle East War, and the long struggle in Vietnam.

At various times, government authorities have used their information resources in other ways to add to the strain, wittingly or unwittingly, on the security system. The most com-

mon, in intelligence parlance, is the "giveaway," in which announcements are made either for attribution or on a background
basis that temporarily shields the source. Then, there is the
"contrived leak," in which a key official may deliberately issue
information to correspondents he trusts in order to discredit a
rival department or military service, attack a policy he dislikes,
or win some political advantage. There also are the inevitable
disclosures of information that come from careless, indiscreet, or
overly vain officials who either talk too much or drink too much,
and sometimes do both. The United States has its share of such
politically appointed or career officials, who probably do more
damage to the government over the long term than the majority
of their associates who walk a careful line between minimal
disclosure and nondisclosure.

The news media, too, have well-tested methods of obtaining sensitive information which, depending on circumstances,
may or may not be disclosed. The most important is the alliance that a powerful correspondent often concludes with various
individuals or groups in the Congressional structure, particularly
those with the right of subpoena in key investigatory committees.
When all goes well, the correspondent gets the information he
seeks and the Congressmen the publicity and editorial favor so
necessary to their careers. As Clark Mollenhoff of the Cowles
Newspapers once wrote: "Without Congressional power to investigate behind them, the reporters in Washington could be reduced
pretty much to the level of the German newsmen who gathered
at the Propaganda Ministry in the 1930s to receive their handouts
from Dr. Goebbels." [62]

The system, of course, works both ways. The Executive Department often finds it expedient to offer information,
openly or by subterfuge, when important Congressional action is
pending. And sometimes, in a lively interchange between the
Executive and Legislative Departments over policy matters, the
public discovers quite by chance that the government is testing
new approaches to foreign or domestic issues. Thus, unintended
or premature disclosure sometimes gives the democratic process
a chance to act which the machinery of government otherwise
would make impossible.

The pressures from the news media, however, have
less attractive features. While the major correspondents in
Washington are very careful for the most part to maintain their
independence, some of the less responsible ones are drawn to

140   particularly powerful officials or members of Congress with the result that they become little more than unadmitted publicity men for their principals. Others, who have very little stomach for the daily strains of news gathering under the scrutiny of a strong government, try to maintain a timid neutrality by giving no offense in the coverage of controversial issues, which is almost an impossibility. As for the potentates of journalism, those with the greatest prestige in the news media, they are courted by the Establishment by all possible means, if there is any hope whatever of winning them over. It is one reason why such correspondents usually have the best sources in government and the most reliable information.

The majority of the Washington press corps, however, can depend neither on undue prestige or undue political favor. The brave and vigorous youngsters—and a few gallant oldsters—practice their craft for the most part in the traditional manner with exhausting legwork at the scene of action, patient questioning of all those involved in a developing pattern of news, and battering-ram assaults on the citadels of official intelligence. It is the most difficult way, but it is frequently the only way for them to do the job.

An emotional foreign journalist, unable to comprehend so pragmatic a system for informing the American public of the acts of its government, once burst out after some slight experience with the complex operation: "One thing must surely be done about the American press and American TV and American movies. They must be censored! They must be controlled by the government!" [63] A more sophisticated foreigner, with years of government service behind him, was taken aback by the ferocious activity in the journalistic jungles of Washington. When he was told that the American government had no official network through which it made known its decisions and its policies, but trusted to the willingness of the independent news media to dispense its views, he asked in wonderment: "Then how can you govern?" [64]

George E. Reedy, President Johnson's first press secretary, gave one answer after leaving the White House: "A democratic society is inconceivable without tension and the objective reporting that democracy requires will always produce tension. . . . We will just have to assume that these tensions are a part of the price that must be paid for values we consider absolute." [65] No responsible official in Washington, and certainly no corre-

spondent of standing, has ever differed with the principle, no   **141**
matter how much both may have quarreled with its execution.
For often, the price that must be paid is very high.

WHEN OPTIMISM DID NOT PAY

Such was the case in Vietnam from the outset of American
involvement. While Presidents Kennedy and Johnson made the
decisions that sent American forces into that unhappy country,
the burden of maintaining public support for the war fell heaviest on Robert Strange McNamara, the Secretary of Defense, and
Arthur Sylvester, who served for six years as Assistant Secretary
of Defense for Public Affairs. Neither, by experience or disposition, was particularly comfortable while practicing the devious
arts of public relations; nor was it possible for them to dissemble
with any degree of effectiveness. Yet, during the initial phases of
American involvement when it sometimes seemed as if nothing
could save South Vietnam from passing into Communist control,
it was their job to keep hope alive and to try to build confidence
in the far from effective South Vietnamese Army. No one has
ever found a way to make a losing situation palatable; certainly,
McNamara and Sylvester could not. Until American troop
strength in South Vietnam passed 500,000, it was even difficult
to sustain McNamara's frequent proclamation that the United
States could not lose the war militarily. The frequent arguments
in which Sylvester opposed some or all of the correspondents
also did not help very much; until his departure from the Pentagon, he remained a controversial figure.

The contrasting personalities of McNamara and
Sylvester, and their varying habits of mind and action, had
something to do with the difficulty of telling the Vietnam War
story to the American public and to the world. As a Phi Beta
Kappa from the University of California, a professor at the Harvard Graduate School of Business, an Air Force Officer during
World War II, and the president of the Ford Motor Company,
McNamara had the credentials of a successful manager. In ap-
plying modern cost accounting principles to the vigorously competitive military services, he revolutionized thinking at the Pentagon. But nothing in his background indicated that he either
knew or appreciated how difficult it could be to deal with the
American and foreign news media in a place like Vietnam.

Sylvester, of course, knew from the outset that he
was in trouble over the Vietnam assignment but apparently re-

142 solved that he would never give an inch to his former colleagues, the correspondents. He had joined the *Newark Evening News* upon his graduation from Princeton, risen through the ranks to become city editor and later Washington correspondent, and at 60 years of age had begun his service in the Pentagon. Although he was technically responsible to a succession of White House press secretaries during the Kennedy and Johnson administrations, he seldom accepted "guidance" except when it came directly from the President or the Secretary of Defense. Tall, red-faced, pugnacious, and often intemperate, he considered an attack as the best defense against the ever critical news media. It was not in him to become an "honest broker" type of public relations man, who served as a kind of mediator between the news media and their sources. He was an all-out advocate of whatever policy the government chose to follow, but his phrasing sometimes complicated his job, as was evident with his pronouncement on the Cuba II crisis: "I think the inherent right of the government to lie to save itself when faced with nuclear disaster is basic." [66] He never modified either his beliefs or his attitude toward news as an element of weaponry in the government's arsenal. While his honesty did him credit, it also complicated his job.

Except for the relatively few news organizations of major importance that gave all-out support to the Vietnam War, the McNamara–Sylvester team from the beginning had a difficult time in establishing a fundamental credibility at home and abroad. To be fair, this was not entirely their fault. They were heavily handicapped by the existing situation in Saigon during the early 1960s, where the charming but inexperienced Ambassador Frederick Nolting and the blunt-spoken General Paul Harkins put all their trust in what they were told by Ngo Dinh Diem. The Saigon dictator, who trusted only his sharp-tongued wife and his wily brother, Ngo Dinh Nhu, was full of glowing claims of victories in the field and in the construction of strategic hamlets that were impregnable to Vietcong attack. At that stage, unfortunately, both the American Embassy and the top-ranking American military believed him.

Consequently, as early as 1962 and 1963, Washington began to entertain visions of victory on the basis of these overly optimistic assessments. When Secretary McNamara went to Saigon himself, he merely heard the same thing at first hand and seemingly believed everything. Thus, in 1962, General Harkins predicted the war would be won within a year; at about the same time, McNamara announced, "We have turned the corner in Vietnam." Early in 1963, Secretary Rusk declared the Viet- cong "look less and less like winners" and proclaimed that the South Vietnamese Army was "on its way to success." On the eve of the military uprising that resulted in the slaying of both the Diems and the exile of Mme. Nhu on November 1, 1963, McNa- mara paid a visit to Saigon and announced on his return to Washington that 1,000 American troops could be withdrawn by the end of the year. He predicted victory by the end of 1965.

There are not many instances in history in which a great power has been made to look so foolish before the world. While some figures in the Kennedy administration were not so confident, one being the ever skeptical Averell Harriman, they made little impression on either the President or the American public. However, a handful of newsmen in Vietnam did tell the truth and their organizations used their reports as early as 1962. They included the dean of American war correspondents, Homer Bigart, and his excitable successor, David Halberstam, both of *The New York Times;* Malcolm W. Browne and Peter Arnett, both of the Associated Press; Neil Sheehan of United Press Inter- national, Charles Mohr and Mert Perry of *Time,* both of whom resigned when their magazine questioned the accuracy of their reporting from Vietnam, and François Sully of *Newsweek,* whose French citizenship led to frequent charges that he was anti-American. What they told the world was that the Diems were incompetent, the strategic hamlet program was a fraud, defeats were being billed as victories, and the war was being lost. In all these matters, they were right; but because they were right, their critics intemperately argued that they had had something to do with bringing about the whole unfortunate situation. It was just another case of blaming the headlines, not the responsible officials who created them.

The American Embassy press officer at the time, John Mecklin, wrote of the episode: "The root of the problem was the fact that much of what the newsmen took to be lies was exactly what the (American) Mission genuinely believed, and was reporting to Washington. Events were to prove how badly the war was going, operating in a world of illusion. Our feud with the newsmen was an angry symptom of bureaucratic sick- ness." [67]

There was no great mystery over where the corre-

144   spondents got their information. Although the angry Sylvester continually charged in Washington that they seldom if ever went into the field to seek out combat with the Vietcong, this was exactly what most of them did do. It was the only way in which they had any chance of finding out what was going on. Halberstam, taking over from Bigart, often became almost apoplectic when he learned that the Embassy was denying stories based on accounts he had picked up from American military advisers in the field after their Vietnam units had suffered serious defeats. To make matters worse, the Embassy started a backfire against the embattled correspondents with the assistance of such allies as *Time*, Joseph Alsop, and Marguerite Higgins. Charles Mohr recalled that Miss Higgins had told him once, "Reporters here [in Saigon] would like to see us lose the war to prove they are right." Before her death, she often repeated her suspicions of the reporters but pleaded that she could not remember having made that particular remark.[68]

Once doubtful of the principal things that were being fed to them by American officials, the correspondents in Saigon began to become skeptical of almost everything—and sometimes with good reason. At the "Five O'Clock Follies," as the daily briefings in American headquarters in Saigon were known, loud and acrimonious wrangles between reporters and briefing officers became the order of the day. It did not help that President Kennedy tried without immediate success to persuade the publisher of *The New York Times*, Arthur O. Sulzberger, to move the controversial Halberstam to another assignment. Other less publicized efforts were made to attack correspondents who were deemed antagonistic to the American war effort in Vietnam, but this particular government line was not very productive. When the correspondents moved out, they did so under their own power or under the direction of their news organizations. The government had no luck in trying to run both the war and the reporting of it, which was just as well.*

NEW METHODS, NEW PEOPLE

It would be pleasant to report that the American news media as a whole made a distinguished effort to right the wrongs that had

---

* Many correspondents shifted in and out and changed employers, as well. Sheehan, Browne, and Mohr joined *The New York Times;* Halberstam, after an unhappy experience in Poland, eventually left the *Times* to write for *Harper's.* Not many of the 1963 group of reporters in Saigon stayed put.

been developing in Vietnam by assigning a large and highly   145
specialized corps of correspondents, but it did not turn out that
way. For the better part of four years, a mere handful of correspondents—most of them quite young—worked under the most
trying circumstances to bring the news of the war to the American public. Even as late as the summer of 1964, shortly before
the Tonkin Gulf attack on American warships, no more than a
score of regulars were on the job. Had it not been for the presence of a small group of able wire service correspondents, the
bulk of the American news media would have been obliged to
rely on the government's version of events.

The situation changed slowly. Sometimes it seemed
to the correspondents in the field that it was not changing at all.
When President Johnson assumed office on November 22, 1963,
after the assassination of President Kennedy, Saigon was in
virtual chaos. Henry Cabot Lodge had replaced Ambassador
Nolting in a shift of policy that made possible the overthrow of the
Diem regime. The first of a dismal procession of Vietnamese
governments was trying to restore order south of the 17th Parallel against Buddhist opposition. General William C. Westmore-
land was taking over from General Harkins amid warnings that
many more American troops would be needed in Vietnam.

In the midst of the 1964 Presidential campaign,
President Johnson chose to move with caution. Lodge did not
remain in Saigon very long, having resigned to make his vain
run against Barry Goldwater for the Republican Presidential
nomination. General Maxwell Taylor had replaced him. But
nothing had happened to halt the disintegration of the South
Vietnamese government. Yet, the American Embassy for reasons
of its own began to ooze optimism.

When Ambassador Taylor returned to Washington
after the Tonkin Gulf episode to report to the President, the
nation was assured on the basis of his brief experience in Saigon
that there was "continued progress" in the war. When Taylor
returned to the nation's capital for another progress report three
months later, he was kept away from the press. Secretary McNamara was later heard telling the President *sotto voce:* "It would
be impossible for Max to talk to these people [the reporters]
without leaving the impression that the situation is going to
hell." [69] For once, the government preferred discreet silence to
phony optimism in a difficult war situation.

New methods and new people were brought into

146 Saigon to keep the American and South Vietnamese governments from contradicting each other so frequently. Here, as in
the Pentagon, McNamara was trying to make everybody "speak
with one voice," which was a sensitive operation in a land where
American troops were not yet being hailed as liberators. As a
result of decisions reached at the Honolulu conference of 1964,
Barry Zorthian, an experienced official of the United States Information Service, was put in charge of all information originating with American sources in South Vietnam. He also maintained close contact with the South Vietnamese, but tried to
leave the impression that they were operating independently.
Yet, since he was Minister-Counselor of the Embassy at Saigon
and the head of the new Joint United States Public Affairs Office
(JUSPAO), it was evident that few Vietnamese except for the
Premier of the moment and leading generals would try to test his
authority.

The Zorthian machine tried to handle everything—
information, propaganda, intelligence, diplomatic background,
economic developments, military briefings, trips to centers of
military action, pacification efforts, and relationships with the
South Vietnamese. Predictably, this amalgamated information
office could not satisfy the veteran correspondents who were used
to fending for themselves and by now mistrusted almost anything
that emanated from the Embassy. But newcomers, ignorant for
the most part of affairs in Asia in general and Vietnam in particular, swarmed to the "Five O'Clock Follies" because they did not
know where else to go at first. Within a relatively short time,
Zorthian had a lot of new correspondents to work with and he gave
them satisfaction. If the old-timers chose to play it differently, he
could not help that.

With the opening of American bombing of North
Vietnam on February 7, 1965, the doldrums induced by the
Presidential election of 1964 ended abruptly. President Johnson,
bolstered by the extent of his victory over Goldwater, moved to
escalate the war in the hope that Hanoi would be forced to sue
for peace. In June, the flamboyant airman, Nguyen Cao Ky, took
over as Premier of South Vietnam with General Nguyen Van
Thieu, head of a military junta, as chief of state. On July 28,
1965, standing before television cameras at the White House,
President Johnson raised the total American troop commitment
in Vietnam to 125,000 and said: "This is really war." At the age
of 63, Henry Cabot Lodge went back to Saigon in August, reliev-

ing General Taylor. And in consequence of all these moves, the   147
news media at last decided that the war was worth covering
adequately. Within a year, nearly 500 correspondents had
swarmed into Saigon and television was proclaiming trium-
phantly that it was covering its first war. It took long enough to
convince television that the war should be covered as a regular
day-to-day matter.

While Zorthian did bring about considerable improvement in his personal relationships with the news media—he was a horse for work and always seemed to be on the
job—the point of view of the most influential correspondents
was slow to change. When Arthur Sylvester journeyed to Saigon
in the summer of 1965 to take a reading on the state of government news-media relations, he ran into a bitter argument with a
roomful of American correspondents. It was a case of overheated
emotions and utter lack of trust on both sides. Sylvester, as
usual, attacked the correspondents for not doing their job properly. In turn, the correspondents accused him of having told
them that the press should be "the handmaiden of government,"
which he denied. It was a thoroughly miserable exhibition, from
which neither the government nor the news media could take
satisfaction. The patient Zorthian had to start all over.

The attacks in which Sylvester had specialized now
were taken up by others. Robert H. Fleming, deputy press secretary at the White House, said, "Some reporters in Vietnam are
inexperienced. We are getting a headline type of coverage." A
State Department official, Eldridge Durbrow, said, "We are getting distorted reports from Vietnam . . . the reporters are inexperienced." General S. L. A. Marshall, one of the most distinguished of military correspondents, wrote of his colleagues, "The
overwhelming majority of correspondents do not get to the front
. . . The American press continues to be derelict in its main
responsibility. The story of the war is not being told . . ." [70]

THE CORRESPONDENTS' ROLE

This kind of criticism was baffling when the public was being
deluged with Vietnam War coverage in the newspapers, in radio,
in television, in the news magazines, and in topical books that
cascaded from the presses. After a halting start, there was no
doubt whatever that television was bringing the war into the
American living room night after night with all its shock and
horror; in fact, the television cameramen and correspondents

148 were often in the forefront of battle, risking their lives with the GIs, the Marines, and the South Vietnamese troops. No doubt this produced a certain amount of sensation for sensation's sake—the blood and gore of combat in an isolated action depicted without any relationship to the trend of events in Vietnam. But since the same thing often has been done in print for nearly 200 years of independent journalism, beginning with the American and French Revolutions, television can scarcely be accused of degrading the role of the journalist. It has actually given him a new dimension for his work, although he does not yet know enough to take full advantage of it. In common with much of journalism today, television's most grievous fault is the tendency to focus on the action and the uproar in the foreground, a relatively uncomplicated process, and set aside or overlook entirely the necessity for reporting on the ideas behind them, which is difficult enough, or attempting to illustrate them, which is often impossible.

In Vietnam, based on the evidence of more than two years of coverage beginning with the escalation of the war, television on balance acquitted itself well. It helped immeasurably to center public attention in the United States on the basis of the conflict and probably did it more effectively than most of the newspapers and magazines. The best of television, certainly, was every bit as good as the best of the correspondence in the published media. In the latter stages of the Vietnam War, because of the combined efforts of all the media, it became impossible for the public to avoid reading about the conflict, and seeing and hearing it, as well. The geography lesson was expensive— more than $25 billion annually once the American commitment to battle rose sharply—but the cost would have been infinitely greater if a determined effort had not been made to inform and involve the public.

Yet, it was a common observation, even after the flow of information about Vietnam became a torrent, that the public was confused by the war. Some in journalism argued that the news media were telling too much instead of too little, that the issues were being oversimplified or otherwise obscured and that the truth, in effect, was generally not being reported in its proper dimension. Undoubtedly, there was basis for such beliefs. But if the public was divided, so was the press itself on more than one occasion.

The extent of the strain within the news media was 149
demonstrated by the bitter arguments over Harrison E. Salisbury's coverage of Hanoi and the surrounding area in North Vietnam for *The New York Times* in late 1966 and early 1967.[71] As
Salisbury himself pointed out, he could not have made the journey if the United States and North Vietnam had formally declared war on each other, for then such an act would have
amounted to treason. But while it was unusual for a reporter to
be behind the lines, it was not unprecedented. During the Soviet
Union's blockade of Berlin, when a great Anglo-American air
fleet was risking war daily to supply the West Germans in their
beleaguered city, American reporters remained on the job in
Moscow and reporters for the Soviet Union were active in Washington. In a war comparable in some ways to Vietnam, and
completely unlike it in others, the British sanctioned reporting
from both sides and the Boers also permitted it.

The State Department, in Salisbury's case, made no
objection to his trip. After some delay the North Vietnamese
gave him a visa. What he did and what he saw bore out observations that had been made previously by French correspondents,
but the publication of his articles in *The New York Times* and
their syndication in other leading American papers created a
sensation. It was the first time the American public had been told
in so authoritative a fashion that the American bombing campaign had not then sapped Hanoi's will to fight, that nonmilitary
targets were being hit and that the North Vietnamese were making rapid repairs to some of the military installations that were
damaged. It was bad news—and exclusive bad news at that—
which raised the hackles of many who had been chanting endlessly of great American victories—or hoping for them. The
Defense and State Departments bristled with angry attacks and
some of Salisbury's rivals pointed out that part of his unattributed information had come from enemy sources. Errors also
cropped up in Salisbury's copy, but not of such magnitude as to
detract from the essential accuracy of his dispatches.

Had Salisbury's mission resulted in the submission
of peace feelers from Hanoi, an unspoken hope when he departed, then he would have been a hero. Certainly, he did everything he could to test the resolution of the North Vietnamese
government and found it unshaken, as other American visitors
that winter and spring also testified. Consequently, he was ac-

150 corded the treatment given to a harbinger of bad news (although he was mercifully spared the ultimate penalty so often handed out in more primitive societies).

No other correspondent who covered the Vietnam War received such treatment, although many were criticized and some were intensely critical of their own work. Frank McCulloch, *Time*'s bureau chief in Saigon for a considerable part of the war, said, "There is an overwhelming conviction that no one on the far end, be he reader or editor, understands what it is the correspondent is trying to say . . . The fault lies with the correspondent." Robert Shaplen of *The New Yorker*, whose acquaintance with Vietnam went back to 1946, argued, "The fact that the United States public is submerged in a constant flow of words and images does not mean clarification but can mean obfuscation." Keyes Beech of the *Chicago Daily News* was more philosophical, probably because he had been covering various wars for most of his career, and observed: "The biggest problem is trying to keep perspective here—not to be in euphoria one week and succumb to despair the next. You have to learn that a situation that seems hopeless on Saturday can seem not so bad next Tuesday." [72]

One of the most active of the Vietnam War correspondents wrote this despairing private assessment of his experience: "America no longer seems capable of functioning as a democracy and the free press itself is therefore obsolete. We still have television, of course. This is a pretty shabby substitute for the written word but it is better than nothing. If you cannot engage a man with a written story, perhaps you may be more successful by bashing him in the face with an impressive picture on the television screen." [73]

It was an extreme view, and one not generally held by either the combative and highly competitive correspondents or the leaders of government. Most of the hammering continued to be concentrated against the government's news policies, with officialdom usually on the defensive. Jack Foisie of the *Los Angeles Times* commented, "Formal censorship would be preferable to news management that squashes information at the roots." The ever critical Charles Mohr charged at one point that information officers in Saigon were more interested in policy than facts—"in the effect of a story rather than its accuracy." Malcolm W. Browne accused the Defense Department of having "deliberately misled American public opinion." [74]

But while the "credibility gap" in Vietnam was much discussed as a political issue, the public on the whole did not seem impressed with the theory that there was a gigantic conspiracy to twist the news. A majority appeared to accept the government's effort to put the best face on the matter, although belief in it was something else again. The big problem was the war, and not the telling of it, which so often depended on a particular point of view and sometimes on semantics. For example, during the summer of 1966, General Wallace Greene, the Marine Corps commandant, suggested to reporters in a background talk at Saigon that "at its present pace the war could last for eight years." Few were disposed to disagree with him; it was, in a few words, not a sensational statement. Forthwith, a number of news organizations reported rather routinely that a "Marine Corps study" had shown the war could continue for eight years at its current level. The President then lifted the offhand remark completely out of routine by denying that any "Marine Corps study" had been made. The embarrassed Marine general relapsed into silence. But nobody denied that the war, at that stage, showed any prospect of ending quickly.

The President made changes. He let Secretary McNamara go to the World Bank. He sent Ellsworth Bunker to Saigon as ambassador and General Creighton Abrams into the military team. He held conferences that seemed endless and staged meetings at the White House that were intended to reassure the public about Vietnam. Sometimes he even held a public catechism for his administrative and military chiefs in an effort to show the public on television that they all agreed with what he was doing. Having done this, he sometimes joked about his credibility problem.[75] True, the press was far from infallible and a substantial proportion of it was aligned against the President and his program in Vietnam. But this did not excuse the administration's repeated miscalculation of enemy intentions.

Long before the end was in sight, Washington gave ample indication that it did not have all the answers to the creation of a peaceful Vietnam and a stable Southeast Asia. So did the government of General Nguyen Van Thieu following the 1967 elections in South Vietnam. Hanoi, Peking, and Moscow all had something to say about it and counted on a confused and divided public opinion in the United States to help them get what they wanted. The continual posture of mutual suspicion between much of the press and government during the war, in this con-

152 nection, scarcely helped the American cause but neither side appeared disposed to do anything to improve the situation.

At a low point in the war, Secretary Rusk confided to a friend: "We are going to go through all hell before we can get Hanoi to come to the conference table. It took a long time in Korea. It is going to take us even longer here, but we're sticking with it." [76] More such blunt talk might have helped penetrate the fog of frustration and highly charged emotion that surrounded the Vietnam issue; however, nothing short of an honorable end to the war would have satisfied a majority of the American public.* It could put up with a "credibility gap." It would not accept defeat.

* On November 8, 1967, San Francisco voters by almost two to one rejected a proposition calling for an immediate cease-fire and withdrawal of American forces from Vietnam.

COVERAGE

10

BY THE HERD

The historian writes for the ages, the journalist for today. It is a mistake to confuse the two, although it is frequently done. Possibly that is because some journalists have become first-rate historians, and some historians have proved that they are capable of superior journalism.* Yet, when the historian contemplates the Negro riots that made a shambles of the ghettos of some of the major cities of the nation

*Allan Nevins and Bruce Catton are journalists who became historians. Arthur M. Schlesinger, Jr., and Henry Steele Commager are among the historians who also are journalists. H. G. Wells was journalist, historian, and novelist as well.

153

154   in the latter 1960s, he coolly studies cause and effect with infinite
patience and in his own good time.

To a journalist, who must go on the air in seconds or
run for a deadline within minutes, such contemplative methods
amount to sheer luxury. For him, they are an impossible dream. It
is his hard lot to determine what is happening as it is happening
and to report on events at once, if not sooner; later, if he has the
will and the wisdom, he may try to get at the meaning of the
news. Therein lies the heart of his problem. For if he has sniffed
danger in advance and made a thorough reconnaissance, he is at
least forewarned if not fully prepared. But more often than not,
he plunges into the swirling torrent of events no more ready to
cope with them at first, despite all advance planning, than the
most innocent bystander.

It is self-evident that the shock troops of journalism,
no less than the police and firemen and the National Guard,
should be in the forefront of any civil disorder if they are to do
their duty. Whether they are generalists or specialists, they must
find out first of all what is going on if they are to present the
public with a fair and accurate and independent report. Unlike
the historian in his lonely search for the truth, they must make a
record in words and pictures—the action they have seen, the
excited second- or third-hand reports of happenings they have not
seen, and the welter of conflicting argument arising from both.
Sometimes it takes a Congressional investigation to sort out fact
from fancy, although the method is not strictly guaranteed.

DO HEADLINES CAUSE TROUBLE?
To anyone who has ever tried to find out what is happening when
a big city is being torn apart by the convulsion of a race riot, it is
sheer nonsense to contend—as some do—that the public would
be better served by restricting the coverage. There is a distinct
difference between mass or herd journalism, concentrated in all
its unlovely strength on a single individual or an isolated event,
and the assignment of news staffs over a considerable area inhabited by tens of thousands of angry or frightened people. The
argument has been put forward, in perfectly good faith, that the
looters, burners, and rioters of Harlem, Watts, Hough, Newark,
Detroit, and a score or more of other places were stimulated by
publicity and emboldened to even greater misdeeds by screech-
ing headlines, excitable radio reports, and gory television coverage. There is no point in denying excesses in such coverage

because such things do happen, although not as frequently today
as they did some years ago. But to blame rioting on headlines, in
print or on the air, is rather reversing the actual order of events.
It is much like the case of the United Nations delegate who
blamed the Korean War on the size of the headlines in the
American press, rather than the Communist invasion south
across the 38th Parallel.

True, the news media have an obligation to guard
against the circulation of false reports that could start a riot or
increase the proportions of a civil disturbance that is already
under way. But every responsible journalist is well aware of this
and does not have to be reminded constantly. After all, in Newark in the summer of 1967, it was word-of-mouth rumor that
police had killed a cab driver which began the actual disorder; by
the time the news media had learned the story was untrue, it was
too late. Those intent on looting, arson, and rooftop sniping
scarcely take their orders from the newspapers, radio, and television. And they do not need headlines or television cameras to
encourage them if they are bent on demonstrating, in other
ways, against ghetto living during the long hot American sum-
mers.

Nevertheless, a number of efforts have been made
by the news media at self-regulation to guard against the excesses that may be attributed, rightly or wrongly, to the presence
of newsmen, still photographers, and television cameramen. The
oldest is the Chicago plan for keeping a lid on news of a riot until
it is under control. Others are procedures followed in St. Louis to
clear all factual material through a police information center
and in Omaha to wait at least 30 minutes before reporting on a
disturbance. Moreover, the Community Relations Service of the
Department of Justice has conferred extensively with the news
media to establish guidelines of a general nature in riot coverage.
And a number of individual news executives have instituted
precautionary procedures in their own organizations. As Richard
S. Salant, president of CBS News, put it: "The real problem is
responsible reporting—making yourself inconspicuous when it
is apparent your camera is encouraging performance and not
'shooting bloody'—gore for gore's sake." [77]

Here, in essence, is the dilemma of the journalist.
By his very presence at the scene of action, wittingly or unwittingly, he becomes a part of the news. He cannot disguise himself; nor, for that matter, can he conceal the cameras that on

156 occasion act as an incitement to demonstrators even if pictures are not actually being taken. Without doing anything, he may be attacked or beaten or robbed of his equipment merely because he is a symbol against which a demonstration may be effectively made. Nor is this limited to rioters in American cities; for years, mobs of paid agitators abroad have learned that it makes headlines in the United States to beat up an American correspondent or otherwise subject him to indignities. It must be admitted, as well, that there are newsmen and cameramen for all news media who, by their conduct or their personalities, make themselves issues and sometimes deliberately provoke incidents; few and scattered though such happenings may be, even one is too many for the good repute of the profession.

Yet, if the journalist gives in to the notion that rioters will calm down if only they are denied the headlines and dramatic television pictures, both he and the public court disaster. Had there been less than complete coverage in the Birmingham riots of the early 1960s, the public might never have seen the visual proof of police dogs tearing at Negro demonstrators that did so much to encourage enactment of civil rights legislation. Nor did the public that saw the shooting and burning and looting on its television screens in later disturbances remain indifferent. Such things are bound to have political consequences when they become known; their appearance in the headlines and on television magnifies and intensifies the reaction but can scarcely be said to have caused it.

It is pure sophistry to contend that turmoil in the American city may be lessened somehow if the newsmen and their cameras will stay away until it is all over, delay their arrival, or censor themselves. The brutal truth is that even where there is partial or total local self-censorship, and it has been done, the news of the rioting is circulated promptly outside the affected area and the playback is sometimes instantaneous. Moreover, there is evidence in profusion to show that rumors, spread by word of mouth and taxicab radios, have caused a great deal more harm in the ghetto than the coverage of the news by trained, seasoned professionals who can distinguish between rumor and fact. On the contrary, there is no evidence to show that the rioting in Watts would have been less severe if the journalist had not been on the job (and for the most part he was, in fact, lamentably late). Nor is there any tangible proof that the

death toll and destruction in Newark and Detroit would have
been smaller if the coverage had been less complete.

Self-regulation is necessary—even imperative—when there is danger that an unimportant incident may be magnified into a widespread disorder if it is publicized in a sensational manner. But once a riot is raging out of control, there is no point whatever to a miserable attempt to keep it a secret from the very people who are in the middle of a horrifying experience. By so doing, the news media can only contribute to their own lack of credibility with the public, for such things cannot be kept secret and it is a mistake to try.

If it were possible by some miracle of official foresight to keep the free-lances and the amateurs outside police lines during a civil disturbance, the professionals might be given more protection. But even this minimal step is open to some objection because it would be difficult to enforce and, even if some effective means of enforcement could be devised, it would make impossible such feats as the color film of the Kennedy assassination taken by an amateur, Abraham Zapruder. The self-defeating nature of censorship, no matter how it is imposed, is beyond argument. Without doubt, there are serious risks to the continued coverage of civil rights disturbances by the news media without major limitations; yet, these risks are unavoidable in a democratic society that is committed to the principle of a free press.

POOL REPORTING

In a number of other areas in the news where mass coverage has proved to be both a blight and an embarrassment, journalists could well yield in their traditional insistence on unrestricted access to the news. The theory has been breached numerous times in the past without dealing a fatal blow to the republic. Certainly, it will be again if the reporting of the weddings of President Johnson's two daughters is taken as a precedent.

As is customary at such events, the clamor for press credentials and picture privileges extends far beyond the regulars of the Washington press corps. A wide variety of journalists, from the Australian Consolidated Press to the editor of the student paper at Davis and Elkins College in West Virginia, discovered urgent reasons for their personal attendance at Luci Baines Johnson's wedding. Some reporters demanded the installation of

158   special telephones in the pews of the Shrine of the Immaculate
Conception in Washington, D. C., so they could dictate their
historic accounts. A television network asked for permission to
fly a blimp over the wedding party for pictures from a special
angle. A news photographer with unsuspected talents as a stee-
plejack proposed to climb the Shrine's tower for competitive
advantage.

It is not surprising, under the pressure of handling
such absurdities as well as the more serious press arrangements,
that the White House ran out of patience. When *Women's Wear
Daily* published an advance sketch of a bridesmaid's gown,
which as it turned out was not entirely accurate, that publication's press credentials were lifted. It was, some zealots cried, an
infringement of the freedom of the press, but not many editors
paid much attention to it. Even they had grown uneasy over the
excesses of herd journalism, as it was then being practiced in the
United States. Although they kept up a steady public opposition
to the imposition of pool reporting and picture-taking, they accepted pool arrangements for covering Luci's marriage to Patrick
John Nugent with good grace.

On the day of the wedding, August 6, 1966, the
representatives of the news media almost outnumbered the
guests, causing the astonished groom to observe, "I've never seen
so many newspapermen in all my life." Had the White House not
taken the firmest steps to control the news, picture, and television traffic, the result might have been utter chaos. As it was,
things turned out pretty well, even though the day was hot and
the interior of the great Roman Catholic cathedral was stifling.

Only 20 pool reporters were permitted to attend the
church ceremonial and the reception, with the remainder of the
press corps observing from a distance. There were about 500
news media representatives in all, including 200 photographers
and 60 foreign correspondents. The President and Mrs. Johnson
headed a list of 700 in the church, including 42 members of the
wedding party. With this kind of a crowd, and room at a pre-
mium, the television crews and the photographers had to be
satisfied with pictures of the President's younger daughter and
the groom entering and leaving the church.

The pool reporting and the closeups of the wedding
party, as seen on television, were spread to the nation with great
professional skill. The reporters of the wire services and the
Washington dailies, with support from news magazine poolers,

made their own work available to the rest of the media. Thus, 159
while nobody had exclusive coverage, everybody was guaranteed
complete coverage under the pool system. It saved the news
media a great deal of time and the White House untold trouble.
Consequently, the same procedure was applied to the coverage of
Lynda Bird Johnson's wedding to Captain Charles S. Robb in
December, 1967.

Yet, despite this and other successful demonstrations of what a good group of pool news and film men can do to
handle a preplanned news event for the multitude, it has been
difficult to dispose of the notion that a journalist must be physi-
cally present at every major event he covers. Even after more
than 40 years of radio and 20 years of television, most self-
respecting newspapers cling to the time-honored routine that
their staff members must be eyewitnesses to events. The practice
has much to recommend it, particularly when events are of a
highly controversial nature; moreover, smaller newspapers and
local radio and television stations that have taken to staff coverage of national and international events are to be commended
and encouraged. No part of an independent system of news
gathering and distribution can afford to abdicate its primary
responsibility; yet, at the same time, due to the increasing
efficiency and lowered cost of jet air travel, it must be pointed
out that the growing numbers of news and film men at major
events often create major problems. Again and again, perfectly
well-intentioned correspondents have discovered that they have
unwittingly become part of the news and even helped make it
merely by being at the scene of action.

THE PROBLEM OF OVERCOVERAGE

It is scarcely a revelation that not everybody who proclaims
himself to be a journalist actually is one. A brief census of the
occupants of any press box in the land at a major sports event
will provide convincing proof that the hangers-on constitute an
embarrassment and an encumbrance to the working newsman,
although he never has found out how to handle the problem. In
addition, at any event where several hundred persons gather
with credentials from various news organizations, it is impossible to separate the correspondent of *The New York Times* from a
hot-tempered youngster covering his first big assignment for a
paper of less renown, or the photographer for *Life* magazine
from the free-lance picture-snatcher who is not averse to creat-

160   ing a sensation. Like any other crowd, a crowd of newsmen often can be stampeded by its worst elements when a news situation gets out of hand.

All this may serve to explain, although it does not excuse, the scenes of disorder primarily caused by newsmen who unintentionally roughed up the Pope and the Beatles with impartial diligence. Neither the feelings of Lady Bird Johnson nor Brigitte Bardot have been spared during photographers' joint efforts to take their pictures. Even Washington correspondents, usually a genteel lot, have been somewhat amazed to find that the viewing public does not take kindly to televised shots of newsmen jumping up at a Presidential news conference and yelling at the President of the United States to attract his attention.

This does not mean, of course, that the American journalist is inevitably destined to act as a rowdy in a group under heavy competitive pressure, although no one has ever accused him of being a Little Lord Fauntleroy. Nor are press photographers and television cameramen, working against each other under difficult circumstances, likely to display the manners of Sunday school characters. The press corps does not exist that meekly accepts news handouts and dictated statements; generally, it is a combative group that responds to provocation in kind. Such attitudes are scarcely calculated to generate sweetness and light on all occasions.

The problem of excessive coverage is not particularly new in American journalism. During the 1930s, Colonel (later Brigadier General) Charles A. Lindbergh, the first to fly the Atlantic alone, bitterly complained of being hounded by the press. On his honeymoon with the former Anne Morrow, a spluttering press motorboat for eight hours circled the yacht on which he and his bride were cruising. During and after the investigation and trial that followed the kidnap-murder of their first-born, the Lindberghs were frequently pursued by newsmen who wanted pictures and interviews. Finally, late in 1935, after a tabloid photographer had forced their nursemaid's auto to the curb to obtain pictures of their second child, the Lindberghs left for England to find a haven from further unwelcome press attention.[78]

With the exception of a brief period in 1940, when Lindbergh himself bid for public attention by campaigning for American neutrality, the press never again forced itself upon

him and his family. The affair, however, meant nothing to a
newer generation of American journalists after World War II. In
the excitement of pursuing new heroes and villains, they forgot
the lessons of the Lindbergh case. Those who ignored the past, in
this sense, were compelled to relive it.

There were complaints against the excesses of news
coverage at such varying events as the United Nations Conference on International Organization in San Francisco in 1945 and
the foreign tours of President Eisenhower and Vice President
Richard M. Nixon in the late 1950s. But by an ironic twist of
circumstance, the issue flared into public attention once more by
the manner in which the news media covered the coast-to-coast
tour of Nikita S. Khrushchev, the Soviet premier, from September 15 to 28, 1959. It was no hero this time, but a favorite villain,
who caused public reproaches to descend on the press.

The whole tour was unruly, despite the efforts of
Henry Cabot Lodge to persuade the 300-odd representatives of
the news media to observe the amenities. But at every stop, their
numbers were swelled by local and regional reporters and photographers who wanted to close in on the Soviet visitor with just as
much persistence as the national correspondents. At length,
much to Khrushchev's amusement, the contest to publicize the
foremost advocate of world Communism in the United States
erupted into the "Battle of Coon Rapids" at Roswell Garst's farm
in that Iowa village. Angered by the badgering of his guest, the
irate farmer pelted newsmen and photographers with silage and
kicked out in all directions with Harrison E. Salisbury as one of
his accidental targets.

"Before the trip was over, I was ducking my press
badge," said Alexander F. (Casey) Jones, the editor of the *Syra-
cuse* (N. Y.) *Herald-Journal.* "I did not want people to know I
was one of the mob of human locusts which acted like a bunch of
reform school characters suddenly released. These big stories are
becoming nightmares. With the advent of television, involving
all the equipment that it does, and the Capone gangster manners
of the cameramen, the free press apparatus has grown to the
point where it is impossible for anyone to think . . . Anything
that happens to us in putting us where we belong from the
standpoint of our manners and deportment is deserved." [79]

It is typical of newspapermen to try to blame television for most of their troubles, but the accusation unhappily does
not square with the facts. There was no television during the

162 circuslike murder trials of the 1920s—and very little radio coverage—but the press managed to outrage a considerable section of important public opinion with its excesses. Certainly, television has intensified the evils of which Colonel Lindbergh and others have complained with considerable justice. But it does seem that all elements of the news media must bear the blame for a rapidly descending spiral of public confidence in the ability of hundreds of news and film men to conduct themselves with professional dignity and competence under competitive conditions.

In the wake of the Kennedy assassination and the Oswald murder, there were numerous proposals for pool coverage of all major stories where it was possible to enforce such restrictions. But not even the prodding of the Warren Commission report produced agreement among the journalists themselves that pooling was always preferable to another such fiasco. The Associated Press argued that it could not depend on a small-town pool reporter, or even three or four who were not familiar with the needs of the AP's thousands of members and clients. Conversely, the smaller newspapers and the local electronic outlets insisted that they were just as entitled to individual coverage as *The New York Times,* the AP, or the *Neue Zurcher Zeitung.* Few were willing to agree in advance to restrictions on major news coverage, except when sheer necessity forced officials at various levels of government to impose reasonable limitations. Then, the news media inevitably protested—a shameful abdication of journalistic responsibility.

"Freedom and public order are usually at war, anyway," wrote Herbert Brucker, the former president of the American Society of Newspaper Editors. "Success lies in a working balance. But the increasing weight and ubiquity of today's mechanics of reporting make the irritation more painful. We of the press will have to find at least a rule-of-thumb answer. So great is the public hostility becoming that if we don't find a way, it will be found for us." [80]

PROPOSALS FOR REFORM

Although there were no demonstrations against the news media outside the ghetto, the public mood in the latter 1960s was unmistakable to those who had spent a lifetime in the study of mass opinion. The problem of herd journalism and its excesses continued to arouse deep concern. Most of the leaders of the news media realized that some important step would have to be

taken sooner or later to stimulate a change in the public's attitude and reduce the possibility of another Oswald case—or
worse.

Well in advance of the 1968 National Conventions,
Walter Cronkite suggested that television should be removed
from the floor of the convention halls. The managing editor of
CBS "News" put it this way: "I heartily believe that in 1968 the
political parties ought to ban television from the floor of the
convention hall. It certainly makes a mockery of the fact that
this is a convention of delegates who are supposed to be listening
to the speeches and tending to some sort of business on the
floor." In an aside, he added, "I'll probably be read out of every
honorary journalism society in the world." [81]

The reaction was quite to the contrary. Vermont
Royster, the editor of the *Wall Street Journal*, declared at once
that the questions Cronkite raised were by no means confined to
television. The issue, as Royster defined it, was "where observation ends and participation begins, where the instruments used
to report what's happening affect the happening." And this, of
course, was and is the crucial point in any consideration of the
effects of massive news coverage.

"Any legislative committee, any corporate board
meeting, any diplomatic conference or any labor bargaining session would turn out differently if every tremor were recorded on
the journalistic seismograph," Royster wrote. "Hence, when a
newspaper gets huffy because its reporter is denied access to an
executive session of a legislature's committee, or when there's a
hassle because Washington reporters are not told what the Secretary of Defense said to the President behind closed doors, it could
be that the journalists do protest too much."

He drew a distinction between the right to sit in the
press or public galleries, writing or commenting on the events of
the day, and the deliberate intrusion on a private delegation
conference on the floor. He was all for aggressive reporting.
"There's no warrant, however," he concluded, "to disrupt needlessly the orderly conduct of affairs. Those who do so, whether
with camera or with pencil, risk making a mockery not only out
of such things as a political convention but of their own duty." [82]

But it was difficult then, just as it is today, to put
over the notion that news coverage could be based on quality
rather than quantity. A Joint Committee on News Coverage
Problems, representing five organizations in the newspaper and

164   broadcasting fields, regarded pool coverage as a dubious substitute for unlimited access to the news by all concerned. While
certain standards for pooling were suggested, it was not done in
such a way as to induce either the news or film man to place
much faith in the system.[83] No less an authority than Pierre
Salinger, during his service at the White House for Presidents
Kennedy and Johnson, complained at one time that there was
too much cheating by pool reporters who held out juicy details
for their own exclusive use.[84]

There was still another reason for the professional
mistrust of pooling arrangements. The pooler could quite unintentionally muff his assignment and leave his colleagues in the
lurch. It happened in New York during the parade that wel-
comed General Douglas MacArthur after his dismissal as the
United Nations commander in Korea. The great Meyer Berger of
The New York Times was chosen that day as the pool representative for several score reporters. He was provided with a jeep and
a driver, given all manner of credentials and placed at the head
of the procession so he could look back at MacArthur. But he had
no luck. At an intersection, uninstructed police forced the jeep
out of line. Had it not been for an athletic journalism student
who jogged the five miles beside MacArthur's slow-moving automobile, the reporters at the end of the parade would have had to
depend entirely on television for their detail.

Both the disadvantages and the benefits of pooling
were even more strikingly illustrated after the Kennedy assassination in Dallas. Merriman Smith of UPI, riding in the pool
reporters' automobile, got the first break—and a Pulitzer
Prize—by snatching the car's portable radio telephone and flash-
ing the news to his office. But thereafter the nation and the world
were well served by pooling arrangements, brilliantly and unself-
ishly executed by the news media, in a situation where the
transmission of quick and accurate news was of the highest
importance.

It is scarcely a surprise therefore that American
journalism has been unable to come up with a definitive solution
to the problems of mass coverage and excessive coverage. Nor
has anybody inside the profession been able to reconcile the
conflicting movements to stimulate greater national and international coverage by local news media and to impose some limitation on the activities of the journalistic herd it produces.
Thoughtful journalists agree that selective coverage by the repre-

sentatives of the national media, plus a few others from prestige   165
newspapers and magazines, can quickly and efficiently blanket
the country with authoritative and independently reported accounts of major news. But it is difficult to decide at all times who
will select the poolers and how it shall be done.

For the short run, every participating news organization takes pride in announcing to its public: "Our man was
there." But for the long run, the outcome may not be very satis-
factory. For the herd, very often, tends to block itself off from
the news. From Cape Kennedy to the Houston Space Center and
from Washington to Saigon, it has happened in the past—and it
will happen again—that the journalists who swarm after the
news sometimes know less than the television-viewing public at
home whom they are supposed to inform. If the President of the
United States goes abroad, the correspondents who accompany
him in the press planes are frequently out of touch with him for
hours. They fly now—and cover the news later. It has happened
that some have been so far behind that they never were able to
catch more than a glimpse of the President during the entire
tour—and this was as true of President Eisenhower as it has
been of Presidents Kennedy and Johnson. Herd coverage scarcely
guarantees good coverage—or in fact any coverage at all.

Once the media managers are able to convince their
representatives in the field that they are public figures who must
be accountable for their public conduct at all times, there may be
some hope of self-regulation. It is not impossible. The visit of
Pope Paul VI to Yankee Stadium in New York City was so well
managed and so beautifully covered that journalists could take a
certain amount of pride in the result. And if there was more of
an edge to the coverage of Svetlana Alliluyeva's first confrontation with the American news media in New York City, it still
went off smoothly and merited the applause it received from all
concerned. Similarly, there were no unpleasant incidents to mar
the excellence of the news and film reportage of the "Glassboro
Summit" when President Johnson and Premier Kosygin of the
Soviet Union conferred in Glassboro, N. J., following the Middle
East War in 1967. What is required of the journalist is the same
sense of restraint, care, and fortitude which he has displayed so
often in covering a natural disaster, a civil disturbance, or a war.

If self-regulation breaks down, then inevitably the
journalist will come increasingly under ever greater official restraints. The White House's pool arrangements are one symp-

166   tom. The United Nations' procedure of setting up categories of correspondents on a priority basis for the coverage of major sessions is another. At all levels of government, both here and abroad, there will always be officials who are anxious to take advantage of the inability of the journalist to control himself by imposing controls on him. Sometimes, they may confer with representatives of journalists; but where journalists cannot agree, and fight among themselves, then the arrangements are going to be made for them. The old rule of "Devil take the hindmost" is not going to be honored much longer by responsible governments when journalists gather in large numbers. Thus, whenever the perils of herd journalism outweigh the advantages, controlled journalism is likely to result.

       Self-discipline, now and in the future, will be one of the journalist's most necessary qualities if he is to maintain his freedom of action.

JUNKET

11

JOURNALISM

$\mathbb{W}$hen General Rafael Leonidas Trujillo Molina was riding high as the dictator of the Dominican Republic, he gained a reputation as a generous and expansive host among the American journalists who were favored with expenses-paid trips to his island stronghold. If some of them were temporarily blinded to his more prevalent image as a tyrant who ruled under a ruthless policy of terror and repression, that exactly suited Trujillo's purpose. He had planned it that way.

The manner in which the Dominican dictator tried to polish up his reputation in the United States did not come to

168   public notice until it was spread on the record of the Senate Foreign Relations Committee. Then it became known that the Dominican Republic Information Center had paid substantial fees to International News Service to gather and distribute material in which Trujillo was interested. It was testified that the project went on for some years and that the news service was paid at the rate of $6,000 for three months, $4,000 of it from the Dominican Republic and $2,000 from a New York publicity agency. Other testimony showed that American journalists had made trips to the Dominican Republic in Trujillo's private plane with their wives on expenses-paid journeys to the island.

The contract ended with the merger of the Hearst wire service with United Press in 1958, resulting in the creation of United Press International. Subsequently, according to testimony at the Senate hearings, UPI did business with about a score of public relations firms that represented foreign governments, some carried over from INS, but gradually abandoned the practice. The investigators were told that the work was carried on by the UPI Special Services Division and did not appear on the daily news file. However, Senator J. W. Fulbright, the committee chairman, was critical of the practice.

When the committee turned to an investigation of the representation of the interests of Nationalist China and the Republic of South Africa in the United States, further details of the practice of junket journalism became known. Hamilton Wright, Sr., the founder of the Hamilton Wright Organization, which for many years represented various foreign nations in the United States, gave his views in a "strictly confidential" letter. It was to the South African Information Service, dated April 12, 1962, and was read into the record of the Senate hearings. These were the significant portions:

". . . It is no trouble to get good editors from good newspapers—[to travel] but it is extremely difficult to get executive editors from the largest syndicates . . .

"We have many friends in all syndicates. We continually extend invitations for themselves and their wives to be 'our guests' on visits to foreign countries. The returns are fabulous. On a recent visit to Mexico one of these editors wrote five stories—used another five written by us and literally flooded the U. S. A. with excellent publicity about tourism in Mexico." Wright, a master salesman, also guaranteed to obtain the Nationalist Chinese $2,500,000 in free publicity for a one-year contract for

$300,000. He even was able to sell one of his staff as a stringer for various agencies that needed Formosan coverage.[85]

The Fulbright hearings disclosed that various other public relations firms also had made it a practice to organize press junkets and other entertainment for newsmen and some even presented gifts and money. The intent of the 1938 Foreign Agents Registration Act, if not the actual letter of the law, was also found to have been breached on numerous occasions.

The journalism junketing continued, however. One of the most active foreign exploiters continued to be the South African Information Service, which in 1965 and 1966 brought a score or more of editors of segregationist and other far right publications from the United States to write firsthand accounts of life in the Republic of South Africa. Many were favorable. But now and then, even a junketeer asserted his freedom. He would, in effect, double cross his expectant hosts depicting conditions as they actually existed in the land of apartheid. South African authorities soon decided that greater virtues were to be found in journalists of demonstrable extreme right convictions. It came to suspect others who might not be as impressed with the beauties of life in South Africa. As for journalists who tried to report with consistent impartiality as resident correspondents, their fate was foreordained. In a typical case, Joseph Lelyveld of *The New York Times* was told that his visa would not be renewed when it expired and he had to leave the country. No reason for the action was given formally, but it was obviously due to the impartial quality of Lelyveld's reportage.[86]

WHEN THE GOVERNMENT PAYS

The efforts to influence the American news media to adopt a more favorable view of various foreign countries have not, on the whole, had a great deal of impact regardless of the claims that have been made by public relations people. What such practices actually do is to strike at the credibility of the media that are involved. Admittedly, the proportion of journalists who accept favors is small; most respectable news organizations insist on paying the way of their representatives if legitimate news is the basic reason for such a journey.

The Vietnam War provided an exception to this general practice. Just before the escalation of the conflict, the Defense Department flew numerous correspondents—some from newspapers of national repute—from the United States to Saigon

170   for 10-day junkets. The cost to the Defense Department was about $1,000 each for the plane fare, and somewhat more than $50,000 was spent. Department officials made no secret of the purpose of the junkets, which was to try to obtain "unprejudiced, independent opinion" on the progress of the war from correspondents who were considered not as contentious as those who were covering the conflict at the time. A random sampling of the Vietnam reportage in some of the newspapers involved failed to disclose any significant change in either the tone or the thrust of the correspondence as a result of the junkets.

    The United States Information Agency also participated in the payment of transportation in order to induce the generally critical Asian and European press to send their own correspondents to Saigon. Such junkets were conducted for 30 to 35 Asians and Europeans, according to testimony by Leonard Marks, USIA director, before the Senate Foreign Relations Committee. He sought to justify the junkets on the ground that many European and Asian newspapers could not afford to send their own correspondents to Vietnam. When Senator Fulbright and others suggested that the USIA was trying to change the generally unfavorable tone of the Asian and European press toward the American war effort, Marks denied it. But Fulbright insistently raised the question, "Doesn't this point to a possible conflict of interest that might compromise the objectivity newspapers owe to their readers?" He pointed out that such great newspapers as the *Toronto Star* and the *Toronto Globe and Mail* had refused the USIA offer of free transportation for their correspondents. The conclusion was self-evident.[87]

    The Vietnam War practices, which were dropped when the coverage reached herd proportions, had been standard operating procedure for years in the American armed forces. Until the Defense Department clamped down as a means of checking interservice rivalry, both the Navy and the Air Force often invited groups of newsmen to their installations for public relations purposes, flew them about the country, or made room for them on Navy ships. On a space available basis, almost any journalist who could drum up the credentials was hauled overseas to tour various NATO and other installations. This was regarded as legitimate public business and was strongly defended by the armed forces involved. The Army, of course, operated at a disadvantage because it did not have the generous resources for transporting correspondents that were at the command of the rival services. But somehow, the Army managed to get its share of correspondents to strategic points where they could see and report on new developments. In short, when it came to promoting junket journalism, the United States was probably more active during much of the 1960s than any other government—and as hard put to justify the practice.

Aside from the political and military aspects of foreign junketeering by representatives of the mass media, the most prevalent manner of promoting free trips today is to write for a travel magazine or the travel section of a large newspaper. The airlines customarily inaugurate new services by throwing parties and lavish junkets for travel editors on an all-expenses paid basis. While Kermit Holt of the *Chicago Tribune* was president of the Society of American Travel Writers, he conceded that sponsors picked up the tab most of the time "because most travel sections don't produce enough ad revenues to make a budget for a writer to go on his own." The *Chicago Tribune,* it should be added, is one of the newspapers that pays its own way when it sends representatives on junkets.

Some junkets, of course, have produced more than mere publicity or other forms of puffery for the sponsors. JETRO, a Japanese government agency for the promotion of foreign trade, brought Sidney P. Allen of the *San Francisco Chronicle* to Japan in 1965, along with a score of others. Allen, a financial writer, did a special series on the Japanese economy and the *Chronicle* published it.

But the admittedly promotional aspects of junketeering usually are dominant. On one such trip, nearly 100 reporters and their wives were flown to Freeport, on Grand Bahama Island, by the Grand Bahama Port Authority and the Holiday Inns of America, Inc. A new inn was being opened and other "news" of a similar nature provided the pretext for the outing. A New York public relations agency, Bell & Stanton, Inc., took satisfaction in noting that 18 "good positive" stories about Grand Bahama Island were published in national magazines and New York dailies. One enthusiastic syndicate writer reported that in six years the magic of American private enterprise had changed an "ugly duckling" into a "preening swan."

Domestically, the competition to play host to a complaisant press is even more hectic. The movies, auto firms, real estate companies, hotels, restaurants, and night clubs from Las Vegas to Broadway, among others, rival each other in offering

172 free excursions for various reasons to journalists with a special interest in their operations. These courtesies are generally rejected by newspapers of stature. If their representatives go on a trip, the paper nearly always pays their way.

A surprising number of other organizations, however, see no harm in junkets for which someone else pays. Warner Brothers was reputed to have spent $100,000 to bring 350 newsmen to Hollywood for the premiere of a movie comedy and a three-day spell of entertainment. When Westinghouse Broadcasting began an all-news program on two of its radio stations, it flew 120 advertising executives, writers, and columnists to London for what it described as a five-day "news seminar." The cost was estimated at $60,000. Schenley's reportedly spent $15,000 for a stunt to introduce its bottled cocktails to the press. As Quentin L. Harvell, executive director of the Public Relations Society of America, explained it, "The competition for exposure is now greater than ever. To create an awareness of the media requires more than it used to—you have to have something special." [88]

THE INDEPENDENCE OF WRITERS

Of all areas of journalism, sports has been most vulnerable in the past to the blandishments of promoters. The most familiar cases are those of some sports writers who acted as paid publicity men for the events their papers assigned them to cover. Editors have done what they can to stamp out the practice, but it still persists here and there. As for the old baseball practice of letting the club pick up the expenses of the sports writers, that has been abandoned for years by the more responsible newspapers. But in professional football, boxing, horse racing, and ice hockey, some of the easy-going practices of the past persist. A number of papers throughout the country cater to bettors and bookmakers with information on point spreads and other gambling data, arguing that it is a "service to readers" and "not illegal." Several papers run the U. S. daily Treasury Balance, knowing perfectly well that the last three figures are the payoff for local numbers rackets.

As for sports telecasts, the practice of permitting clubs to let their own men announce the details of a game has brought about obvious conflicts of interest, particularly when the network has a contractual involvement with the club or owns it

outright. That problem will not be resolved until television acts   173
decisively to remove from itself the suspicion that is still attached to the sports sections of some otherwise responsible newspapers. The only way to do it is to guarantee the independence of
the sportscaster.

As for the critics and reviewers, the best ones have
always insisted that tickets to shows and concerts on which they
sit in judgment are a legitimate charge against their own news
organizations. Generally, the leading news media agree with
them. But literally hundreds of ersatz critics from the backwash
of journalism daily violate all ethical considerations by demanding tickets to leading attractions. In New York, such things can
be resisted but promoters are not such free agents elsewhere.
The pretended journalists in this shadow area create the same
problem in the coverage of the arts as they do in the political,
diplomatic, and military field. Often, those unfamiliar with the
mores of journalism suggest that the licensing of the journalist
by one means or another would dispose of the difficulty. The
trouble with licensing, of course, is that it also would sound the
knell of free journalism. The only way of dealing with the ragtag
and bobtail element is to judge each case on its merits. That, by
and large, is how the needs of the critics and reviewers from less
affluent news organizations are handled.[89]

Kenneth MacDonald, the editor of the *Des Moines
Register* and *Tribune*, spoke for the strictest managers in journalism in outlining his policy toward junketing and free-loading,
saying, "We pay our own way to fashion and food shows, on
baseball trips, to new auto model unveilings, etc., and we frown
on passes for staff members other than those who have a professional reason for accepting them. I do not believe that responsible newspapermen are influenced by gifts, at least not in the
direction anticipated by the giver . . . This does not mean that I
condone gift-giving. Except for minor items at Christmas time,
etc., I think gifts should be rejected."

The equally ethical Royce Howes of the *Detroit Free
Press* thought the damage was primarily moral. "The undeniable,
flagrantly free-loading situation is about as bad a thing as can be
for the dignity, and hence for the reputation, of the participant—
and doubtless more especially if he is a newspaperman," he said.
"Whether it has a consequence to him in any other respect, I'd
question . . . My observation is that the beneficiary of a free-load-

174 ing is often quite cynical about the merits of his hosts. This does not in the least diminish the damage to professional stature that lies in unabashed exploitation."

However, many editors and managers in American journalism have adopted a more permissive attitude. They do not often object to free trips, parties, and even small gifts for their associates and their employees as long as publicity payoffs are kept out of the newspaper. One justification for this is a kind of ceremonial politeness to those who do business with the newspaper—advertisers, news sources, and others of influence in the community. Many an editor, for example, feels he cannot in good conscience refuse to attend a cocktail party or dinner given by a major advertiser or an influential political figure. For the same reason, the chief of a Washington or United Nations news bureau appears at numerous diplomatic receptions, the least newsworthy of functions, rather than offend important people. When a journalist ascends into the rarefied atmosphere of a Walter Lippmann, he is able to overlook the mundane considerations of party-hopping and other purely public relations functions. But in the workaday world, even those with the noblest attitudes find it necessary, as Royce Howes once said, to "show the flag" on occasion.

One of the most sensible newspaper executives, Harry Montgomery, assistant publisher of the *Arizona Republic* and *Gazette,* put the problem in this fashion: "Telling a reporter he can't let a promoter or a public relations man buy him a drink or give him a pass would be about as effective, in my opinion, as telling him to go forth and sin no more. I attend quite a few cocktail parties. Even when I know their purpose is promotion of a firm or product. I don't feel the least bit obligated or contaminated, and I don't believe reporters do, either. If the promoter wishes to spend his money for that sort of thing, it is his business." [90]

Clifton Daniel, managing editor of *The New York Times,* was equally blunt. The *Times,* he explained, always offers to pay "but we don't refrain from covering the news because we might have to accept a free meal or an occasional trip in the process." The *Portland Oregonian,* too, accepts trips "when a commercial interest and a legitimate news interest coincide." The *Pittsburgh Post-Gazette* was the frankest of all, ruling out only the obvious publicity gimmicks, but permitting reporters to go on trips where there was news interest. "If we had a larger

news budget," said William Block, the publisher, "we might ban   175
the trips entirely." [91]

THE HIGH PRICE OF JUNKETS

The acceptance of gifts poses another ethical problem for the journalist. At Christmas time, in the offices of news organizations that welcome the largesse of public relations men, everything from liquor to food baskets comes to editors and reporters alike. The more important the journalist, the more attention he receives. It is scarcely a secret that less scrupulous members of the profession, particularly in the sensational area of the press, think nothing of compromising themselves by accepting gifts of considerable value. But in the higher echelons of journalism, the line is strictly drawn. A Roscoe Drummond or an Arthur Krock may accept a gift necktie, a bottle of Scotch, or a box of apples without causing talk. And even Drew Pearson may accept a Christmas turkey from Lyndon Baines Johnson (who stopped sending them after he became President). But there are also a number of journalists who would not even accept a bottle of liquor from a home-town Congressman. No publisher can have much confidence in editors who take whatever they can get, and no responsible editor likes to see his staff members flaunting gifts from public relations offices.[92]

The junkets and the gifts, regardless of their extent, are symptomatic of the critical malaise in American journalism—the resolute refusal to do anything of a substantive nature to enforce professional standards. Occasionally, the philosophy of accepting something for nothing has produced scandals. At least 32 Illinois newspaper editors and publishers were disclosed to be on the Illinois State payroll in 1949 in an exposé by the *St. Louis Post-Dispatch* and *Chicago Daily News*. In 1963, the Securities and Exchange Commission showed that several financial editors had been profiting from the selection and the play of business news. In retrospect, Peter Bart, a financial writer at the time, warned that editors must "deal sternly with reporters who do favors for friends and help plant dishonest stories." He added pointedly, "They must also bar junkets for reporters and for financial editors." [93]

It does not often work out that way, however. As it was explained by James McCartney of the *Chicago Daily News*, a former Nieman Fellow at Harvard, "No reporter can operate successfully without friends. But being objective about friends

176   can be as difficult as being objective about one's wife . . . The
price that the press, and perhaps the country, pays for reporters'
vested interests can be high." It was McCartney's thesis that, in
too many instances, reporters identified their own interests with
those of the primary sources on whom they depended for news.
They were the "in" group, as opposed to more objective or "out"
groups that did not hesitate to attack a news source if it became
necessary. Some of the most influential reporters in Washington,
he maintained, "have deep vested interests in their beats or in
their specialties . . . The problem is undoubtedly universal in
the news business. When national news is involved, its import
may be magnified." [94]

Such influences go beyond an occasional gift of a
bottle of Scotch for a political reporter, a new hat for the columnist on the women's page, or a trip to Las Vegas for a tired editor.
They go to the root of the independent practice of journalism as
surely as the pressures that are so often applied from outside the
profession.

In the early part of the century, when the journalist
was poorly paid and indifferently educated on the whole, it was
said that the conditions of his work made the newspaperman a
ready target for special influence. But such views are outdated in
an era when the return for the leading figures in journalism is
commensurate with that in other professions and the competent
journeyman's pay exceeds a minimum of $10,000 a year on the
nation's best newspapers, with television and the news magazines often paying at least 50 percent more for the same type of
help.* Almost universally, the better news media now expect
their staff people to be college educated and are willing to pay
them accordingly.

The journalist, however, can scarcely aspire to the
same public respect that is accorded the physician, the lawyer,
and the clergyman in the United States without devising a
professional method for dealing with cases of gross misconduct.
The adoption of high-minded statements of principle, without
provision for enforcement, makes a mockery of the organizations that sponsor them. Where cases of misconduct reflect on
the entire profession, the responsibility goes beyond any individual or single news organization. The operation of an unofficial

* The top minimum in *The New York Times* Guild contract after 1970 will be
$275 a week.

blacklist in some places is not enough. The public has a right to   177
expect that the journalist will apply to the suspected wrongdoer
in his own profession the same function of investigation and
critical comment that the news media apply to American society
in general. Yet, just about the only time such things happen is
when the top officers of the American Newspaper Guild or the
electronics unions decide they will have to make an example of
someone for strikebreaking. And most of these actions are both
pathetic and self-defeating. Nor do governmental appeals and
threats to curb foreign travel to save currency promise any change
in junketeering.

True, the journalist still has a rousing sense of
moral indignation on occasion. After the Fulbright hearings into
junket journalism, Norman E. Isaacs, executive editor of the
Louisville Courier-Journal, exclaimed, "There is too much pa-
laver in editors' speeches and in their articles about our rising
standards and our desire for clean, honorable, objective reporting—and too little done about getting these things into practice."
But few journalists who remain active in the profession have
been willing to date to brave the wrath of their associates by
devising a punishment to fit the crime, much less see that it is
carried out.

It is not enough for the independent journalist to be
resolute in defending himself from the forces outside his profession that threaten to encroach on his liberties. Whether such
encroachments are fancied or real, he can scarcely be criticized
for not letting down his guard. The history of the twentieth
century is full of instances of great independent newspapers in
Europe, Asia, and Latin America that have been too weak or too
complacent in the face of determined opposition and have fallen
victim to ruthless foes. But the journalist's vigilance against the
outer enemy must be matched by his determination to deal cou-
rageously with those who betray his profession from within. Because he has refused to do so thus far, he has paid dearly in
terms of his standing with the American public.

UNDERDEVELOPED

12

JOURNALISM

Several thousand travelers annually visit one of France's celebrated shrines to tourism, Mont St. Michel in Normandy, in the vague hope that it will be worth the effort. Many of them in past years have been Americans who have turned from the sales pitches in the guidebooks to consult travel sections, special pages and columns in the American press for the unadorned truth. Usually, from everything the casual reader is able to learn from these sources, the trip to Mont St. Michel is a must.

Yet, toward the end of a recent travel season, Hor-

ace Sutton in the *Saturday Review* called the celebrated abbey a 179
"tawdry tourist mess, unsightly and, certainly, considering the
religious aspects of the place, untasteful." The holes around the
face of the ancient Rock, he wrote, had been designed so that
boiling oil could be poured on the invading British of another era
but "they might be better used on the profiteers and those in
charge of a national monument who have let it degenerate into a
popcorn stop for rubbernecks." [95] Whether or not the French
have made sufficient repairs since to satisfy the critic is beside
the point. What merits deeper examination is the policy that
animates the journalist who deals in such departmental news as
tourism, which is generally published outside the main run of
the news.

It is an easily observable truth that reputable newspapers and news magazines, in their general news sections, do
not have a holy regard for the tourist shrines; embarrassing
incidents, criticism, and the like are published and, where there
are decent local television news staffs, broadcast along with the
rest of the day's grist. In Honolulu, capital of Pacific tourism, the
Honolulu Advertiser broke the routine of a recent summer rush
of tourists by publishing a full page of largely critical comment
from visitors under the eight-column headline: "Waikiki: Pleas-
ure or Pandemonium?" [96] It was the clamor of construction in the
famous beach area that bothered those interviewed, and apparently some of the *Advertiser*'s editors as well, but such a display
and such doubts could rarely be found in the fat travel sections
or special foreign travel columns of the American press, even
after the government tried to cut down the spending of U. S. tourists abroad.

This curious dichotomy is, of course, not confined
either to Hawaii or the news of tourism. Very often, there is a
discernible difference between the treatment of departmental
material outside the main news section and the breaking news
itself. While there are a number of exceptions, many of them
praiseworthy, the comparatively stringent scrutiny that conscientious editorial managers devote to the content of the main
news section is not often steadily applied to the rest of the
newspaper. Partly, this may be attributed to a slap-happy journalistic tradition, long since dumped by news magazines, that
the general news section counts for much more than departmental material in a newspaper. But partly, it is also due to the
old-time form of editorial organization, which still exists on

180   many papers although it is unequal to the test of modern conditions. Under this setup, a single managing editor, with one or two assistants, assumes the tasks of supervising production of the newspaper, the work of the news editors and city editor, the direction of all other departments and the necessary liaison with the paper's nonnews executives. This regimen obviously taxes the ability of the most competent managing editors, and all too few of them are around.

There are some who suspect the existence of a kind of journalistic conspiracy on some newspapers, in which the news sections do a relatively honest job and the puffery is deliberately left to the departments in an effort to please the advertisers. Such suspicions generally rest only on circumstantial evidence which, in newspapers as well as in a court of law, can be most deceptive. Actually, the way the system works is that an able, efficient, and imaginative departmental editor often can demonstrate to the satisfaction of a timid proprietor that good journalism is good business. But where a department is run along lackadaisical and traditional lines, without any relationship to the news of the day, it can sink pretty low without any particular conspiracy. Then, it is up to the managing editor to do something about his particular area of underdeveloped journalism or, if he is either too lazy or irresponsible to do so, suffer the consequences in declining morale. For such things can never be kept a secret from any newspaper staff.

TRAVEL NEWS: FANTASY AND REALITY

There has been a considerable reform in recent years in departmental editing on the better American newspapers, primarily because of the development of a broader and more realistic editorial management at the top, but somehow it has not reached many travel sections or special pages. Here, as may be easily established through any random check, much of the copy is almost as rhapsodic in tone as the advertisements it supplements, either by accident or design.

With more Americans traveling each summer than ever before, the central purpose of a number of travel editors and writers seems to be to stimulate the urge to see the world or, at stated periods of the advertising season, the United States. In this their desires coincide with the fervent wishes of the airlines, the shipping companies, the foreign departments of tourism, the hotels, restaurants, auto rental companies, and all

the others that ride the tourist flood with great profit to themselves. It is a difficult combination to oppose in a special section
devoted to travel, unless the proprietor and his principal editors
lay down and support a hard-fisted policy against sugar-coating
the news of tourism. Where it happens, it is most effective.

But all too often, the news on Page 1 bears no relation to the world of the travel sections. As an excuse, it has been
argued that this is because they are produced far ahead of time. In
the case of the six-day Middle East War of 1967, when tourism
to Arab lands and to Israel was abruptly suspended, there is no
doubt that travel sections and columns were caught. But despite
a Communist summer-long terror attack in Hong Kong that year,
the familiar travel section articles about that tourist shopping
paradise still appeared; in fact, short announcements also were
published in scattered news sections that travel agents were still
taking bookings from travelers who were unimpressed by the
headlines.

During the Army-led backlash against an abortive
Communist coup in Indonesia, while hundreds of thousands of
people were being killed in that unhappy land, the travel copy
still insisted that tourists must visit Bali, the enchanted isle.
Great American airliners continued to swoop down regularly at
Tan Son Nhut Airport in Saigon with apprehensive contingents
of tourists until the escalating American forces in South Vietnam reached such proportions that no space was available for
tourism. The travel editors plugged the Angkor Wat in Cambo-
dia, blandly overlooking the unpopularity of Americans in the
country,* and mourned only that Burma—for a time—was
barred to visitors from the United States. From Japan to Aus-
tralia and from Tahiti to India, the Orient was "in" so why was it
necessary to stress the unpleasantness of news in certain areas?
In the travel sections, for the most part, the world looked different, then and now.

Thus, outside the metropolitan areas of the country
where information on foreign parts is more available, the unini-
tiated traveler from the United States usually has had scant
notion of what to expect. And this is true whether he ventures
into newly popular tourist areas like the Orient and the Iron
Curtain countries (now politely called Eastern Europe in the

* Mrs. Jacqueline Kennedy's visit there in November, 1967, gave them unexpected assistance.

182   travel ads) or the older strongholds of tourism in Great Britain and Western Europe. Certainly, the average newspaper often does little to prepare him. For with comparatively few exceptions, there is less space for foreign news in the bulk of the American press than there is for the bumper crop of travel news which breaks up the mass of advertising in the special travel sections or pages.

If the American press as a whole published a respectable quota of foreign news, it could be contended that there is no necessity for smaller newspapers to duplicate the more ominous catalogue of events in the news sections or to publish some of it with the more saccharine travel copy. But except for the better newspapers and travel writers like Horace Sutton and Dick Joseph, the bulk of travel news is generally bland and uninformative and seldom takes current world conditions into account. For the most part, it is left to the government to warn Americans not to travel in certain danger areas or, in extreme cases, to forbid them to go. As one editor put it, necessarily retaining his anonymity, "We've regularized our puffs by publishing special sections." [97] In many travel sections and pages, it is a particularly sad truth.

THE BLIGHTED REAL ESTATE SECTION

The real estate sections, pages, and columns of a number of less carefully edited American newspapers constitute another area of underdeveloped journalism although the situation is better than it used to be. Journalists who grew up in the newsrooms of the 1920s learned to dread the dull periods of the day when an unfeeling deskman would parcel out a stack of real estate publicity to be edited (checked for spelling and grammatical errors, but not substantially changed) or perhaps rewritten into a long combined "lead story" for the real estate section, with every advertiser favorably mentioned. It was part of the routine of the era in large cities and small; where newspapers insisted on producing their own real estate copy, and they were few, they were looked upon as paragons of virtue.

As in the case of the travel copy, the improvement that has been noted is primarily in the handling of real estate developments in the news section. As for what happens in the real estate sections, an expert and impartial witness, Ferdinand Kuhn, made this observation: "In all but a few big city newspapers, one has only to look to know that the press adulterates its

news with unlabeled advertising. The line between news and
salesmanship is hard to find in the pages and sections that deal
with food, fashions and travel. In the real estate pages, the line
has almost diasppeared . . . I have asked editors how they explain or justify this kind of copy. One of them told me it was only
'shinplaster to keep the ads from bumping.' " [98]

Consequently, while conscientious editors lead
newspapers of consequence in campaigns for bond issues to fight
urban decay, many of their fellows see nothing wrong with
skipping the issue in the real estate pages. Nor do the real estate
sections, in all save the better newspapers, do very much about
such Page 1 news as the destructive riots in the ghetto, the drive
for open housing legislation, the difficulty of obtaining sufficient
schools for new communities, and the ever present problems of
soaring tax rates. Too often, the "news" of real estate—in its own
page or section—consists of undisguised pap, much of which
obviously comes from interested companies that may or may not
have advertised on that particular day. Whenever there is a
substantial investment of real estate advertising, such as a special section in behalf of one builder or one important project, it
appears almost to be taken for granted by some newspapers that
textual material will accompany the paid material in the news
columns. Editors justify such practices on the ground that the
addition of a new building or store or theatre in the city is news.
That is true enough, but very often the news is saluted at such
extravagant length that it becomes difficult, if not impossible, to
determine what difference there is in the advertising and editorial approach.

"Real estate editors," Kuhn wrote, "find no difficulty
in switching their love from apartments to houses from one week
to the next. If the section features advertising for houses rather
than apartments, the editor will be glad to conform in his news
columns. Conflicting advice poses no problems. If a city happens
to have competing newspapers, the reader can enjoy contradictory advice on the same week-end, as I often do in my own city of
Washington." [99]

With the quickening interest in urban affairs, particularly in universities that have established special centers for
the study of the problem of urban decay, it is heartening to
observe that a new kind of specialist, the urban critic, has gained
influence in American journalism. His numbers still are comparatively few, but his prestige is growing wherever he is allowed to

184 operate effectively. In San Francisco, for example, Allan Temko has been published by the *Chronicle* with benefit to the city; in several instances, his criticism of architectural plans of projects ranging in importance from bridges to cathedrals has resulted in substantial changes. Ada Louise Huxtable, in *The New York Times*, has been given such a free hand that she did not scruple to denounce the design of the new Metropolitan Opera House in Lincoln Center, one of the show places of the city. Over the years, her opinion has been both feared and respected by the architects and builders who are constantly making over the metropolis, sometimes not particularly for the better. In St. Louis, George McCue's criticism in the *Post-Dispatch* has been equally valuable during the course of the city's long effort at urban renewal. And in Washington, Wolf von Eckardt in the *Post* has won a wide following for his intelligent and perceptive criticism of the urban renewal campaign in the nation's capital as well as his determined battle against dismal plans for still more historical monuments.[100] In Los Angeles and Boston, Milwaukee and Louisville, Chicago, Cleveland, and Phoenix, as well as a scattering of other cities, similar critical efforts are being encouraged by perceptive editors.

But except where the old puff-laden real estate section has given way to a modern, realistic treatment of urban problems, the best work of the critical correspondents is carried up front in the general news section or, if it belongs there, on Page 1. For the vast area of American newspaperdom, the relegation of a staff member to the real estate section is considered to be a sentence to a journalistic Siberia from which there is often no return. And that, in itself, is an attitude that must be changed through more enlightened editing if real estate news is to be improved.

WHAT EVERY WOMAN KNOWS
There is somewhat less excuse today to include the women's pages of newspapers in the sorry catalogue of underdeveloped journalism, primarily because of the determined efforts of a number of talented women editors who have decided they no longer will stand for the puffery and payoffs that once were fairly general in this area of the press. In Washington, for example, it is frequently true that the women's pages are read with greater care than any other part of the paper except Page 1 because that's where much of the news may be found. In New

York, a hardheaded reporter, Charlotte Curtis, has established a
very high standard for the coverage of social events and made
herself must reading even in a man's world; nor can it be said
that her elevation to the dismaying job of editing a women's page
for *The New York Times* has made her writing less sharp. On
such equally successful papers as *Newsday,* in Garden City,
N. Y., and the *Los Angeles Times,* the old-time women's page has
become indistinguishable in quality and news treatment from
the rest of the newspaper. Such subjects as alcoholism among
housewives, the use of "the pill" in birth control, prostitution,
prison reform, and sex crimes are now treated with unabashed
frankness on women's pages of better newspapers in such places
as Atlanta and Detroit, Seattle and San Francisco, Des Moines
and Minneapolis, Miami and Louisville, and Charlotte, N. C.[101]

It would be pleasant to report, in view of the
strength of the reform movement, that all the old objections to
women's pages have now disappeared but it would not be true.
One of the best known women's page writers of recent years,
Marylin Bender of *The New York Times,* has charged, for example, that some fashion writers still accept clothes made available
at wholesale prices—or given to them. She also believes some
fashion editors are "snobbish" about accessories because they
sometimes get them at cut rates. As Miss Bender put it, "In
coordinating an outfit, a fashion editor is considering her assignment, which is usually to take a nondescript dress and give it
impact in a photograph. Accessories help to do this. But also
fashion editors can get their own clothes at wholesale prices—or
sometimes at no cost at all. They can afford to be as snobbish
about shoes and handbags as an electrical appliance sales manager's wife is about her kitchen." [102]

Another disagreeable feature of some of the wom-
en's pages is the product plug—a free and usually laudatory
mention of a commercial product. In an informal survey of
editors, one replied under cover of anonymity, "Product plugs
don't sneak into our news columns any more; they march in with
banners flying, trumpets blaring and drums beating. I'm thinking of building a moat around the building and issuing Sten
guns." Moreover, one discouraged women's page editor admitted
in the same survey that her section was the weakest in the
paper.[103]

Evidences of commercialism, sometimes entirely innocent of advertiser pressure, may be noted in any sampling of

186 women's pages. A bundle of 30 such sections from all parts of the country, collected at Columbia University, produced such examples as the following:

A large mid-Western newspaper, saluting a new building for a fashion house, presented a three-quarter page picture layout of dresses. The editor, in large type, enthusiastically lauded the manufacturer, saying that "she has put her taste, elegance and femininity, for which she is famous, into the selection of distinctive gowns designed exclusively for her." The reader then was advised of the exact floors in the new building where the gowns could be seen and purchased.[104]

A large New England newspaper published a picture layout of men's fashions with an article that began: "What kind of fashions are zooming ahead non-stop? Men's . . ." The readers of the women's page then were told that a large store was "aware and attuned to the important changes" in men's apparel and had "wisely staged a show of updated men's fashions" exclusively for women. The show was described in lavish detail.[105]

A large New York newspaper published a handsome four-column layout of picture and story about a woman with an important husband and great-great grandfather, celebrating her appointment as district manager for a Southern apparel house. She was shown, handsomely modeling a coat (about $150) and dress (about $75) in the line she was merchandising.[106]

Such examples may be multiplied in various sections of the country. In fairness to the women's page editors, many of them have been under the impression for years that this is the way to give service to their readers and few editors or publishers have tried to disabuse them. The women's magazines and fashion magazines do it at much greater length, so what's wrong with it? Now, at least, the forward-looking women's page editor has an unparalleled opportunity to decide for herself what is right and what is wrong. The old ways could change—and there is hope that they will.

In the society sections, change is bound to come with much greater deliberation. For many years, they have been edited for the most part in accordance with the standards, preoccupations, and prejudices of an all-white, middle-class America. The constant reader of society news in the average American paper, in essence, is rarely able to detect the presence in the community of a substantial proportion of women who belong to labor unions, associate with nonconformist groups, or happen to be Negroes or Puerto Ricans. In such papers, the first generation of foreign-born usually is represented by displaced nobility, sometimes of dubious lineage, and diplomatic visitors. Generally, one has to be "in"—or a freak—to be noticed by the more rigid grand dames of the press. The situation is such that in many communities, North and South, a woman has a better chance of dying respectably on the obit page than of being born on the society page. The probability also is greater that she will attract more notice by being divorced than by being married.

Many Northern newspapers for years have accepted a policy of not identifying persons by race or national origin unless it is germane to the story. That is the way it is done in their news columns, at least; but in the society news, the problem seldom comes up because a distinct minority of social items is likely to be concerned with such things. True, an occasional picture or story about a nonwhite woman or family may be noticed on the average society page outside the deep South as a sign of the paper's lack of prejudice. But the evidence, in reality, is pretty slender even on the better papers.

Southern editors, of course, have a much larger problem to handle; but at the same time, they are generally much more frank about their limitations. "Our customs, call them prejudices if you like, date back much further and are deeper rooted," one Southern editor said. "These traditions are changing, but like the church, what is happening in the social realm seems to be the least changing. This is reflected in the women's sections of Southern newspapers. Pictures of Negroes here are about as rare as a Negro worshiper at a Southern Baptist prayer meeting." Another gave this view: "Society pages present a special problem and in my opinion that lily white bastion will be slow to fall. It will come, however, and the only thing I know is to practice gradualism. We will have to do it that way or suffer the loss of a great many white readers."

The gradualness of the process was illustrated by two surveys taken four years apart. The first, by Ernest Gueymard of Baton Rouge, La., in 1961 showed that almost no Southern newspaper he studied, and very few in the North, mixed white and Negro social news on the same page. The second, by Tenney S. Griffin of Valdosta, Ga., in 1965 reported that almost half of those surveyed in the South now integrated their news—but there was no indication of the volume. Of 91 editors questioned, almost equally divided between North and South,

188   Griffin found 24 Southern editors whose newspapers refused to publish Negro society items and 23 who did; among Northern editors, only one said his newspaper would publish no news of Negro society.[107]

There were conscientious newspapers that went to a great deal of trouble to record vital statistics, knowing of the interest that many readers take in them. The *Wilmington* (Del.) *News* and *Journal* published a daily record in agate type of marriage licenses, births, and deaths. The *Houston Chronicle* ran a "Lifebeat Page" with similar statistical reports. The *Providence* (R. I.) *Journal* and *Bulletin* specialized in such reportage, using 60 percent in agate and the remainder in body type.[108] But for notice in the women's page or the society section, the gatekeepers measured individuals in the 1960s by a sense of news values that often appeared to differ substantially from those that were applied to products. Had it not been for the leaders, particularly in the women's pages, there would have been little progress. Nor will there be for the future unless a lot of old ideas and taboos are dropped.

BUSINESS, GOOD AND BAD

It is difficult to include the business and financial sections in the generally sick area of underdeveloped journalism because so much of the stimulus for journalistic reforms has come from economic specialists. And yet, aside from the leading newspapers and magazines in the field, any survey will show that there is an appalling nakedness about the average financial and business section which cannot be disguised by the expanse of stock market tables. There are very few newspapers that can pretend to rival the *Wall Street Journal* and *The New York Times* for completeness and authority in the financial field. However, in a number of less impressive sections, there are knowledgeable financial editors and writers who give the public substantial assistance. As for the rest, the wire services provide decent financial coverage even if it is not often as effectively used as it could be.

In view of the presence of 20 million shareholders in the United States, with the number increasing on the average at the rate of 1 million a year during the boomtime 1960s, it is surprising that so many financial sections are comparatively neglected. While the financial news columns are not as riddled with material originating from public relations sources as travel and real estate, many a financial page or section is demonstrably stuffed with special pleading. The "musts" from the business office (material sent to the editorial department with orders to publish) may be fewer than in recent years, but recognition for advertisers in the financial news columns has not vanished.

J. A. Livingston, the Pulitzer Prize-winning financial editor of the *Philadelphia Bulletin,* puts it this way: "I think it's fair to say that on many newspapers—especially those outside the large investment and industrial centers, and I don't exclude all of these—financial is a stepchild department . . . The managing editor can help, can inspire, but he has to have more than a clod as a financial editor to get response. He has to have somebody who has a greater interest than piecing handouts together and tacking on a byline as a frame for his half-column cut in the format of a column." [109]

The competence of some of the financial writers and editors also is questioned by William A. Paton, professor emeritus of accounting and economics at the University of Michigan. "It is a truly sad state of affairs," he observed, "when we see financial writers who can't even tell the difference between the distribution of corporate assets in the form of securities owned—accrued dividends—and a split of outstanding shares, an entirely unrelated phenomenon and completely counterfeit as far as dividend action is concerned." [110]

Part of the explanation for such errors is, of course, the mistaken effort of small financial staffs to make speed rather than accuracy their prime motivation. The rest is due to the inevitable publicity handout, few of which ever could win prizes for accuracy. Gerald M. Loeb, a veteran stockbroker, once noted an error in a financial section he read regularly and asked the editor, a friend, how it had happened. The editor said, "We haven't enough people to take the time and meet our deadline. Most often we have to rely on the press release." [111]

Relying on the press release can be a dangerous business. In a survey of 162 business and financial editors, 22.6 percent said that "as a matter of routine" they were obliged "to puff up or alter or downgrade business stories at the request of the advertisers." The pressures, the editors added, came to them primarily through their own advertising departments. It is all too rare that an independent-minded journalist like Sylvia Porter

190   can break through this maze, making her way from a $20-a-week
wage to an income of $250,000 a year and a total circulation of
20 million for her financial column.[112]

Thus, in financial journalism, there are examples of
sheer brilliance at the top and pressure and sheer incompetence
at the bottom with a great grey area in between. Most journalists
of consequence acknowledge that some of the most welcome
innovations in writing for daily publication have come from
specialists in the dismal science, economics. Much of the writing
in the *Wall Street Journal* is both original and effective, paying
scant attention to the faded blueprints of journalism. The same
is true of specialists and columnists who write on economics for
the weekly news magazines, the business press and some of the
daily financial sections of consequence. While none of them
adhere to a formula, which is their principal strength, they all
appear to stress investment news over company news, the interest
of people rather than of the advertiser, and the basic necessity of
trying in nontechnical language to explain the complicated trends
of the times. Not everybody has to be a John Kenneth Galbraith to
do this kind of work. But in addition to bright people with a good
economic background, what is required is a decent amount of
effort, encouragement from top management, and a sufficient
budget to do the job. Where these four factors are present, improvement may be expected; where they are missing, the financial
section is going to amount to a dead loss except for the stock
market tables.

THE SPECIALISTS

Confronted with the requirements of an age of specialization, too
many editors still hold to the quaint notion that an ignorant
reporter—quickly briefed by an ever present and good-natured
expert at no expense to the news organization—can best explain
abstruse problems to an uninformed people. Once, just before the
opening of a complicated United Nations debate, a reporter had
the bad judgment to enter a New York City newsroom with a
load of books and settle down for a cram course. His editor was
impatient at the unusual spectacle of a reporter reading a book
on company time. "Just get over there and write what you hear
and what you see, and never mind about what's in those books,"
were the classic instructions.[113]

The wide and sometimes disheartening variation in
media coverage of such specialties as economics, science, educa-

tion, and religion is due in part to the difference between such editors, who retain a powerful influence, and the media leaders, who insist on using well-qualified specialists whenever they can. There is a middle way, the specialists whose work is offered on every conceivable occasion by the wire services, but editors who "just print the news" will spike that kind of copy as fast as they will the slightest hint of interpretation. Old ways die very hard.

A case in point was the coverage of the religious controversy centering on the "God Is Dead" theology, which made so many headlines in the latter part of the 1960s. The Ecumenical Council at the Vatican had served to make usually indifferent editors aware that there was a very special kind of news in modern religion. When ecumenism was succeeded by the much-publicized doubts of a relatively small number of American theologians, the media at first were not quite certain how to handle it. Some newspapers delicately decided to forget about the whole story because of the offense it might give to devout readers. But *Time* magazine went all out with a sensational cover featuring two-inch red type on a black background: "Is God Dead?" It wound up reassuringly with a father's plea to Christ: "I believe; help my unbelief." [114] The electronic media, with very few exceptions, walked on tiptoe around the whole puzzling business.

While both the "God Is Dead" controversy and the far more significant ecumenical movement pointed up the need for specialists in the field of religion, there was no notable rush to the seminaries or the universities to find well-educated writers capable of backgrounding the subject. Local sermons, occasional midweek interviews on a dull news day, and the regular offerings of the wire services sufficed for the bulk of the American news media. "For years—and I imagine this is still the case on some newspapers—getting the religion beat was something akin to being assigned to the paper's Siberian bureau," one specialist on religion news said. "Reporters sought to remove the albatross of religion writing as quickly as possible. Some . . . have prided themselves on how rapidly they could be relieved of the assignment. They would do as poor a job as possible for fear that if they performed well they might keep the beat indefinitely." [115]

As for science, the flight of the first Soviet Sputnik revealed the unpreparedness of the American news media to interpret science in meaningful terms to the American public. The science writers still in service were, in the main, the veter-

192 ans who had struggled through the depression and a world war on a mere handful of publications outside the specialized field. Just as the first Sputnik led to a great deal of introspection in the field of education, the journalist also began to take stock of his shortcomings. As a result, for the first time since William L. Laurence's flight over Nagasaki during the last atomic bombing raid of World War II, science writers were in demand. But there were precious few of them who were prepared to do the job. It was one field in which the news media were ahead of the universities in demanding trained people. Even television decided that it might be well to have a commentator with a reasonably good scientific background, instead of an actor, discuss the space race. Thus, Jules Bergman won his chance on the American Broadcasting Companies' network and set the style for literate science reporters on television. Attracted by the glamor and the excitement of the race to the moon, and the space shots that punctuated it, editors of most self-respecting newspapers did not have to be convinced any longer that they needed science writers. It became, next to foreign correspondence, the most popular of all the specialties and still retains its hold on the imagination both of the public and the media proprietors.

In education, however, the old-time "school reporter" is still operating at the bottom of the journalistic totem pole in many parts of the country. The newspapers are eager to attract young readers with their "Teen Pages," few of which seem to mean very much to the average teen-ager, but there is no discernible mass movement to give education the kind of coverage it should have. Outside the better papers and the news magazines, news of education is too often considered dull stuff. Consequently, it is only the well-staffed metropolitan dailies and a few smaller newspapers that have been able to replace the downtrodden "school reporter" with qualified writers on education.

Yet, even among the leaders, the habit of ignoring colleges and universities as centers worthy of a full-time reporter from the regular staff continues to permeate some of the greatest newspapers in the land. In New York City during most of the 1960s, for example, not a single newspaper (and certainly none of the electronic media) would have dreamed of assigning a staff reporter to give regular and detailed coverage to such institutions as the City University of New York (100,000 students), New York University (60,000 students), Columbia University

(25,000 students) and the burgeoning State University of New York which was celebrated with a *Time* cover story in 1968. Each of these is larger than many a state capital and generates a considerable amount of news week after week. But the various university publicity departments are left with the burden of alerting the news media whenever something of major interest develops; the rest, unfortunately, is coverage by handout. In some university centers, notably Minneapolis, the dismal normal order of journalism in education has been reversed. There, the *Minneapolis Star* and *Tribune* took the initiative by assigning a staff reporter to interest the university in making more of its activities known to the people of the community.

But in education, as in the other underdeveloped areas of journalism, progress as a rule has come with terrifying slowness—even in New York City and Washington, D. C. It takes the shock of a Sputnik, and worse, to cause a very large section of the press and its electronic rivals to adjust to a new phase in history.

THE AMERICAN

13

CULTURAL

REVOLUTION

O ne of the more agreeable features of this rude and dangerous age in the United States, allowing at once for an outraged dissent by heavy-handed intellectuals, is an awakening mass interest in the arts. It is quite a distance from the Notre Dame football team to the New York Philharmonic and Carl Yastrzemski to Rembrandt, but middle-class families with time on their hands are trying to bridge it. If this tends to confuse teen-agers who would rather learn more about the Watusi or its newest equivalent than the uses of chia-

roscuro, probably it is good for their souls. Everybody else is
more or less confused in these times. Why exempt the young?

Necessarily, this determined march upon the arts by a very large and newly enthusiastic public presents American journalism with problems in expanded coverage and criticism of a subject area that has been neglected far too long by a considerable part of the news media. After all, how many editors can tell the difference between a Picasso and a Pollock? It is no base canard, but a verifiable truth, that Auguste Renoir (1841–1919) was listed on a newspaper's society page as one of the guests at a tea party; in fact, when a shocked art critic made a correction deleting the French painter from the living, the composing room loftily ignored it. On another occasion, when a local museum acquired a full length painting of a reclining nude, the managing editor of the paper ordered it reduced to a one-column cut. "Which half?" demanded the art critic. Still another editor decided that he could not afford to give Rembrandt much space and ruled that a mug shot of one of his portraits was good enough. And in one hilarious instance, a managing editor solemnly transformed a perfectly contented police reporter into an instant art critic by giving him the title.[116] Under this formula, some curious but undoubtedly interesting results might be forthcoming if a night rewrite man became a music critic and was assigned to cover Vladimir Ussachevsky's latest electronic concerto. In the less sophisticated precincts of the American news media, it is clear that culture has its moments but there are very few of them.

SAUK CENTER AND LINCOLN CENTER

Newspapers that are on a self-improvement jag, and even a few of the local electronic media that are not completely committed to the glorification of the pow, the bam, and the zowie would like very much to do more with the arts than they have in the past. But there is an immediate obstacle. Journalists who are competent in this burgeoning field are in extremely short supply, primarily due to the magnificent disinterest of most universities in popularizing the arts, and always have been. Furthermore, the care and feeding of a critic is somewhat more complicated and more expensive than the assignment of a reporter to cover a two-alarm fire.

There is, of course, an even larger roadblock in the

196   press's meandering processional along the cultural byways. It is, to put it very plainly, the mental hazard. While the established leaders of the press have always tried to do a careful and conscientious job in the coverage of the arts, a lingering remnant of an old and persistent anti-intellectualism among journeymen has inhibited more general progress until fairly recently. To the average editor, who does not want to be bothered with anything except the breaking news (which radio and TV are the first to report), any critical or artistic effort for many years has been automatically disparaged as "long hair"—the ultimate in journalistic damnation. Consequently, it has not been easy to bring about a change in the historic posture of mingled press hostility and condescension toward the arts. That change is in evidence now may be more of a tribute to advancing public interest than to either intellectual or editorial leadership.

But neither a somnolent press, which has to be baited with Andy Warhol girls to bestir itself, nor a passel of mourning intellectuals, who predict that the masses will cheapen sensitive artistic standards, can stop or divert the American public's response to the arts. The American cultural revolution, as it is imprecisely known, has swept aside the protests of claques and coteries. Suburbia, swollen by throngs of well-heeled refugees from the turmoil and decay of many of the nation's inner cities, now shelters many self-contained artistic groups with strong ties to the metropolitan centers of the land. While Sauk Center is not about to turn into Lincoln Center, and Main Street is scarcely an extension of Broadway, millions of small-town citizens have learned to appreciate the art treasures and other cultural attractions of the big cities and no longer are willing to do without them.

Nearly every large city in the nation today either has a center or a hall for the performing arts and at least one tolerably good art museum or aspires to build them. Symphony orchestras, community theatres, and art exhibitions—some with impressive records of achievement and others with unfulfilled promise—are spreading rapidly. Publishers, with a record production of 30,000 new hard cover and paperback titles a year, are selling more than $2.5 billion in books annually and expect to increase their output. In four hours on a single Sunday recently, 59,000 persons crowded into the Metropolitan Museum of Art in New York City—more than the attendance at many a World Series baseball game. And despite continual caterwauling

over the decline of the American theatre, those who inspect the
state of the drama on Broadway, off Broadway, and off-off Broadway run into the millions each year. It is safe to say that the arts,
on the whole, draw consistently larger audiences than sports
across the country. But a large section of the news media still is
not entirely convinced of it, as is evidenced by the comparatively
great attention paid to sports and considerably less to the arts.

BOOKS IN THE NEWS

What has happened to books, the most pervasive cultural symbol
in the United States, is fairly typical of what has happened to the
arts in general in the arid sections of the American press. Less
than 20 percent of the nation's daily newspapers carried book
reviews to the extent of a weekly book column or page during
much of the 1960s and there were less than a dozen daily book
reviewers, including those of the syndicates and wire services.[117]
The book sections, headed by *The New York Times* Sunday
Book Review, could be found in only a few leading newspapers.
There were also reviews in the news magazines, mainly of books
that were likely to interest a mass audience. Otherwise, only
magazines such as *The New Yorker*, the *Saturday Review*, and
small competitors in the weekly field, and such monthlies as *The
Atlantic, Harper's*, and a few others gave books the recognition
that was due them. New ventures, such as *The New York Review
of Books*, were events in American literature.

The enterprising Michael J. Ogden, executive editor
of the *Providence Journal-Bulletin* and a past president of the
American Society of Newspaper Editors, conducted his own unscientific survey into this state of affairs. He discovered, to nobody's surprise, that comparatively few of his fellow editors read
books, pleading lack of time. Ogden himself disarmed suspicion
that he might be guilty of softness toward literature by remark-
ing that he had to pay a $2 overdue fee at the local library when
he borrowed "The Art of Rapid Reading." [118]

Granville Hicks maintained that the low repute of
book reviewing was in part deserved in the space age. "To prove
it," he wrote, "you have only to borrow from a publisher his file of
reviews of a book that you know. You will find, the chances are,
that a quarter to a half of the reviews have been written by
persons who haven't read the book or, at any rate, needn't have,
since what they say is borrowed from the blurb. You will then
discover that a large proportion of the reviewers who express

198 personal judgments have read the book so carelessly that they make serious mistakes in describing its contents." [119] But an author has no recourse. A letter to the editor, except in extraordinary circumstances is filed and forgotten with a light shrug of a secretarial shoulder. Since when has an author been right and a critic wrong? The ancient rule of the newsroom still holds good: "You can never win an argument in the other guy's newspaper."

Allan Keller, a New York author and critic, also testified to the generally shoddy state of newspaper book reviewing. "As an author," he recalled, "I saw 200 to 400 reviews and out of them 90 percent were written by people who had the effrontery to copy six paragraphs from the dust jacket and book publishers' releases. Where does justice lie? I am convinced that 80 percent of the reviewers are activated merely by getting a free book, or 300 of them would not use the same lead."

One of the most eminent and productive of American literary critics, John Barkham of the Saturday Review Syndicate, argued that the low standards of most book reviewers were likely to eliminate possible readers of books rather than increase their numbers. "We need to wean people to book reading," he said. "We are a reading nation but there are not enough book readers. Some of the fault lies with us because we reviewers do not persuade our readers to read the books we write about." Another, W. G. Rogers, who for many years conducted a daily book column for the Associated Press, felt that reviewers were generally too kind.[120]

It was *The New York Times*, finally, that placed the responsibility where it really belonged—on the newspaper publisher himself. Summing up the complaints after a symposium on book reviewing in New York, the *Times* commented editorially: "In a nation that has over 1,700 newspapers, wasn't it sad that only 310 carried book reviews? Was it not a fallacy that book readers did not exist in sufficient numbers outside the Eastern and Western seaboard areas to warrant wider and better book coverage? And wasn't the newspaper publisher being short-sighted in ignoring the value of cultural stimulation through the book page? One looked with new eyes on the previously berated out-of-town reviewer: It was a wonder he existed at all." [121]

Yet, it was a time when the critical function was urgently needed in American life. The frequently false values of mass culture were being merchandised in the United States on a vast scale, particularly on television, when the steady plugging of a book by a leading personality could send sales into the millions. Book publishers were bemused by the kind of sales that could result from the appearance of an author on a program such as NBC's "Tonight" show.[122] The television promotion effort, consequently, took on the appearance of a crusade; but if ever a volume was seriously criticized outside the narrow orbit of educational television or an occasional Sunday afternoon show, the viewing public was sublimely ignorant of it. Books existed on television to be sold or adapted to the needs of the medium, seldom to be criticized.

Irving Howe complained, "In fiction, the movies, television and journalism—in every channel of mass communication—there has been a flood of shoddiness, some of it brutal and vulgar (see the cheap paperbacks) and some of it fashionable and slick (see the playboy magazines). In response to all this, the work of serious critics has taken on a tone of urgency, even of combative gaiety. Critics . . . have analyzed and attacked the falsities of 'mass culture,' doing battle against the smooth descendants of the Philistines and barbarians who first aroused the ire of Matthew Arnold in the late 19th Century. (And doing battle, incidentally, also against certain kinds of newspaper reviewers who write not literary criticism but undiscriminating puffery.)"[123]

THE EMBATTLED MOVIE CRITIC

If puffery was difficult to guard against even in the most reputable book pages and sections, it amounted to a way of life in the entertainment sections of all but the strongest and most vigilant newspapers. The root of the problem was in the motion picture industry, where several generations of particularly ruthless advertising and promotion men had operated on the principle that a movie review existed primarily to be quoted in the advertising. In much of the nation's press, it was common to see favorable canned reviews of movies, sometimes sent out by the companies themselves, or a mere news report that a new movie was being shown with a brief description of the plot. Serious movie criticism was, with few exceptions, almost a lost art.

The instances of intimidation of movie reviewers were numerous and the sad part of the situation was that much of the arm-twisting was successful. One New York critic had to

200   write a favorable review of a bad movie after he had published
an originally honest review. Another saw a headline over a critical article changed between editions to indicate that a star per-
former "rates a rave" when he rated almost anything else. "The
studios' dirtiest tactic," wrote William K. Zinsser after his retirement as a New York movie reviewer, "is to try to have a critic
fired, or transferred to a job where he can do less damage. This
tactic is used habitually, and there is good reason to believe that
it has dislodged several New York critics in the past ten or fifteen
years . . ."

Archer Winsten of the *New York Post* concurred. "It
is my firm belief," he said, "that there are many ways of neutral-
izing, softening and counteracting the opinions of movie critics,
and the movie companies know them all, and use them whenever it seems advantageous to do so. I don't blame them, though I
think they're short-sighted in trying to reduce the New York
movie critics to the status of unpaid press agents. I do blame
those, including myself, who have failed to bring to public attention every slightest indication that there is something rotten in
the state of New York City movie reviewing in the daily papers.
This is a fight that should never have been allowed to remain in
the undergrounds of rumor, insiders' stories, and the cynicism of
those who profit by killing integrity."

The in-fighting occasionally burst into public view.
When Bosley Crowther attacked a United Artists movie, "Tra-
peze," the movie company withdrew its advertising from *The
New York Times*. As the *Times*'s critic, Crowther's influence was
great and his independence a matter of continual annoyance to
the movie promotion people who tried to sway the reviewers. His
newspaper stood by him, ignoring United Artists' move. After a
suitable period, the company's advertising appeared again in the
Times without any change of heart by its movie critic.[124] However, there were not many Crowthers and the original one became a critic emeritus in 1968. Where newspaper editors were
craven, fearful, or simply indifferent to what was going on in
their entertainment pages, the movie promotion men more often
than not were able to get their way. The estate of the movie
reviewer, in consequence, was probably lower than that of any
other in the arts.

Ezra Goodman, a former critic for *Time* magazine,
summed up, with considerable distaste the old battles that movie
reviewers had lost in New York more often than they had won

and commented: "These, mind you, are the New York newspapers, generally considered among the best and most powerful in
the country. The situation is worse in other cities where newspapers are even less independent and usually have lower journalistic and critical standards." [125]

CRITICISM: A DYING ART?

In drama, music, and art, there were fewer problems because
there were lamentably few first-rate critics in any of these important fields. In the drama, the lack of critical talent was understandable because New York City had been the historic center of
significant American theatre for more than a century. But even
in the metropolis the shortage of drama critics was so marked
that *The New York Times* had to try three times after the
retirement of Brooks Atkinson until a suitable replacement was
found—Walter Kerr of the defunct *New York Herald Tribune.**
Moreover, it was a sorry observation on the profundity of New
York drama criticism that at least one of its long-time practitioners had never, apparently, seen a bad show and several were
accustomed to praise poor plays in a bad season. The public as a
whole learned only after the conclusion of the first season of
theatre repertory at Lincoln Center that much of it had been an
artistic disaster.

There were only a few newspapers outside New
York that supported critics who concentrated on the drama by
making periodic trips to Broadway and Off-Broadway theatres.
Where such critics functioned across the land, they were widely
and often eagerly read, for a large part of the New York theatre
audience habitually came from out of town. Its continued faith-
fulness to the stage in the face of successive indifferent to poor
seasons in the 1960s was a tribute to its persistence and its
courage, but relatively few newspapers and magazines contributed to an effort to develop an American theatre worthy of its
patronage.

No such limitation existed in serious American
music. The holy triangle bounded by New York, Boston, and
Philadelphia, to which American musical accomplishments had
for so long been confined, was considerably expanded in the
1960s. First-rate orchestras could be heard in several other cit-

* Beginning with the 1967–1968 season, the *Times* rationed Kerr's reviews by
mutual agreement, running his critical comment on Sundays and assigning an
erstwhile dance critic, Clive Barnes, to do the daily drama reviewing chores.

202   ies; moreover, the development of music centers in some of the universities outside the eastern seaboard contributed to a new spirit that was notably absent from the ever commercial theatre. The faithful reader of newspapers and magazines often looked in vain, however, for critics who could assess these truly striking developments in American music. There were only a few here and there—perhaps two or three in New York and others scattered in solitary splendor from Boston to California. The situation was such that the New York Music Critics' Circle disbanded in the mid-1960s, saying it did not have the facilities to keep up with new performances and could not even award its annual prize.

The art critics in daily American journalism were even lonelier than their associates in music and drama. Emily Genauer, of *Newsday*, who had served the defunct *New York World Journal Tribune*, liked to recall that nearly every New York newspaper had at least one weekly page on art—and sometimes two—in the 1920s. But with the coming of the great depression, the rise of the electronic media, and the constriction of the press, art news and criticism were major casualties. Despite the growth of museums, art galleries, and special exhibitions in the United States, the American press as a whole remained stubbornly indifferent to the public interest in art. *The New York Times,* the *Washington Post,* the *St. Louis Post-Dispatch,* the *Los Angeles Times,* and a few others made a specialty of art coverage and art criticism. As for the rest, it was something that fell within the province of the women's page or the society section—and that was it. The news magazines, on the whole, did a much better job with minimal staff and rock-bottom expense.

THE ELECTRONIC CRITICS

In the electronic media, culture was something that usually seemed to matter only when a suitable sponsor could be found. An unexpected nationwide public response to Arthur Miller's "Death of a Salesman," when it was produced on the Columbia Broadcasting System network, resulted in a rush by all networks to present original drama during succeeding seasons. Playwrights were signed up to produce miracles for the home screen, but of course they did not come off. As for electronic criticism of the drama, it was crammed into one-minute spots in the late newscasts on local television—a remarkable journalistic stunt for those who were assigned to perform if not to criticize. What

saved the experiment from turning into a farce was the good   203
humor of those who suddenly found themselves functioning as
electronic drama critics. Edwin Newman, critic-at-large for
NBC News, described his operation as follows:

"What is usually thought of as the most question-
able part of having plays reviewed on television actually seems to
me the factor that contributes most to the reviews' value and—to
make a large assumption—their influence. That is the brief time
the critic is given in which to make his views known. In my case,
it is a minute, which is between 180 and 200 words, depending
on how many are polysyllabic. There is nothing like it to sharpen
the thought and clarify the point of view, to bring forth, in short,
an opinion that is definite and plainspoken." [126]

There were no known regular book or music critics
who served the electronic media at that particular time. The
National Broadcasting Company did engage an art critic, Aline
Saarinen, but her appearances were not regular; since there was
no opposition, the theory evidently was that the viewers would
never miss her.

But if television's attitude toward the critical function was puzzling, the attitude of the press toward the criticism
of television was even more difficult to understand. As late as the
mid-1960s, the leading practitioner in the field, Jack Gould of
The New York Times, estimated there were no more than ten
critics on all daily newspapers in the nation who were, in his
words, "paid to examine TV both esthetically and sociologically."
He stressed the need for the development of local criticism for
the community in which a newspaper was published, but most
editors blithely continued to ignore him. They used the wire
service or syndicate critics; when challenged, they frequently
pointed out that it made no difference to television ratings
whether newspapers criticized TV or not. The very worst shows
could become hits. Some of the best could be snuffed out for lack
of viewer interest.

"Sooner or later," Gould wrote, "some elements of
the press also will have to cease pussy-footing around a disturbing conflict of interest. Newspapers and news magazines constitute one of the largest individual groups of TV station owners.
The most hilarious and hypocritical incident in the celebrated
quiz scandal was the boasting of some newspaper chains that
they were aware of the rigging all along. They conveniently
neglected to tell their readers that their TV stations were among

204   those contributing to the deception of the country. Newspapers owning TV stations have a special obligation not to extend to the home screen the Fourth Estate's traditional reluctance to review and discuss its own behavior." [127]

Beginning with six stations serving 8,000 families in 1946, television within 20 years expanded so rapidly that in 1966 it was reaching 54 million homes or 94 percent of all family units. There were 67 million sets receiving programs from 700 stations, with another 124 under construction and 179 added applications on file with the Federal Communications Commission. Families averaged 5½ hours of daily television viewing on a year-round basis, with a peak of 6½ hours a day in midwinter. They spent $27.5 billion on their receiving sets. But the TV broadcasters, with an $800 million investment in transmitting equipment, realized enormous gains. In fact, the National Association of Broadcasters estimated that by 1970 television's gross income from advertising would exceed $3 billion. [128] This was the giant that virtually escaped serious criticism in all but a few of the nation's most powerful independent newspapers and magazines.

Ernie Kreiling, a television critic, agreed with Gould that American newspapers generally had failed to develop "a significant body of informed, penetrating and effective criticism of television." * But he also observed that the newspapers, too, were "serving as the TV industry's principal means of promotion and exploitation." Kreiling was referring here to the program schedules, which even the poorest dailies felt they had to publish as a service to their readers, and the seemingly endless feature stories about television personalities. He pointed out that in Hollywood alone the three big networks maintained publicity staffs of more than 100 persons in the 1960s and spent $1.6 million on their public relations annually. "Until American newspapers decide how far they are going in promoting television to the relative exclusion of examining it," the critic concluded, "ABC, NBC and CBS will continue to be grateful for their all-out support and active, uncritical cooperation." [129]

Still another critic, Hal Humphrey of the *Los Angeles Times*, argued that television is more than a medium for advertising, show business, and news; it is, he insisted, a part of

---

* Radio and television, for that matter, generally abdicated their function of criticizing newspapers. The late Don Hollenbeck of CBS alone did a decent job.

American culture. Consequently, he maintained that newspapers should give it "constant dispassionate reporting and evaluation" for the benefit of a public that was "too easily mesmerized by it." [130]

Such pressures as these have generally caused a good many editors to reassess their position. It is readily demonstrated that the newspapers with reasonably well-staffed pages and sections devoted to the arts are also the ones that try to do a decent job of criticizing television. As for the rest, the reaction falls into two categories that are fairly clearly defined. One is the group that volubly protests it is doing a simply tremendous job in publicizing and criticizing the arts without substantial evidence to support its case. The other is represented by the thoughtful editor or critic who would like to do more but privately recognizes his limitations. "To get competent help," one commented, "means spending $8,000 to $12,000 a year for one critic. Most newspapers . . . cannot afford to hire two critics, perhaps even one. Syndication seems one answer, but an unsatisfactory one . . . Criticism at the local level is difficult. If it's too severe, it stifles local talent. Again, it's often unqualified to deal with a visiting artist." Another wrote, "Everybody knows that as a whole, the American press devotes little (and often incompetent) attention to literary, theatrical, musical and other artistic enterprises. But . . . there are a lot of oases, and they're not all in New York, Boston, Philadelphia, Washington and the Athens of the West, Los Angeles. To overlook the territory in between is misleading." [131]

It would be equally misleading to try to call the roll of the newspapers and the few electronic media "in between" that do a comprehensive job of covering the arts in their communities and providing adequate criticism of them because, almost certainly, some of the good ones would be left out. But among the oases, where cultural journalism is vigorously practiced, are New Orleans, Louisville, Denver, St. Louis, Dallas, Houston, Buffalo, Milwaukee, Cleveland, and San Francisco. To understand how this works in a medium-sized city, Paul E. Neville, managing editor of the *Buffalo Evening News*, gave the following explanation of the coverage of the performing arts:

"In order to understand our staffing, one should know something about our problem. Buffalo is a leading new-music center, home of the Rockefeller Foundation and State University sponsorship of the Center for the Performing Arts.

206   Under Lukas Foss, the Philharmonic is among the 30 orchestras
designated by the Ford Foundation as 'major orchestras.' The
area has long nurtured chamber music and the Budapest Quartet
is the resident university quartet. The music year, now extended
to 11 months, embraces more than 300 events. The Studio Arena
Theatre is a bustling regional theatre with a resident company of
21. There are a number of highly competent nonprofessional
theatre groups to which we give attention.

"Assigned to music is our No. 1 critic, an Eastman
School graduate, who also covers the dance. He has an assisting
critic who covers secondary events. Our record columnist also
covers the area of entertainment music in the theatres, clubs,
etc. Drama is covered by our No. 1 critic, who also does occasional movie reviewing. His assistant critic does movie and some
live drama reviewing on the local drama scene. If there is a
heavy run of drama or cinema openings on the same day, we
assign a city-side reporter to help, one who has an interest in the
state." [132]

Thus, the critical contribution may be modest in this
and like-minded newspapers published in cities of medium size
but it has undoubted value for the community. To have performances criticized rather than merely reported on is an advance
in itself. Moreover, such activity helps to give Buffalo the air of a
growing cultural center instead of the somewhat dubious destination of an ancient vaudeville routine, "Shuffling off to Buffalo." Neither lack of space nor lack of desire nor fear of additional cost (which at the privately quoted rates above seems
pretty low) should prevent newspapers from making a more
serious attempt to cover and criticize the arts in communities
that have made an effort to lift themselves out of the ruck.

Sweetness and light are all very well, but few newspapers and critics have been able to subsist on good cheer. There
is more substance, and a lot more honesty, in a critique such as
the following by Walter Kerr in *The New York Times* at the end
of a disappointing year in the drama: "This isn't a bad season.
It's never got up enough energy to be bad. To be bad, you must be
bold, you must aim high and nosedive hard, you must want to be
big and blow apart with the effort. This is a limp season . . ." [133]

New York may not be the only place in the nation
where such criticism is done well. But despite all its failings it
still sets the standard, for whatever it may be worth.

THE ILLS OF

14

PHOTO

JOURNALISM

When the United States Air Force sent its newest bombers nonstop around the world, its own exclusive color picture of the conclusion of the flight appeared on the cover of *Life* magazine. The opposition magazines, newspapers, and photo agencies protested this handsome display of government largesse, but the damage had been done. The Pentagon apologized. Shortly thereafter, an Air Force officer who had taken part in the unusual transaction was assigned to duty at Wheelus Air Base in Libya, where the temperature reaches 125 degrees at times. And soon the rumpus subsided

208 without any indication that the public either had noticed or cared.

In retrospect, the Air Force officer—a combat veteran and no journalist—should not have been judged so harshly for apparently misunderstanding the functions of photo journalism. For promotional values are an intrinsic part of the topsy-turvy world of pictures. With a blizzard of prints descending daily on the glutted marketplace, commercial interests often overwhelm the standards of both news and art. To an unthinking syndicate editor, sales can mean more than the public interest. And the covers of *Look* (7.5 million circulation) and *Life* (7.2 million circulation) can be made to seem more worthy of attainment than fidelity to principle.

For too many years, the photo journalist has been judged primarily by his greatest feats—the superb flag-raising on Iwo Jima caught by Joe Rosenthal's camera for the Associated Press, the frozen horror of Robert H. Jackson's photograph of the assassination of Lee Harvey Oswald, taken for the *Dallas Times-Herald,* and the heroism and self-sacrifice of three generations of combat photographers in the wars of this century. There is little doubt that Malcolm W. Browne's Associated Press picture of a Buddhist monk's flaming suicide on a Saigon street helped bring down the Diem regime and that the shocking photos of strife in the nation's cities galvanized the American public. Who can forget the exultation of Harry S Truman holding a *Chicago Tribune* election extra with an erroneous banner proclaiming a Dewey victory in 1948, John-John Kennedy saluting at his father's funeral outside St. Mathew's Church, John Glenn's triumphant return from the first American global flight in space? These are a part of the heritage of the age.

PICTORIAL VALUES

It is not so pleasant to meditate on the meaning—and the waste—of the publicity photos that inundate the newspapers and the magazines from every self-seeking source. In the entertainment sections, the women's pages, society, real estate, travel, and other parts of the press outside the main run of the news, the self-serving picture may frequently be seen. On occasion, when the new automobile models are about to be unveiled, the commercial spirit invades the news sections as well. There can, of course, be no objection to the publicizing of actresses or

automobiles when they are news, but the excuse of news values
inevitably covers a multitude of pictorial sins.

The case against commercialism in photo journalism was best stated by no impractical reformer but one of the most respected figures in the electronic industry, Dr. Frank Stanton, the president of the Columbia Broadcasting System. In addressing the American Society of Newspaper Editors, he said:

"Some of the most eloquent protests against trivia on television come from newspapers the front pages of which have been ablaze with hot 'inside' stories on personalities whose sole contributions to television are light entertainment. Some of the most sensitive attention to decolletage on television has come from newspapers of well-earned specialized reputations for warmly imaginative photographs of richly endowed actresses. . . .

"I have seen too often in newspapers the well-articulated conviction that the trouble with television is that it worries too much about the size of its audiences and not enough about fulfilling its high promise. And yet, I am continually struck by the fact that you, too, are supported by an advertising economy; that you, too, must entertain as well as inform and edify; that you, too, have the problem of providing something for everyone."

Dr. Stanton, with some justification, might have elaborated on the tendency in a backward section of the press to glorify violence in picture and text just as television does, to resort to every dubious technique of shock and sensation to attract public attention, and to treat the necessary but less saleable pictures of the day as a pack of stencils. But he turned instead, as leaders of journalism will on occasion, to the less controversial topic of freedom of information, leaving his auditors to meditate on the parallels between the ills of television and the ills of pictorial presentations in the press.

Like almost everything else about the news media, the problems of photo journalism are primarily national in scope. While there are some good local cameramen who operate for television, the picture syndicates, and the newspapers, the preference is for individuals or teams with demonstrated ability to serve a national audience. In the case of the great Alaska earthquake of 1965, for example, NBC went to the unusual length of flying a photo team from Tokyo for its television cover-

210   age; whenever possible at major events outside the main population centers, similar television coverage is arranged through
New York and a few other major cities. It is also true that when a
President travels, the principal news organizations in Washington prefer to send their regularly assigned White House cameramen instead of depending on local talent.

Naturally, this is bound to offend both newspaper
and local television executives outside main population centers
who have faith in the demonstrated ability of their own photographic staffs. All of them argue in public that they are "as good
as New York, and sometimes better," whatever they may say in
private. But a survey of 200 Associated Press members receiving
Wirephoto Service provides a realistic assessment of the photographic capabilities of the American newspapers at the local
level, and it also shows the extent of the problem. Out of 156
replies, 5 newspapers reported having no staff photographers, 11
others used reporters as photographers (and in one case an
engraver was also a picture-taker), while the greatest number of
respondents said they had three photographers. A minority of
newspapers in the survey accounted for a total of 883 photographers, with 26 in one morning–evening newspaper combination.[134]

It is reasonably clear therefore that the concentration of professional talent in photo journalism—even more so
than in reportorial coverage—is on the staffs of the Associated
Press, United Press International, the national and international
picture syndicates, the larger and better staffed newspapers, the
news and picture magazines, the electronic media, and the advertising and public relations agencies. The leading picture
newspaper, the *New York Daily News,* can draw on a staff of 60
photographers and send teams to all parts of the nation, a practice that is also general on the services and well-equipped magazines as well as the electronic media.

Consequently, there is no great mystery about the
mass of photographers who materialize seemingly out of nowhere at every major news event. For the most part, they serve
either the national media or the agencies that must ceaselessly
vend their wares. While local agency bureaus and smaller newspapers are able to compete with the leaders in some instances,
they are exceptions. It is no wonder therefore that most of the
American press depends on the agencies for its national and
international picture coverage and welcomes publicity pictures

with local appeal. Often, the smaller newspaper has no choice; the weakness in the system is at the local level.

THE QUESTIONABLE PICTURE

The news agencies handle everything from the President of the United States lifting his pet beagle by the ears to the opening of the new Metropolitan Opera House in New York, from the latest television starlet marrying an aging Hollywood actor to the agony of rioting in the cities and battle pictures in Vietnam. They must do the job quickly and professionally, adjusting pictures to the news, and providing both color pictures and black and white. One Midwestern newspaper ordered a transparency of the Mona Lisa from the Associated Press, expressed indignation because it was made from a copy rather than the original, and copied its own shot out of an art book.[135]

The wonder is not that there are inevitable drawbacks to the agencies' service, but that they are able to perform as well as they generally do. If the instinct for the flashy spot news shot and the commercially usable picture dominates the daily photo file, the agency editor can scarcely be blamed. He has learned to provide the kind of service his clients demand; if he does not, someone else will. Being on the inside, he is more aware than any nonprofessional of the extent to which editors determine the kind of picture service they get by the quality and type of pictures they use. Consequently, if there is to be less commercialism in photo journalism and more consideration of the public interest, it will have to start at the level where the pictures are used.

Not every editor is addicted to the old insistence of yellow journalism on "blood, money, and broads." Nor does he believe that all notions of journalistic illustration begin and end with pictures of pretty girls, babies, animals, and sports pictures, with an occasional mug shot of a captain of industry to add tone to the paper. Oxie Reichler, the editor of the *Yonkers* (N. Y.) *Herald Statesman,* a newspaper that is more than 90 percent home-delivered, has long repressed the familiar editorial weakness for shock, leg art, and the overexposed bosom.

"Should I be ashamed," he once asked, "that we go to great pains not to print words or pictures that might make a reader sick to the stomach if she happens to be reading our paper at dinner?" [136]

The *Los Angeles Times* has printed its share of pic-

212   tures illustrating some personal tragedy, but it drew the line at
some gruesome photographs of three girls, tied up in a desert,
which were taken by their demented captor just before he killed
them. Other newspapers in the area did not hesitate to publish
the madman's work. "I guess the only answer to how we handle
pictures of people in their darkest moments is that we more or
less muddle through," said Nick Williams, the *Times*'s editor.

Michael J. Ogden, the executive editor of the *Providence Journal-Bulletin*, argued for a policy against printing the
pictures that serve no conceivable use except to capitalize on
someone's grief. "I can understand the printing of an auto accident picture as an object lesson," he said. "What I can't understand is the printing of pictures of sobbing wives, mothers, children . . . What is the value of showing a mother who has just
lost her child in a fire? Is this supposed to have a restraining
effect on arsonists? I am sure that those who don't hesitate to
print such pictures will use the pious pretense of quoting Charles
A. Dana's famous dictum that he always felt that 'whatever the
Divine Providence permitted to occur I was not too proud to
print.' Which is as peachy a shibboleth to permit pandering as I
can imagine."

Vincent S. Jones, the executive editor of the Gannett
Newspapers, saw little merit in publishing pictures for their
shock value. "I, for one, feel strongly that we should not use a
picture which makes the reader feel that he has intruded upon
grief which, except for circumstances beyond the subject's control, would—and should—be completely private," he explained.[137]

Few editors are able to fall back today on the excuse
that such pictures must be used because of the requirements of
competition; nor is it at all logical that newspapers should seek
to be measured by the more liberal standards of self-expression
that apply to the stage and to fiction. A newspaper edited by
Norman Mailer or Jack Kerouac would be just as incredible as a
modern novel, written in the vulgar idiom of the day, by someone of the stature of Erwin D. Canham of the *Christian Science
Monitor*. The newspaper is not a theatre or a work of fiction
(although sometimes the public has its doubts) and it cannot
rightfully claim to be judged by such standards. Not many editors would seriously advance the proposition, in any event.

What is somewhat more to the point is the increasing modern development of the laws governing the invasion of

privacy, a doctrine that is relatively new to the American public. **213** The defense of truth, which is nearly always an absolute safeguard against libel judgments in the United States, does not apply when damages are claimed for the invasion of privacy, except in matters of public or general interest. It is an area in which the unauthorized personal photograph is particularly vulnerable. As S. D. Warren and Louis D. Brandeis wrote more than 70 years ago, "Instantaneous photographs and newspaper enterprise have invaded the sacred precincts of private and domestic life . . . For years there has been a feeling that the law must afford some remedy for the unauthorized circulation of portraits of private persons . . ." [138] In view of the United States Supreme Court's efforts to protect the right of free trial from undue publicity and its other strictures against the excesses of journalism in the reporting of crime news, the press will proceed at its peril with gross violations of the right of privacy. The day of judgment will come when the high court defines the new doctrine and the responsibility of the news media in relation to it.

It is true, of course, that intensely personal pictures of human tragedy have won numerous prizes, but standards for even the highest awards change with the times. Moreover, prize-winning, commendable though it may be, is not the primary purpose for which a newspaper is published. If there is a point at which public policy departs from the vital necessity of protecting personal privacy, it is in areas that affect people generally—war, strikes, civil disturbances, natural disasters, wrecks, and the like. Joseph Costa, executive editor of the *National Press Photographer* and himself a veteran photographer, took a perfectly sound position when he said, "I believe that the yardstick on which to base a determination is the importance and the social, economic, cultural or educational significance of a story, and whether the picture helps bring all the facts in their correct perspective." [139]

Even when the picture has great significance, however, there is no easily available set of standards by which it may be approved for use by the news media. *The New York Times* did not use the first picture of a Buddhist monk who burned himself to death; yet, many months later when the *Times*'s own opposition to the Vietnam War grew more vehement, the photograph of another such suicide was used by the newspaper. Morley Safer's CBS report of the burning of Cam Ne in South Vietnam, illustrated with televised film of a Marine setting fire to a hut with a

214   cigarette lighter, created a backlash of controversy. The murder of Malcolm X, the first advocate of Black Power, gave UPI a picture scoop, while AP had to apologize to its members for not giving them sufficient "protection" on a photograph of the victim's body being borne from a Harlem hall. *Life* had an even more gory picture, taken immediately after Malcolm X was shot.

The massacre of white hostages by beleaguered rebels in the Congo produced some of the most barbaric pictures since the opening of the Nazi concentration camps by Allied troops. When friendly troops finally reached the scene and came across the bodies of the victims, television and still photographers recorded the details for history—and their clients. The body of the most prominent victim, Dr. Paul Carlson, was shown with sightless eyes open in a photograph printed by *Time* magazine. However, only one out of six editors of the mass media, with a particular interest in pictures, argued that it should not have been published.

Joseph Costa said, "This picture . . . made a statement that pin-pointed the savagery of the Congo more eloquently than could have been accomplished by words alone. The emotional impact of seeing this great man, lying dead, his eyes sightless, could not have been conveyed in any other way."

Similarly, only one out of six editors had any scruples against using a picture of a Congolese rebel being stomped to death by a soldier. It was an AP cablephoto which appeared in the *New York Daily News* and a number of other client newspapers. Vincent S. Jones, who would not have used the *Time* magazine shot of Dr. Carlson's body, argued in favor of the stomping photo. "I would print this picture," he said. "No other medium can convey the brute savagery of this kind of warfare." [140]

As for the photographers, there is no record extant of any professional who stood, camera in hand, while dramatic action developed before him and failed to take as many pictures as he could. As Malcolm W. Browne said when he was once asked why he did not try to stop the suicide of the Buddhist monk in Saigon instead of taking the picture, "Frankly, it never occurred to me to interfere. I have always felt that a newsman's duty is to observe and report the news, not try to change it. This attitude may be subject to criticism, but that is how I reacted [in the case of the Buddhist fire suicide] and how I would react again. As a matter of duty, I photographed the whole horrible sequence . . . and relayed the pictures and story as fast as

possible into the Associated Press network. It is difficult to con- **215**
ceive of any newsman acting otherwise." [141]

TRUTH AND PICTURES

Wherever American interests are involved in the revolutionary
tide that is sweeping over much of Asia and Africa, it may be
taken for granted that the emotion-laden picture will be offered
to the mass media. Some may be loaded with propaganda values.
Others may intrude needlessly on private grief. Even the most
competent, conscientious, and experienced editors may not agree
very often on what should and should not be used; now and then,
they may even reverse themselves as they have done in the past.
What is in the national interest is exceedingly difficult to define.
It is so today and it has often been so in the past.

One of the most sensitive of American editors and
publishers, former Governor James M. Cox of Ohio, used to go
over the pictures in his newspapers during World War I and
circle the body of any American soldier that appeared. He did not
want such photos used. Once he circled the foot of a dead soldier
sticking out of the end of a truck. "Let's not publish such pictures," he would say to his editors. "It causes needless worry to
any woman with a son at the front." He was not a particularly
sentimental man, but he had a strong sense of propriety.[142]

Oliver Wendell Holmes had an entirely different
reaction after seeing the pictures of Antietam that were taken by
the first great combat photographer, Mathew Brady. "Let him
who wishes to know what war is look at this series of illustrations," Holmes wrote. "These wrecks of manhood thrown together in careless heaps or ranged in ghastly rows for burial were
alive but yesterday . . . Many people would not look through this
series. Many, having seen it and dreamed of its horrors, would
lock it up in some secret drawer, that it might not thrill or revolt
those whose soul sickens at such sights. It was so nearly like
visiting the battlefield to look over these views that all the emotions excited by the actual sight of the stained and sordid scene,
strewed with rags and wrecks, came back to us, and we buried
them in the recesses of our cabinet as we would have buried the
mutilated remains of the dead they too vividly represented. Yet
war and battles should have truth for their delineator." [143]

The problem of how much truth the public can
stand is one that inevitably worries editor and government
official alike. During the bitter rioting that swept major Ameri-

216 can cities in the summer of 1967, the inflammatory oratory of the champion of "Black Power," H. Rap Brown, thundered from the nation's television sets and appalled the sensible leaders of the country, white and black. But there was no alternative to turning Brown on and showing the televised scenes of looting and thievery that accompanied the rioting in the Negro ghettos. To have done otherwise would have been to concede to the public that television was less honest than the press, which carried the worst that happened in thorough detail and accompanied it with the attacks on United States "imperialism" by Stokely Carmichael from his temporary sanctuary in Cuba.

Similarly, in Vietnam, there could be no muffling of the truth. The bravery and daring of both the still and television cameramen often produced pictures that aroused the public. Very often, after a particularly stirring newsfilm that did not show American interests in a particularly favorable light, the Pentagon would protest directly to the networks. While Arthur Sylvester was Assistant Secretary of Defense for Public Affairs, he sought to justify his position as follows:

"Pictures have an impact that words seldom have. They are immediate, vivid and produce non-verbal and emotional reaction. Within minutes the viewer may be on the telephone, or dashing off a letter to his congressman . . . I can tell you quite frankly that this immediate response to a partial story causes no end of problems. The letters start coming in. Program viewers think they know what is going on. But what they have seen is usually part of the picture. To give them a complete picture in words is a contradiction in itself . . ." [144]

Yet, Stendhal, writing of the Battle of Waterloo in "La Chartreuse de Parme," was able to convey some of the confusion and disarray and senseless horror of war by using such techniques as only a master novelist can. In the modern framework of television, Morley Safer had this response to the Pentagon's view: "American soldiers are not always 100 percent sterling characters, just as American policy is not always exactly what is right for the world or for Vietnam's smallest hamlet. The unfavorable has always been reported along with the favorable—but television tells it with greater impact. When the U. S. blunders, television leaves little doubt. So when a government official, either in Saigon or Washington, denies what television plainly reports and then attempts to give verisimilitude to

his denial by damning the reporter—at best this is pure hum-   217
bug." [145]

The ills of photo journalism are many. Sometimes, because the photo journalist in all his roles is intensely human and the most combative of the journalistic breed, his faults may even overshadow his virtues. But neither talk of codes nor voluntary regulations will work any miracle cure. The problems of photo journalism are caused in the main by the world it tries so painstakingly to reflect, not by faulty techniques or surly temper. But a better understanding both of the world and of the uses of pictorial journalism is manifestly necessary in a time of turmoil at home and abroad.

The art of the camera, no less than the art of the writer, is not easily mastered; in both fields, geniuses are few. Outside a comparatively small number of newspapers, the weekly magazines and television, not many editors really are abreast of the newest and the best in pictorial journalism. Moreover, in all areas of the news media, the editors who combine a keen knowledge of national and international affairs with an expert background in photo journalism are pathetically few. On 147 newspapers in an Associated Press survey, only 44 had picture editors and 103 did not. Of the 44, less than 30 selected pictures for publication and assigned their own photographers.[146] The ratio for the bulk of the American press is probably lower, thus confirming the general suspicion that in too many cases the assignment and selection of pictures are added duties piled on some editor who has no special qualifications in the field.

It is, of course, an impossibility to ask a small newspaper to engage or even train specialists in photo journalism, or to expect its photographers to display the qualities of a David Duncan. But at the metropolitan level, some soul searching is in order. Not many newspapers can display pictures with the quality and imagination of the picture magazines. Even more important than both personnel and techniques, however, is a better understanding among those who take and edit pictures of the kind of world they are trying to reflect. That is, for the long term, the key to the development of photo journalism as a more powerful element in mass communications.

THE SHAPING

PART 3

OF PUBLIC

OPINION:

THE ENDLESS

STRUGGLE

POLLS AND

15

POLLSTERS

The age of the computer has created more problems for American journalism than it has
solved. Probably the most controversial is the almost habitual use
of the public opinion poll and the projection of its results through
the computer. With each succeeding national campaign its political importance and its prestige have increased despite its admitted
errors and other limitations. And on many an election night, in
the most dazzling feat of all, pollsters have announced the outcome of elections on the basis of less than one percent of the vote
as projected through computers.

222   While the public was once dubious of the statistical validity of basing a national trend on a few thousand—and sometimes a few hundred—interviews, such doubts have long since been dissipated among the more sophisticated elements. The pollsters have succeeded in creating the impression that only a dunce would question their methods and procedures. In dealing with more competent critics, the line changes to one of polite character assassination such as this: "Of course, he doesn't really like public opinion sampling because he doesn't know anything about it." The whole effort in the past has been to surround the pollster with the aura of a Sir Galahad seeking the Holy Grail when he is, in reality, a fallible human being working with sensitive instruments to try to plumb the depths of the human mind. It has been argued in his behalf that computers do not lie; however, it is also true, as Samuel Lubell has frequently pointed out, that the information to be analyzed is fed into computers by human beings who are somewhat more subject to error.

        The triumphs of the pollsters have been exaggerated almost as much as their errors. Some of the more enthusiastic supporters of current methods of public opinion sampling have been heard discussing in hushed tones the possibility that American citizens soon will be helpless before some Big Brother who will manipulate 200 million people with consummate ease. For them, 1984 is as real as LSD—and as fascinating. They brush aside the somewhat less than brilliant results achieved by such manipulators as Mussolini and Hitler, arguing that these dictators were mere amateurs.

        Such exaggerated notions have hurt the pollster far more than they have helped him. The fact is that his empirical art has developed rapidly in a quarter-century in the United States and is today a useful and necessary part of American journalism, as long as it is applied with some knowledge of its limitations. Neither politics nor economics nor the social revolution that is sweeping the nation can properly be assessed without a decent sampling of public opinion at regular intervals. Moreover, the modern entrepreneur who does not analyze his potential audience before starting a new publication or television station, or substantially changing an existing one, is bereft of his senses. The sampling of public opinion has won public recognition. It cannot from now on be easily disregarded as a force in American life.

        That does not mean its bad results, bad habits, or

bad manners, where they are in evidence, must be excused or   223
even tolerated. Nobody in journalism is exempt from criticism,
as the pollsters have discovered over the years. Consequently,
they have no more right to publicize their triumphs in runaway
elections as marvels of science than they have to excuse their
failures by blaming editors for drawing false conclusions from
their statistics. The best ones do not. They invariably point out
that it is generally the better part of wisdom not to use a random
public opinion poll as the basis for a firm forecast of the outcome
of an election.

THE POLLSTER AS ORACLE

The fascination of President Lyndon Baines Johnson with both
polls and pollsters has been a major factor in their public acceptance. Regardless of the uses to which he put the findings, tire-
lessly quoting the ones that pleased him and rejecting the rest, the
President focused popular attention on the polls because of the
power of his high office. When he engaged his own private poll-
taker, the quiet and serious-minded Oliver Quayle of Bronxville,
N. Y., he created a White House precedent. The President's poll-
taker, like the President's press secretary, was bound to become a
figure of consequence because what he did had national repercus-
sions.

Quayle, who had predicted the outcome of the 1964
election with remarkable accuracy on a state-by-state basis, con-
ceived it to be his duty to "tell the President how he is communicating with the people." He and his organization continually
surveyed the nation on various topics, reporting to the President
every week or ten days. Mostly, he used housewife–interviewers
as an inexpensive source of parttime labor and equipped them
with questionnaires on cards. For the tabulation and analysis of
results, he trusted no one except himself and a few close associates.

Quayle's services to the President had several notable effects. When the oil storage depots at Hanoi and Haiphong
were bombed in 1966, dismaying the doves in Congress and in the
press, the White House attempted to offset criticism with a Quayle
poll that registered 85 percent approval of the raid by the American public. He thus ably reinforced the President's faith in the
Vietnam War escalation policy of that particular time.[1] At another
period, Quayle's polls in advance of the 1966 Congressional elections flashed a warning signal that helped send the President into

224 action—although it did not seem to change the outcome in many cases where Democrats were in trouble. In any event, Quayle's recommendations generally received the most careful consideration at the White House during the time when he was in high favor. He talked a rough, pungent language that most politicians understood.

It is amply clear that such influential pollsters as Quayle have a multiple effect on public opinion in addition to sampling it, just as a reporter sometimes affects the news merely by the process of covering it. The pollster's political clients often force him into the role of a soothsayer who professes to interpret the public will. (The astrologers of New Delhi who have been consulted by some of the elite in the various Indian governments of the 1960s often exercise a similar authority, although the outside world does not take them as seriously.) When the pollster's findings are made public, they are amplified through the news media and reflected back on their supposed source with results that are difficult to determine. It would be a brave pollster who would undertake to find out how much the public is influenced by reports of what it is supposed to be thinking. Records of such an exercise are not prominently displayed in the voluminous literature of poll-taking if, indeed, they exist at all. Finally, neither pollsters nor journalists nor those who practice both callings profess to know how much a poll's predictions of victory for a particular candidate influence his chances in a close race. Some, like James Aloysius Farley, have always argued that there is a "bandwagon vote" that will automatically go to a likely victor. But such likely victors as Thomas E. Dewey, beaten in 1948 by President Harry S Truman, have always found it hard to believe.

Most poll-takers have few illusions about the public with which they maintain such close contact. They know quite well that most people are eager to give their opinions on almost any subject, whether they know anything about it or not. It is, in fact, one of the disagreeable parts of poll-taking that the field workers never know when, merely by asking questions, they encourage the expression of opinions by people who had not previously held them. Thus, the formation of an instant public opinion because of a pollster's activity is not an inconsiderable hazard of his work.

Almost all pollsters will concede privately that, in most surveys of public attitudes, about 20 to 25 percent of the responses are based on appalling ignorance. Such findings as *The New York Times*'s celebrated revelation that 25 percent of

those polled did not know Berlin was behind the Iron Curtain
come as a shock to the public at large, but not often to the
pollster. One of them has an unflattering name for such respondents—"slobs." [2] It is, perhaps, one of the reasons for the "adjustment" of raw polling statistics in many political campaigns; the
"slob" vote, improperly projected, could create difficulties.

THE LIMITATIONS OF POLL-TAKING

On the whole, both clients and public have come to expect far too
much of the poll-takers. The findings are often not as clear-cut as
press releases make them appear. An amateur pollster, Representative Charles A. Mosher, an Ohio Republican, received
nearly 5,000 replies in 1966 to a questionnaire sent to his own
district, in which 54.4 percent of the respondents agreed it was a
mistake for the United States to be in the Vietnam War but 47.8
percent called anyway for an expanded war to defeat Hanoi. On
the basis of this split image, Mosher concluded: "Our military
course is now set . . . The American people will not accept any
result there which may be labeled 'defeat.'" [3] Commenting on
another poll in 1967 which showed 76 percent of Americans
supported the Vietnam War but only a bare plurality approved of
the way President Johnson was handling it, *Newsweek* observed
in despair: "For sheer complexity, the country's present political
mood has no parallel. Nothing follows logic, or even common
sense." [4] Most pollsters agreed the problem would become worse
and they were, of course, right.

Louis Harris, who like Quayle established his reputation with Elmo Roper Associates, was quick to concede that
polls—even in the age of the computer—could run into serious
trouble. In President Johnson's landslide victory over Senator
Barry Goldwater in 1964, Harris and other pollsters found that
they still could not accurately estimate the percentage of voters
who would go to the polls—a crucial statistic in any election.
"We're still plagued in polls by turnout," he said. "We didn't
estimate the turnout correctly in the South . . . We did not catch
the falloff in the Republican turnout in the Northeast." In his own
defense, he again raised the familiar plaint that polling is useful
in establishing issues but that the press is to blame for publishing
"how the election is going to come out before the fact." *

---

* Most public opinion analysts agree that a margin of error of at least 3 percent
on either side of a prediction should be allowed in any sampling, which negates
any finding of a victory prediction by a smaller percentage.

226   Yet, Harris is the proud author of the useful Vote
Profile Analysis of the Columbia Broadcasting System, which
attempts to project an election result on the basis of a small
percentage of votes counted on election night. Here, he does not
protest that the press twists the results but argues: "We are in
the computer age and we must use polls along with computers in
our projections. But these projections really must be accurate
in terms of having the courage to say we won't call the election, as
well as saying we will call the election." [5] The pollsters, in short,
have become infected with the political spirit and would like to
have things both ways.

          The story of Vote Profile Analysis, one of the sys-
tems popularized by television and quickly picked up by some of
the leading newspapers in the land, is typical both of the successes and the risks that are inevitable in the age of the computer. In the 1964 Presidential election, VPA did extremely well.
But in some less important elections thereafter, it showed that it
was fallible. For example, in a New York City primary election
on September 14, 1965, VPA made an early forecast of victory
which the opposition candidate and his managers refused to
accept despite much talk by television reporters about bowing
to the dictates of "science." The opposition candidate, as it
turned out, was right and VPA was wrong, causing the Columbia
Journalism Review to comment caustically: "Television news
should remind itself that it covers elections; it does not sponsor
them." [6]

          One of the greatest feats of any poll-taker, as it turns
out, antedated VPA and other devices of a similar nature. This
was Harris's accurate and keenly analytical polling service for
John F. Kennedy throughout the Presidential campaign of 1960.
His work was credited with influencing to a large degree the
successful strategy of the Kennedy campaign staff. It was, for
example, a Harris poll that led Kennedy to stake his primary
campaign on the outcome of the voting in West Virginia's Presidential primary election, which proved to be decisive. Harris, too,
developed the information on which Kennedy based his position
on several major issues during his televised debates with Richard
M. Nixon. As a result, after his election, President Kennedy
became a polling enthusiast.[7] When Quayle thereafter became
President Johnson's poll-taker, what had been regarded as an
esoteric art became a political necessity.

          Some of the most intelligent criticism of poll-taking,

in all its aspects, comes not from the intellectuals in the universities or the working press but from within the ranks of the pollsters themselves. Samuel Lubell, the rugged individualist among
poll-takers of national repute, has noted the changes in the work
which he has conducted with considerable success from 1952 on
and seems not to care for the new direction of public opinion
sampling. "The competition between the parties and the reporting of this competition has changed," he wrote. "The focus has
tended to be less and less on issues and more and more on what
is often termed 'image-making.' Because I oppose using the study
of public opinion as a means of manipulating voters, I do not like
this trend. Nevertheless, we should not underestimate its force."

Lubell has little respect for what he calls the aura of
mystery that has been erected about the computer and the manner in which it is used by irresponsible television commentators.
For it is clear that not every station that invokes the reputation
of the computer on election night actually practices the art of
vote projection as advertised. For some, good guesses rather than
the inexorable laws of science, so-called, are the payoff. Astute
political writers for newspapers have done this kind of thing for
years—without computers and without television's ballyhoo.
Consequently, the practice of trying to call the winners almost
immediately after the polls close has its difficulties for all concerned. As Lubell wrote:

"In many situations, the decision on calling the election winner is largely a subjective one and should really be
classified as a human 'stunt' rather than as the 'computerized'
equivalent of an official count. The fact that a computer is employed may mislead the public by creating the illusion of mechanical efficiency when the performance is strictly human." [8]

The uses of public opinion polls during a campaign
are of even greater concern to a considerable proportion of their
clientele—the editors who use them. In a post-mortem on the
1964 Presidential election, 66 percent of the editors who responded to a questionnaire said they firmly believed that polls
influence elections, although they were not certain exactly how
this was done. In analyzing the results of the questionnaire, Don
Carter,* chairman of the Campaign and Election Committee of

* Carter, managing editor of the *National Observer* at the time of the questionnaire, later became executive editor of the *Record*, Hackensack, N. J., and the
Bayonne (N. J.) *Times*.

228   the Associated Press Managing Editors, reported, "We have editors who argue that in close elections, opinion polls stimulate interest, but in landslides they make voters apathetic. Another contends that polls, responsibly done, help clarify what the nation thinks is important at a given time. The real sleeper in all this is the effect of opinion polls on candidates themselves. What influence this information may have in leading one candidate to step up his campaign, or vary his tactics, is hard to measure. But we're convinced that the potential is there and the end results may be greater than we think."

THE PRESS AND THE POLLSTER

The stress on the potential of the movement to analyze public opinion is what has led the more venturesome editors to experiment with such systems as the CBS Vote Profile Analysis and the rival NBC Electronic Vote Analysis. If they have generally disappointed the electronic media by not placing primary dependence on this kind of forecasting, it is usually because they have a somewhat more sophisticated view today about the importance of being the first to proclaim a victory—or seeming victory—at the polls. In the era of newspaper primacy on election night, this kind of journalistic brinksmanship was widely practiced and the results were even more dismaying, sometimes, than those on television. Since they now can no longer be first with the news, it follows that responsible newspapers have reached the unspectacular but obvious conclusion that they must be sure to publish correct information and do it in depth that is impossible for the electronic media to duplicate. The press, on the whole, is therefore less worried about repeating the mistakes of 1916 and 1948, which are ancient history, than in picking up some of television's errors. Hence, the cautionary attitude toward vote projection systems.[9]

        There is somewhat less reserve about the press approach to the use of readership studies conducted by public opinion analysts, although even here no pell-mell rush has developed. This was generally due to the expense involved rather than lack of faith or lack of interest in the results. However, there are intensely suspicious editors who find it impossible to trust a pollster even when he is being highly paid for his work and has a national reputation to protect. One such editor assigned reporters to follow the poll-taker's staff and conduct identical depth interviews to check on the information that was being gathered.

William P. Steven, who had used readership surveys extensively during his successful regimes as editor of the *Minneapolis Star-Tribune* and later the *Houston Chronicle*, frequently pleaded with his associates to do more with readership surveys. "An editor who operates without them," he said, "is like a butcher who operates without scales. Having reliable information as to what your readers prefer among the things you offer should neither hurt your pride nor divert your purpose." [10] But a more typical attitude was expressed by Frank Eyerly, managing editor of the *Des Moines Register-Tribune*. "Surveys can be a useful tool," he conceded, but added quickly, "But they can also be an impediment. If a survey suggests that only 20 percent of your readers use part of your content, are you going to cut that portion to ribbons so that you can use more space elsewhere? . . . If one comic shows 75 percent readership and another shows 50 percent readership, are you going to kill the second comic and go on a hunt for something that hopefully will register 75 percent readership?" [11] And the ever careful Michael J. Ogden, executive editor of the *Providence Journal-Bulletin*, concluded, "We have done everything there is to do with surveys except, possibly, make extensive use of the results." [12]

Dr. Chilton R. Bush, the director of a center for research sponsored by the American Newspaper Publishers Association, realistically set limited aims for his work in view of the essentially conservative nature of his clientele. His steering committee, he said, doubted that research in itself could point the way to a new type of newspaper. He himself warned that research was no substitute for news enterprise or editorial judgment, a rather painful truism. But such disclaimers were apparently thought necessary to disarm suspicion of the center at the outset and make it possible to function.[13] It was only a beginning, albeit a small one.

Here and there, individual publishers have shown that they are ahead of the rank and file in the use of public opinion studies, whether for good or ill. It was, after all, a survey of the actual and potential readership of the *New York Herald Tribune* that finally led to the decision to suspend publication. The finding was that there would be heavy—and probably insupportable—losses in both circulation and advertising if the paper resumed publication once the strike against the parent newspaper ended. In effect, that decision by the publishers foreshadowed the demise of the *New York World Journal Tribune*, the

230   successor organization.[14] Under less dramatic and more favorable circumstances, surveys were also used in preparing for the establishment of at least two new newspapers, the *Suffolk Sun* in eastern Long Island and *Today* in Cocoa, Fla., plus any number of radio and television stations.

Such developments, naturally, have added to the credibility of the public opinion survey among journalists when it is conducted by experienced and responsible organizations. The electronic media, as always, continue to be the principal patrons of the poll-takers, although most of the news and picture magazines and several of the more progressive newspaper groups are becoming increasingly active in the field. The chief holdouts continue to be the tradition-bound newspaper publishers, basically because only a few of them have significant competition at the local level and they can continue to put out the kind of publication they think their publics want. But with the passage of time, their numbers are dwindling.

No matter how much progress he makes, however, the pollster is never going to overcome completely the inherent skepticism that is attached to any effort to gauge public sentiment in the mass. As Samuel Lubell once observed in a cynical mood, "I believe that no one paying for a poll will release it except in a way that will give him some advantage." [15] He referred to politicians and others dependent on public favor who make it a practice to hire pollsters to conduct studies for them, after which they issue the good ones and sit on the bad ones. It is a form of news management, in the main, and is no more disreputable than a lot of other news management practices at high government levels. Moreover, the same philosophy may be applied to many a publication in the heat of an election campaign; in numerous cases, by remarkable coincidence, polls favoring a paper's candidate are featured on Page 1 and adverse polls either are glossed over or lost entirely in the editorial shuffle. Only papers of stature regularly publish polling reports showing that their candidates are trailing and even permit their political writers to predict, the day before election, that their candidates are likely to lose.* Less altruistic publications, with perfect propriety, defer conceding victory to the opposition until after the votes are counted. While such tactics invariably lead to charges

---

* The *New York Daily News* poll in 1966 picked the Democratic candidate, Frank O'Connor, over its own candidate, Governor Nelson A. Rockefeller, Republican nominee for re-election. Rockefeller won anyway, aided by *News* editorials of October 18 and November 5, 1966.

that unfavorable polls are being suppressed, there is no known method in an American election of preventing a candidate from proclaiming far and wide that he has knowledge of an opposition poll in which he is leading.

It is in the universities, surprisingly enough, that the reputable poll-takers are encountering a somewhat greater threat to their credibility. This is one of the penalties of their success, for today the nation is being deluged by academic questionnaires on every conceivable subject—and many of them are amateurish in both concept and execution. But it is the fashion. Faculty and students seem to feel themselves under compulsion to present documentation for beliefs and attitudes that would have been advanced in other years on the basis of logic and reason. Since these qualities are currently in short supply in the United States, the computer and the slide rule have been seized upon as a substitute for thought. The survey is "in." It is so prevalent that the American Psychological Association has concluded that the nation is suffering from "survey sickness." [16]

Unhappily, there is little that the professional poll-takers can do to keep the amateurs from wholesale poaching on their territory. The news media, never in particular favor with intellectuals, are besieged with demands to submit to questionnaires. A thoughtful editor or publisher is asked to check a yes or no box on such questions as the following: "State whether . . . big business competition is destroying personal journalism and making the existence of small but independent newspapers impossible." While many such effusions come from students who want editors to help them with everything from class assignments to doctoral dissertations, a few do make serious and responsible attempts to examine the state of American journalism. Yet, in view of the time that would be required to service the amateur pollsters, most editors and commentators simply give up. One of them wrote in explanation: "A number (of these questionnaires) do come from press agents operating under the guise of research agencies to discover 'the majority opinion of the American press' for purposes dimly stated . . . Rare is the newspaper that is equipped with the staff to provide the answers." [17]

THE CREDIBILITY FACTOR

Finally, the credibility of the public opinion survey as an independent, scientific instrument is inevitably affected by the continual argument that wells up over television program ratings.

232   Although the Madison Avenue advertising agencies and the electronics industry both accept and defend the system, many inside the Establishment do not disguise their doubts. Moreover, the slender shaft of newspaper criticism almost always touches the ratings as a weak point in the selection of programs. Few outside television accept the argument that the system is not perfect, but is the best that can be devised to fit the circumstances. Even fewer would agree that the current method of ratings contributes to the elevation of television's standards, whatever may be said about its measurement of the money-making potential of a particular program. Senator A. S. (Mike) Monroney of Oklahoma was not alone when he argued in the Senate against the "mumbo-jumbo cult of TV ratings" and charged: "The laws of the nation . . . are reversed and negated, because the network presidents supinely bow to this fictitious god that tells America what it may hear and see." [18]

Despite the restlessness over the workings of the rating system, there is scant likelihood that it will undergo major change unless a national scandal is uncovered in connection with its operation. The rating companies escaped the Senate investigation of the television quiz scandals that rocked the industry in 1958. Five years later, when a House subcommittee considered their work, very little of consequence emerged. The House group did question the reliability of the procedures, but added scant factual background to justify its doubts. Little else happened to disturb the equanimity of the A. C. Nielsen Company, largest research organization in the business at the time, or its rivals. Arthur Charles Nielsen, the boss of the firm, saw no reason to change his method of checking the "Audimeters" attached to television sets in 1,200 selected homes throughout the nation and projecting the results to indicate the approximate size of audiences for network programs. He claimed neither infallibility nor exact accuracy, but his application of the principles of statistical sampling continued to hold the confidence of the industry as a whole.

A despairing critic, Richard K. Doan, wrote: "In settling for Nielsen's mechanical devices as a preferred method because they eliminate human guesswork about set usage, the industry settled for half a loaf. The other half is knowing whether anybody really is watching or how closely. The networks analyze ratings information 60 ways constantly. There is a method in this confusing madness. It supplies them with con-

trived alibis for programming defeats as well as contrived   233
grounds for claims of superiority." [19]

There is no apparent limit today to the growth of
public opinion sampling because it has become an industry virtually without regulation. Responsible firms and rank imposters
operate in the field with impunity. Advertisers, always the most
timid and conservative of all business groups, fear to do anything that will upset a system that has worked well enough for
them in the past and is likely to fulfill their most pressing needs
in the future. But the public interest will not be served by a
continued "hands-off" attitude by government. Both the reputable practitioner and the public have much to gain by the application of the same scrutiny of polling that federal regulatory agencies give to most other forms of trade and communication in the
nation.

The news media themselves have not been able to do
the job thus far of closely examining the work of the poll-taker
except in isolated instances. Whatever their objections, whatever
their doubts, they have in effect accepted a practice which, with
rare exceptions, they are unable to change. In a number of
important instances, it is a fine question whether the news media
do more to reflect public attitudes than to shape public opinion.
Certainly, one of the unintended results of the growth of poll-
taking is to disclose in unflattering detail the limitations of the
news media as leaders of public opinion. Too often, the media
are disclosed to be in the unenviable situation of a general who is
not quite sure what his army will do when he gives the command
to advance.

FREE PRESS

16

AND FAIR TRIAL

The press and the bar have been assuring each other for years, in rare moments of good feeling, that there is no essential conflict between the exercise of the rights of a free press and the preservation of the right to a fair trial. This is a beautiful theory, to which all right-thinking constitutional lawyers and editorial page editors wholeheartedly subscribe. It is a part of the American dream that all good things can be achieved at the same time without too much of a struggle.

Unfortunately, in practice, it often happens that a conflict does exist between the enforcement of the guarantees of

234

individual liberty laid down in the First and Sixth Amendments.
The administration of justice requires a certain amount of secrecy
in the investigation of a crime, in the consideration of indict-
ments by a grand jury, and in the deliberations of a trial jury.
And while the press may agree that these and other restrictions
are both wise and necessary, at least for the ordinary run of
cases, the extraordinary event nullifies the best of intentions.

It is then that the press, as a matter of public policy,
proclaims its right to penetrate the secrecy of both the police and
the judiciary, if it can, to insure that justice is properly being
done. Consequently, the interest of bench and bar to conceal and
the interest of the press to reveal come into conflict and it is right
and proper that this should be so. For there is no built-in assurance that errors in the legal process are self-correcting any more
than there is a guarantee that the press at all times will conduct
itself in a fair and proper manner. The two processes, if carried
out in good faith, should operate as a mutual check and balance
upon each other. Very often they do. When they do not, much
more than the First and Sixth Amendments is affected. The
whole of the democratic system in the United States inevitably
comes into question, for it cannot operate to the satisfaction of
its citizens unless both sets of rights are safeguarded.

Although the American Bar Association and the
American Newspaper Publishers Association in recent years
have taken a doctrinaire approach to the whole matter of free
press and fair trial, with each insisting that the other make
insupportable concessions, this has not been the prevailing mood
at the working level. Here, the police, the prosecutors, the defense attorneys and the judges must operate with the news
media in some semblance of harmony or let law enforcement fall
into utter disarray. Reporters have always been well aware that
there are laws in many states forbidding them from gathering
certain kinds of information, but they have been able to perform
their duties despite that because officials concerned with law
enforcement in most instances have granted necessary data vol-
untarily even though they had the right to withhold it legally.

In the face of a movement led by Justice Paul C.
Reardon of the Supreme Judicial Court of Massachusetts to impose punitive sanctions on court officers or police who issue
unauthorized information, the instances of voluntary cooperation between press and bar have grown steadily. Just before
the American Bar Association gave its final approval to the

236   Reardon Committee's program to try to effectively hobble the press, voluntary press-bar committees were at work in 21 states to initiate joint programs and lay down voluntary guidelines. In nine of the states, successful working agreements were in operation; in eight others, specific details were being considered, and the remaining four were in the beginning stages of such discussions.[20] There is every indication that the cooperative campaign will expand, although, as Justice Reardon has somewhat sourly observed, a substantial part of the news media is unlikely to go along.[21]

There is still another facet of the new relationship between press and bar, and in the dealings of each with the police. That is the decision of a number of individual newspapers and a part of the electronic media, notably the Columbia Broadcasting System, to abide by guidelines they themselves have set. But it should not be imagined that these or other peace offerings by the news media have made the legal establishment any less determined to maintain the right of fair trial by judicial fiat if necessary. It is true that Justice Reardon's original decision to press for contempt actions against noncooperating news media was abandoned when a report of the Association of the Bar of the City of New York questioned the constitutionality of such sanctions. But the distinguished chairman of the New York City Bar committee, Judge Harold R. Medina, drew immediate dissent from his colleagues when he argued that editors had the right to disregard voluntary guidelines and print otherwise prohibited information in cases of "overriding public need."[22]

If this indicates the stiffness of the position of bench and bar, the following from the American Newspaper Publishers Association shows the quality of the press's resistance to judicial regulation: "The people's right to a free press which inherently embodies the right of the people to know is one of our most fundamental rights and neither the press nor bar has a right to sit down and bargain it away."[23] Despite the broad evidence of cooperation at the working level, the hard line at the top indicates that the contest is likely to continue for a long time with results that are far from predictable. Only one thing is certain: that an increasingly skeptical public is likely to view the more sanctimonious pronouncements of both press and bar with scant evidence of belief.

It is a temptation to observe, in view of the rising pressures of press censorship outside the United States and for

greater press conformity inside its borders, that the legal offensive against the news media as a whole is in keeping with the
repressive spirit of the times. However, such an interpretation is
not competely justified, for the excesses of the news media have
greatly contributed to the legal moves that have been undertaken
within recent years. It is useless to try to blame television, in one
instance, or the press, in another, or for the rival portions of the
news media to blame each other; for, in all truth, the public does
not separate the two. If anything, the press is given a greater
share of the blame in the public mind because its voice is far
stronger and more independent than television's, even if television's impact sometimes is greater.

THE DEVELOPING CONFLICT
There has always been a certain amount of concern in the
United States over the compatibility of free press and fair trial.
But following the assassination of President Kennedy and the
murder of Lee Harvey Oswald in Dallas, public attention was
focused on the issue as never before. For if the quick and accurate coverage of the Kennedy tragedy marked a high point in the
history of American journalism, the fatal shooting of Oswald two
days later before 50 million television witnesses was a new low.

The sight of the strip-tease operator, Jack Ruby,
lunging gun in hand toward his victim caused millions of Americans to turn from their sets in mingled shock, bewilderment, and
anger. They had never seen anything like it before, nor did they
want such an outrage to happen again. Consequently, with the
publication of the Warren Commission's report on the assassination, bench and bar received wide initial public support for their
campaign to restrain the news media in reporting some aspects
of the administration of justice.

The reaction of the news media was predictable.
The press—with television in low-keyed obbligato—responded
with a chorus indicating grave concern. Committees were appointed to report on what should be done, but little of a positive
nature was recommended. In the immemorial tradition of the
journalist, his committees could summon up no enthusiasm for
studying the past; instead, they wanted to go ahead, untram-
meled, to cover the next big story. Some of the more defiant
editors at once raised the cry that all this investigating was
damaging the cause of the free press, thus joining the issue.

Without doubt, the cause of the free press has been

238   damaged to some extent with the rise of the campaign for regulation, either from within journalism by agreement or from outside by force. But there are no particular devils to blame. For well-nigh two centuries, American journalism has had to put up with a spirit of philosophical anarchy in which its less responsible elements prefer to operate. Those who have counseled moderation and common sense, all too often, have been regarded with suspicion by their colleagues. The upshot has been an almost total failure, until recent years, of the necessary functions of self-denial and self-restraint within a large section of the American press. In retrospect, the Oswald case was the watershed from which a stream of reform began to flow.

It is regrettable that the reform movement, as it gathered strength, threatened to go too far, but that was inevitable under the circumstances. Some of the most powerful forces in the American system had been released and they would not easily be contained. That was made evident by the actions of the Chief Justice of the United States, Earl Warren, who was a prime mover in both the Kennedy-Oswald inquiry and in subsequent cases involving the conduct of the press that were decided by the Supreme Court. In the report of the Commission of which he was chairman, Justice Warren and his six colleagues were unsparing in their denunciation of the role of the news media in virtually forcing the police to bring Oswald before the television cameras in Dallas. It is worth recalling the substance of the report, for it set the tone for all that happened afterward in the press-bar controversy:

"While appreciating the heavy and unique pressures with which the Dallas Police Department was confronted (on November 22, 1963) by reason of the assassination of President Kennedy, primary responsibility for having failed to control the press and to check the flow of undigested evidence to the public must be borne by the Police Department. It was the only agency that could have established orderly and sound operating procedures to control the multitude of newsmen gathered in the police building after the assassination.

"The Commission believes, however, that a part of the responsibility for the unfortunate circumstances following the President's death must be borne by the news media."

The charges in the bill of complaint included unruly conduct by some 300 reporters and photographers who swarmed into Dallas Police Headquarters, badgering of witnesses, pressure on the police to disclose evidence, and interference with the rights of the prisoner himself. "The Commission believes," said the report, "that the news media, as well as the police authorities who failed to impose conditions more in keeping with the orderly process of justice, must share responsibility for the failure of law enforcement which occurred in connection with the death of Oswald . . . The promulgation of a code of professional conduct governing representatives of all news media would be welcome evidence that the press had profited by the lesson of Dallas.

"The burden of insuring that appropriate action is taken to establish ethical standards of conduct for the news media must also be borne, however, by state and local governments, by the bar, and ultimately by the public. The experience in Dallas during November 22–24 is dramatic affirmation of the need for steps to bring about a proper balance between the right of the public to be kept informed and the right of the individual to a fair and impartial trial." [24]

The Commission's view was quickly echoed by the American Civil Liberties Union, which said, "In our view, Oswald's killing is directly related to the police capitulation to the glare of publicity." The *Dallas Times Herald* agreed that the prisoner's murder was made possible by the effort of the police "to accommodate the press in announcing the time of Oswald's transfer [from his cell]." *The New York Times* formally apologized for having referred to Oswald as "President Kennedy's assassin," and added editorially, "The Dallas authorities, abetted and encouraged by the newspaper, TV and radio press, trampled on every principle of justice in their handling of Lee H. Oswald." Herbert Brucker, then the president of the American Society of Newspaper Editors, concluded, "It will be a long time before the full story of what happened in Dallas is told. But there seems little doubt that TV and the press must bear a share of the blame." [25]

In self-defense, the spokesmen for the press took several different lines but none indicated that there was overwhelming sentiment for the kind of positive action the Warren report had proposed. What happened in Dallas, some editors pointed out, was an extremely rare and unusual event from which too many conclusions could not be rightfully drawn. They argued that the press was highly competitive, and that aggressiveness and excesses by several reporters ultimately were bound to be matched by others. Alfred Friendly, then the managing

240   editor of the *Washington Post*, put it this way: "The press was
not pretty in Dallas. But it may not be fair to accuse it for failure
to embrace a system that was not its to prescribe." Still other
editors complained that it was unfair to accuse the newspapers
of responsibility for sins that mainly were television's, and that
television had in a sense paid penance for its sins by giving up
four days of advertising worth an estimated $30 million in order
to bring all facets of the Kennedy tragedy to the American
public.[26]

The American Society of Newspaper Editors finally
adopted a report of its special committee rejecting the proposal
for a code of conduct and warning against the pell-mell rush for
voluntary self-regulation. The ASNE report declared it was
proper for the press to resist regulations of the bar and law
enforcement agencies that "would black out large areas of information from the moment of an arrest to the beginning of a trial."
The editors contended, "The democratic community is not
merely entitled to know promptly the facts about crime and the
progress of law enforcement and the administration of justice;
democracy's successful functioning is endangered by the lack of
such knowledge."

The report rejected the notion that the press should
be bound by the same regulations that govern the operation of
law enforcement agencies and the courts. It held that the Warren Commission's complaints against the press were "unfair and
the assertions in large part ungrounded." Except for an offer to
confer on the subject, to rededicate itself to the principle of
safeguarding the rights of defendants and to reaffirm its determination to give full reports on the administration of justice, the
report stuck to the traditional journalistic line. It opposed the
suppression of information. It warned that voluntary codes could
be "more harmful than the evil complained of" because they
could prevent the press from doing its duty. "We are persuaded,"
the report concluded, "that no set of specific rules can be written
into a code of press conduct that will not do more harm than
good." [27]

THE BACKGROUND

It was therefore apparent that nothing at all would have happened to change the conditions of journalism in the aftermath of
the Kennedy tragedy had it been left to the journalists themselves. To a very large extent, that had been the history of

previous arguments over free press and fair trial. The American 241
press, unlike the British, has never been under restraint in the
coverage of news of crime or court proceedings as long as the
news meets the fundamental tests of truth or privileged publication based on proceedings of public record.

In an outburst of sensationalism in the twenties,
when tabloid journalism made a shambles of judicial procedure
in a series of show trials, bench and bar could scarcely claim
immunity from blame. In such cases as the Hall-Mills and Sny-
der-Grey trials, the excesses were shocking. Nor could it be
argued that the circuslike publicity was necessary to the administration of justice. It was, primarily, a contribution to the raven-
ous appetites of sensational editors for ever larger circulations.

Of all the celebrated murder trials in this century,
however, none became more of a hippodrome than the case of
Bruno Richard Hauptmann in Flemington, N. J., in 1935. Because he was accused of the kidnap-murder of Charles Augustus
Lindbergh, Jr., the infant son of Colonel and Mrs. Lindbergh, the
laconic Bronx carpenter became an object of scorn and even
derision to many of the newspapermen and radio broadcasters
who swarmed to the old Hunterdon County Court House. For six
weeks, the trial was an unparalleled spectacle for notoriety hunt-
ers. Motion picture actresses and their friends from cafe society
in New York attended with such regularity, mysteriously finding
ways to get into the small and crowded court, that they were
dubbed the "mink coat brigade." Hauptmann was photographed,
sketched, and sometimes even interviewed under prejudicial circumstances. It was scarcely a surprise when he was found guilty
of murder in the first degree and sentenced to death in the electric
chair.

The American Bar Association, at its 1935 convention, received a committee report condemning the Hauptmann
trial as a "public show," the effect of which was to "cheapen life
itself by causing people generally to undervalue the life of the
criminal and to increase the morbid desires of sensation seek-
ers." Two years later, the ABA adopted its Canon 35 largely as a
protest against the excesses of the news media at the Flemington
hearings. It read (as amended in 1962): "Proceedings in court
should be conducted with fitting dignity and decorum. The taking of photographs in the courtroom, during sessions of the court
or recesses between sessions, and the broadcasting or televising
of court proceedings are calculated to detract from the essential

242   dignity of the proceedings, distract the witness in giving his testimony, degrade the court, and create misconceptions with respect thereto in the mind of the public and should not be permitted." However, the press set up such a protest against Canon 35 that it was by no means universally applied in the United States and frequently was ignored. It was reasonably effective in 28 states.[28]

Even more honored in the breach than in the observance was the ABA's Canon 20, warning lawyers against making prejudicial public statements with regard to pending or anticipated litigation. When the New York State Bar Association sought to strengthen that rule in an effort to obtain broader compliance in 1957, the effort was widely criticized. "If publicity is important at time of arrest," wrote J. Russell Wiggins, editor of the *Washington Post*, "it is also important at subsequent phases of the process of determining the guilt or innocence of an accused person . . . Even statements by prosecutor and counsel concerning their intentions, although occasionally prejudicial to a case, have in some instances exposed to the community, in advance of trial, weaknesses in a case or unfitness in a prosecutor." [29]

THE COURTS TAKE ACTION

In the aftermath of the Warren Commission's report, the press found there was considerably less public sympathy for its all-out resistance to change in its coverage of the administration of justice. There were caustic remarks from outstanding legal authorities throughout the land. Arthur J. Goldberg, while an Associate Justice of the Supreme Court, said that the American press commonly uses "labels such as 'killer,' 'robber,' 'hoodlum'. . . to describe the accused weeks before and even on the eve of the trial." [30] Judge J. Skelly Wright, of the United States Court of Appeals for the District of Columbia, warned the American Society of Newspaper Editors that it was "very important that certain information is not published before a man is tried, at least in a context where it may come before a jury." He added drily that if the press would do something about this, "all of these efforts that are presently being made to control the press would disappear, as they should." [31]

In the absence of substantive action by the press, the New Jersey Supreme Court on November 16, 1964 ordered prosecutors, police, and defense counsel not to issue prejudicial

statements to the news media before and during trials. These
included references to a person's prior police record, statements
that a case was "open and shut," and "alleged confessions or
inculpatory admissions" by an accused person.[32] While the court
obviously had the power to enforce its decision against defense
counsel and prosecutors in the course of a trial, its authority over
what police officials said and did was regarded as dubious and it
had no way of acting against the news media other than to
extend citations for contempt of court, which it was reluctant to
do.

The New Jersey action touched off a new phase of
the struggle to curb the press. The Philadelphia Bar Association
approved similar guidelines for its 3,700 members, precipitating
a bitter wrangle with the newspapers. In Massachusetts, when a
Press-Bar Guide was issued, the press to a large extent also
opposed it. However, in other New England states, Kentucky,
and the Far West, similar action was discussed. Eventually, the
Department of Justice issued its own guidelines which followed
the general pattern. And in the United States Senate, Senator
Wayne Morse of Oregon threatened to fight for a new law which
would make it unlawful for any federal court employee, defendant, or defense counsel "to publish any information not already
on file in court or admitted as evidence." [33] He did not go through
with it.

The Supreme Court in 1965 struck hard at the use
of television in court trials in its reversal of the fraud conviction
of Billy Sol Estes, the Texas fertilizer tycoon, in a Texas state
court.[34] The case which did not affect Estes' federal conviction
set constitutional limitations on the use of electronic and photographic equipment in the courtroom. In effect, it checked a
sporadic movement that had been spreading at the local
level—and in some nationally prominent cases as well—to permit televised trials. To bench and bar, the suspicion was widespread that the television camera was in the courtroom for sensational purposes alone and did nothing to advance the cause of
justice. In all candor, television did little to refute this impression; consequently, there was little outcry over the Supreme
Court's action in the Estes case although the fight against restricting information to the news media went on.

It soon developed that the First and Sixth Amendments meant different things to bar and press. The lawyers,
characteristically, gave the broadest interpretation to the Sixth

244 Amendment and the narrowest to the First. They argued that the press had no particular rights under the Sixth Amendment: "In all criminal prosecutions the accused shall enjoy the right to a speedy and public trial, by an impartial jury . . ." The trial, the lawyers pointed out, was for the benefit of the accused and not the press. John Foster Dulles's celebrated dictum (in defense of the government's ban on American correspondents entering Red China in the 1950s) was revived in an effort to show that the First Amendment's guarantee of a free press—to use Dulles's words—related only to "the publication and not to the gathering of the news." [35] Justice Reardon, in fact, bolstered the position with a citation from a United States Appeals Court decision: "Even were we to assume the First Amendment protections from unreasonable restraints upon the dissemination of news information extend by implication to the gathering of such information as well, it still could not be successfully urged that the right to gather news is unconditional." [36]

Journalists, of course, refused to accept such an interpretation of the First Amendment, regardless of how it was applied. Arthur B. Hanson, general counsel of the American Newspaper Publishers Association, fired back at an American Bar Association convention: "I would remind us all that the guarantee of the Sixth Amendment for 'a speedy and public trial, by an impartial jury' contains those words which the bench and bar of our country have held to contain implicit within them the guarantee of a 'fair trial.' We would all agree, however, that the specific wording 'fair trial' appears nowhere in our constitutional documents." [37]

The frequent admiration expressed by the American bench and bar for the so-called British system also aroused a contrary feeling among the American press. The journalists held British procedures, if applied in the United States, would violate the First Amendment. The British, it was pointed out, historically permit publication of only the basic facts regarding the arrest of an accused person before trial and punish any further publication with severe sentences for contempt of court. Notations of a defendant's prior criminal record, alleged confessions, or the citation of incriminating evidence all are contemptuous in the British legal system. So is prior comment on the correctness of judicial procedure, the supposed guilt of a defendant or other views that may be considered prejudicial to a fair trial.

The issue was dealt with, in part, by the United

States Supreme Court in the *Los Angeles Times* case in 1941 when the newspaper editorially attacked a lower court's decision to put two convicted union leaders on probation, called them "gorillas" and demanded that they be sent to jail. A Bar Association group succeeded in having the *Times* held in contempt but the high court, in a 5–4 ruling, set the judgment aside. Justice Hugo L. Black, in the majority decision, applied Justice Oliver Wendell Holmes's test of a "clear and present danger" to the supposed obstruction of justice and found that none existed.

Accordingly, the American press regarded the *Los Angeles Times* case for many years as its justification for asserting the right to comment on the proceedings of a criminal investigation and trial. The *Times* case also was conceivably one factor in causing the Reardon Committee and other bar groups to drop plans to apply punitive sanctions to the press and concentrate instead on disciplinary action against the officers of the courts and police.

The British experience, in consequence, seemed then and now not to be precisely relevant to the current problems in the United States. For the United States, with nearly four times the population and 30 times the area of the United Kingdom, has a far greater incidence of crime, a less incorruptible judiciary, and 51 different brands of justice—the 50 states and the federal government. It has been on the basis of such differences, as well as the varying concepts of press responsibility, that the American news media historically asserted their will to act with great freedom, and at times even with license, in reporting and commenting on the administration of justice. Only after the Dallas tragedy in 1963 did sober second thoughts make a profound impression on many editors.

Through its stout defense and its modest and limited offers of cooperation with bench and bar, however, the press did seem to be riding out the storm as the critical year of 1966 began. The comparatively restrained coverage of the Candace (Candy) Mossler murder trial in Miami in that year showed the news media to be eminently capable of self-discipline in court coverage. Just before the jury came in with a verdict of acquittal for the blonde widow and her nephew in the alleged murder of her husband, Judge George Schulz announced: "I thought the press conducted itself in an exemplary manner. There were times when I asked them not to publish certain things, such as the names of jurors, and they complied . . . Perhaps this trial may

246   have contributed to a better relationship between the courts and the news media." To add to the press's mood of euphoria, an AP survey of 112 newspapers during the seven-week trial showed that on one day 35 had used nothing, 12 had stories on Page 1, and 65 had buried the case inside with short accounts. A Page 1 headline in the *Bulletin* of the American Society of Newspaper Editors asked, "Is The Big Murder Trial Passe?" [38] Then the roof fell in.

THE SHEPPARD CASE

With a blast at the press for "virulent publicity" and a "carnival atmosphere" that had made a fair trial impossible, the Supreme Court in an 8–1 decision struck down the 1954 conviction of Dr. Samuel H. Sheppard of Cleveland on a charge of murdering his wife. In the decision handed down on June 6, 1966, Justice Tom C. Clark spoke for the majority in warning: "The trial courts must take strong measures to insure that the balance is never weighed against the accused."

It was small comfort to the press that the presiding jurist, Circuit Judge Edward Blythin, who had since died, was primarily blamed for "the massive, pervasive and prejudicial publicity that attended" Dr. Sheppard's prosecution. "Trials," said the high court, "are not like elections, to be won through the use of the meeting halls, the radio and the newspaper." It censured Judge Blythin for announcing he could not restrict prejudicial news accounts and made this reference to the power of the court to issue contempt rulings: "The carnival atmosphere at the trial could easily have been avoided since the courtroom and courthouse premises are subject to the control of the court."

The State of Ohio had demanded a first degree murder conviction and the death penalty in the Sheppard case, but the defendant had been convicted of second degree murder and sentenced to prison for life. The conviction was later affirmed by the Court of Appeals and the Ohio Supreme Court. But after serving more than nine years in prison, Sheppard was granted a writ of habeas corpus by Federal District Judge Carl Weinman on the ground that excessive publicity had denied him a fair trial. The Federal Circuit Court of Appeals reversed the lower court but, when the case went to the Supreme Court, Sheppard won both freedom and a new trial. Later that year, at a decorous second trial, he was acquitted.

In view of the final outcome of the case, the Supreme Court's decision became an enormous influence on bar-press relations from that time on and was frequently cited by both sides. The press found solace in this section of Justice Clark's opinion, laying down the basic principle under which it operates in American courtrooms: "The principle that justice cannot survive behind walls of silence has long been reflected in the 'Anglo-American distrust for secret trials.' A responsible press has always been regarded as the handmaiden of effective judicial administration, especially in the criminal field. Its function in this regard is documented by an impressive record of service over several centuries. The press does not simply publish information about trials but guards against the miscarriage of justice by subjecting the police, prosecutors and judicial processes to extensive public scrutiny and criticism.

"This court has therefore been unwilling to place any direct limitations on the freedom traditionally exercised by the news media for 'what transpires in the courtroom is public property.' The unqualified prohibitions laid down by the framers [of the Constitution] give to liberty of the press . . . the broadest scope that could be countenanced in an orderly society. And where there was 'no threat or menace to the integrity of the trial,' we have consistently required that the press have a free hand, even though we sometimes deplored its sensationalism."

Having reasserted its support of the free press, the high court proceeded to recommend to trial judges its own concept of guidelines for press conduct. Among these were a limitation on the number of reporters in the courtroom at the first sign of disturbance; restrictions on photographers; protection of witnesses against premature disclosure of their testimony; control of the release of information by counsel for both sides, police officers, and witnesses; and a warning to reporters against the use either of inaccurate stories or material not introduced in the proceedings.

"From the cases coming here," the Clark opinion went on, "we note that unfair and prejudicial news comment on pending trials has become increasingly prevalent. Due process requires that the accused receive a trial by an impartial jury free from outside influence . . . Of course, there is nothing that proscribes the press from reporting events that transpire in the courtroom. But where there is a reasonable likelihood that preju-

248   dicial news prior to trial will prevent a fair trial, the judge should continue the case until the threat abates or transfer it to another county not so permeated by publicity."

In an interpretation of the guideline section of the Sheppard decision before the National Conference of State Trial Judges, Justice Clark made his meaning crystal clear and it was not flattering to the press. "I'm not proposing that you jerk a newspaper reporter in the courtroom and hold him in contempt," he said. "We do not have to jeopardize freedom of the press. The press has made sure our democracy works as it should." But he quickly added that he would tolerate no prejudicial press behavior, saying, "If doubt comes to our court that a defendant's rights have been jeopardized, I'm going to vote to reverse." [39]

Once more the press argued in its own defense that an "extreme case" had been cited in order to impose new and onerous strictures against the news media in their coverage of the courts. The plea was made that, with a crime rate that increased 73 percent between 1955 and 1965, the public had a right to know the immediate state of the administration of justice instead of being obliged to wait until the conclusion of a court trial. It was also argued that less than 10 percent of the cases referred to the courts ever go to a jury trial, and a far smaller number ever receive notice in the press. As for complaints of prejudiced trials because of undue publicity, it was contended that out of 51 such complaints in 1964–1965, only three were the basis for actual reversals.

"It appears clear," said Robert C. Notson, the then president of the American Society of Newspaper Editors, "that if the newspapers are muzzled in publication of pre-trial information, especially at the time of arrest, the vast number of criminal cases will be disposed of with little or no public knowledge. I can think of no surer way to invite corruption among our law enforcement officers and to bring the courts into disrepute than this proposal for exchanging open justice for closed justice. The public has a right to distrust justice administered in secret." [40]

Such criticism was intensified when the Supreme Court, in the Miranda case, freed a suspect in an Arizona rape case because he had not been advised of his right to be silent and to be represented by a lawyer at his interrogation. The high court's majority opinion held that from the moment a person is within police custody—that is, denied liberty of movement—the Fifth Amendment privilege against self-incrimination takes effect. In consequence, it was held that a suspect's confession before trial may not be used against him unless the police have notified him of his rights. The minority in the high court termed the doctrine "dangerous," a view with which many editors agreed.

The police and prosecuting authorities, some of whom had been accustomed for years to announcing confessions and other damaging admissions by prisoners after prolonged secret questioning in station house "squeal rooms," were almost as despairing as the press had been over the Sheppard verdict. Those who had become accustomed to acting as inquisitors, rather than accusers, did not quite know what to make of the new dispensation. As for the news media, the sensation-minded, who had never seen anything wrong with publicizing a police-announced solution of a crime in advance of trial, expressed professional outrage.

THE JUDGE AS EDITOR

Soon enough, the standards that had been proposed by both the Warren Commission and the Supreme Court were put to the test. On July 13, 1966, eight nurses were killed in Chicago by a man who invaded their quarters, bound and gagged them, and escaped after the crime. The lone survivor, Miss Corazon Pieza Amurao, a Filipina who was working in South Chicago's Community Hospital, was able to give the authorities a description of the murderer. Police also found fingerprints at the scene of the crime. As a result, Police Superintendent Orlando W. Wilson issued an alarm for a 24-year-old seaman, Richard Franklin Speck, as a "wanted" man. When he was captured as a direct result of the description the police had broadcast of him, Wilson announced, "Yes, I feel that we have enough evidence to convict him. We have physical evidence placing him in the building and we have positive identification from an intended victim. As far as I am concerned, there is no question that this is the man."

In other respects, the police superintendent adhered to the guidelines. He obliged newsmen to leave the corridor of the hospital where Speck was held. He did not permit police to question the suspect before a court-appointed lawyer could be present. As for the press, its treatment of the shocking case was far more subdued than could have been expected under the circumstances. True, there were excesses. The *Chicago Sun-Times* in one edition published a piece by Jimmy Breslin in which

250   he wrote of Speck: "With an acne face and a bent mind, he crawled out into the life that others lead and he killed eight young nurses with a knife and with his hands." In the next edition, the sentence was edited to read: "He was accused of crawling out . . ." And the *American*'s Harry Romanoff, at 67 years of age still a good mimic, posed by telephone successively as a coroner and a lawyer to obtain information from gullible sources. It was part of an older and racier Chicago tradition when newspapering was still referred to as a "game" and newspapermen were "boys."

But neither Superintendent Wilson nor the press had any apologies to make. "I think the information I gave to the Chicago public was the information they should have and I saw no reason for withholding this information," Wilson said. "He [Speck] is the killer." *Editor & Publisher* commented plaintively, "Is the press supposed to report the news of a crime and the identity of the major suspect [when known] in order to bring about his arrest and then forget the whole thing—even forget there was a crime and sufficient evidence to link one man to it—when that man is caught? Can the public be expected to forget eight deaths in such a hurry? It sounds a little unrealistic." [41]

Unrealistic or not, the Speck case illustrated the complex responsibilities of the press in the reporting of the administration of justice under the new dispensation. With a change of venue, Judge Herbert C. Paschen ruled at Speck's trial that the press could not obtain official transcripts of the proceedings and could not publish the names of prospective jurors even after they were sworn or dismissed. He also laid down other and less onerous regulations. But the *Chicago Tribune* and other Illinois newspapers, in an appeal to the Illinois Supreme Court, succeeded in forcing the abandonment of the two severest restrictions, although the rest remained. In this strained atmosphere, Speck was convicted. [42]

The bench and bar did not distinguish themselves with examples of moderate conduct on all occasions any more than the press did as the tension between them increased. The *Denver Post* had to fight for the basic details of a campus murder at Boulder, Colo., in which the district attorney and the police refused to give substantial information even though they had no suspect in custody at the time. In reporting on a murder defendant's plea for release on a habeas corpus writ, the *Phoenix Gazette* and *Arizona Republic* were obliged to defy a contempt

order aimed at suppressing what went on in open court. Later,   251
the Arizona Supreme Court upheld their position. In Wake
County, North Carolina, two Superior Court judges demanded
the suppression of almost all police news, which the police took
to include even reports of automobile accidents, but the authorities could not make this ridiculous news ban stick.[43]

The pressures against press misconduct, however,
continued to rise in the courts. Nearly three years after Jack
Ruby's television murder of Lee Harvey Oswald, the Texas Court
of Criminal Appeals threw out his conviction and death sentence
at a time when (although the court did not know it) he was
dying of cancer. It ruled that there was so much prejudice in Dallas County that a "fair and impartial trial" for the defendant had
been impossible. Thus, in the face of incontrovertible evidence
that Ruby had murdered Oswald, the court let its concern over the
right of fair trial lead it to adopt an academic position, which was
beyond public understanding. Certainly, it did not add to public
faith in the good sense of its court system. While Ruby's death on
January 3, 1967 ended that particular controversy, it scarcely
solved the larger aspects of the problem.[44]

THE REARDON RESTRICTIONS

The bar placed its faith in the Reardon Report's restrictions. As
amendments to the Canons of Professional Ethics of the American Bar Association, departmental rules of law enforcement
agencies and rules of the court, wherever appropriate, these
strictures invoked the most formidable powers of enforcement.
With threats of judicial punishment of noncomplying police and
officers of the court, and the additional possibility of disciplinary
proceedings or even disbarment against attorneys, the Reardon
rules called upon both to withhold the following information in
criminal cases from the time of the arrest of a suspect until the
end of his trial:

A defendant's previous criminal record.

The existence of a defendant's admissions or a confession.

Identification of prospective witnesses.

Results of tests taken by a defendant (such as lie
detector) or his refusal to take such tests.

Discussion of the merits of the evidence, including
the possibility of a guilty plea.

The police were given permission under these regu-

252   lations to announce only the fact and circumstances of an arrest, the seizure of evidence, the text of the charge, the identity of the arresting officers, and the length of the investigation. The prosecuting and defense attorneys, in addition, were authorized to quote without comment from public records of the court in the case or to announce the scheduling or result of any stage of the judicial proceedings.

There were holes in this legal charade, as both lawyers and journalists were quick to point out. For example, while a defense attorney could not speak for his client publicly under pain of judicial or professional action against him, the defendant at all times could speak for himself and authorize whatever publicity he chose to seek. And while court officers and police were forbidden to issue past records or other details of a defendant's background bearing on a case, the news media naturally could use their own material in their libraries or even obtain the necessary records from sources not directly involved in a proceeding. Finally, there was every reason to believe that the background procedure, which was so popular in Washington and in foreign capitals for formally concealing the source of an announcement, could be successfully invoked to circumvent the Reardon regulations. The extralegal "leaking" of information thus became a part of American jurisprudence and American journalism as well.[45]

The press entered still further objections to the regulation of news of criminal matters by the police and the courts in the wake of the rioting that swept the Negro ghettos of major American cities in the summer of 1967. Speaking for the American Society of Newspaper Editors, J. Edward Murray posed the following problem for the bar: "Picture, if you will, a busy Detroit police chief . . . telling reporters and broadcasters what to say about the character and past reputation and past history and prior criminal records of the suspects arrested for sniping and arson and looting. Does that make any sense? How can the bar ask the press to ignore all prior criminal records at a time when recidivism is probably the main factor in the rising crime rate, when something over half of all offenses are committed by repeaters? Concerning confessions, the press has moved far toward the bar's point of view. Nevertheless, there are times when the general public has a right to be informed of legitimate confessions."[46]

It is therefore abundantly clear that the unilateral

attempt to impose restrictions on the flow of the news, however   253
high-minded the purpose, will be the source of endless controversy between press and bar. The chances are, therefore, that
minimal enforcement of a strengthened Canon 20 is likely except under extreme provocation. Under these circumstances, the
individual decisions of the news media themselves to abide by
certain self-imposed restrictions and the even broader and more
hopeful movement toward cooperation between press and bar
make a great deal more sense to the public at large. It is self-
evident that there will always be extremists on the bench, eager
to strike at the press under any pretext that comes to hand, and
sensationalists in the news media, determined to swing for the
big picture or the big headline regardless of cost to the nation's
system of law enforcement. But in a very real sense, the
press-bar controversy has served to usher in a new and more
promising relationship between them and the public they both
serve.

VOLUNTARY PRESS CURBS

There is no better example of a disinterested press than in
Toledo, Ohio, where the *Blade* and the *Times,* both owned by
Paul Block, Jr., have imposed on themselves a code to limit their
news reporting of criminal proceedings to protect the rights of
the accused. The American Bar Association has paid special
tribute to the Toledo voluntary code, which lays down the following conditions of publication:

Before trial, only the name, age, and address of the
accused; the circumstances of the arrest; the charge; and the
identity of the complainant will be published. Action by a grand
jury will be limited to a report that an indictment has been
returned and a trial date set. Except under special circumstances, reporting of the trial itself will not include prior criminal records of the accused, any confession or other admission, or
statements by lawyers that may be prejudicial to the rights of the
accused. The names of jurors and arguments or evidence submitted to the court in the absence of the jury will not be
published.

Since they have no competition except from radio
and television, the Toledo newspapers have good reason to believe that they can fulfill their commitment. Yet, they also leave
themselves free to publicize all necessary details of any case at a
time when further publicity will not endanger the rights of a

254   defendant. They point out, too, that it might be necessary in the event of a wave of violent crime to publish additional material as assurance to the community.[47]

There are equally responsible agreements between press and bar groups throughout the nation that have been worked out on a cooperative basis, among the most notable being those in Washington, Oregon, Missouri, and Kentucky. The Washington agreement is a model, described as "noteworthy" in the Reardon Report, which sets up the following guidelines:

Information may be issued on a defendant's biographical background without restraint other than to conform to accuracy, good taste, and judgment; on the substance or text of the charge and the identity of the complainant; the identity of the investigating or arresting agency; the length of the investigation; and the circumstances immediately surrounding the arrest.

Precautions should be observed in considering the publication before trial of opinions about a defendant's character, his guilt or innocence, his admissions, confessions, or alibis; references to tests or statements concerning the credibility or anticipated testimony of witnesses, opinions concerning evidence or argument in the case, and prior criminal charges and convictions of the accused. In addition, it is held to be improper for members of the bench-bar-media or law enforcement agencies "to make available to the public any statement of information for the purpose of influencing the outcome of a criminal trial." [48]

In essence, what the Washington plan seeks to do is to place the responsibility for insuring both fair trial and free press on those who have the greatest stake in protecting them—the press and bar. In any voluntary agreement, violations are likely; however, such a risk is preferable to the kind of guerrilla warfare that is built into any disciplinary system which one side tries to impose on the other. It is manifestly true that in an older era, when newspapers were engaged in cut-throat competition and depended in the main on street sales and sensation for their well-being, with some prestigious exceptions, such cooperative agreements as the Washington plan would have been instant failures. But today, when newspaper competition exists in only a few major cities and most of their circulation is home-delivered, they have everything to gain and nothing to lose by coming a little closer to the public's notion of the function of a free and responsible press. The same is even more true of television, despite the more vigorous competition of the electronic media at the national and key local levels.

    For the future, the rule of common sense seems to be a good one to follow.

RIGHT TO KNOW

17

VS. NEED TO

KNOW

L ike home, motherhood, and the American flag, freedom of information has its band of vigilant and hardy defenders. At any journalism convention of consequence, a resolution vowing to fight to the bitter end for FoI, to use the characteristic headline abbreviation for the Cause, is bound to be submitted with a flourish and unanimously agreed upon as quickly as possible. After all, who can be against virtue in journalism?

In many ways, it is a pity that so important a matter is usually discussed in clichés appropriate for a Fourth of July

celebration at Center Moriches, N. Y. For the issues that are
lumped together under the symbol, FoI, are real and vital and
very much worth careful examination. Contrary to the rather
bored public impression of this long and persistent exercise of
journalistic rhetoric, it is no sham battle that is being waged by
self-appointed crusaders for murky and ill-defined goals. Practical ends are being sought—and in part achieved—by perfectly
hardheaded, tough-minded men.

What they seek, when they talk about "the public's
right to know" as opposed to the military intelligence standard of
"the public's need to know," is more access to information of
public concern and more legal protection for the journalist.
Judged by any form of measurement, their achievements have
been impressive. Currently, through the passage of laws of varying effectiveness, "open records" are available in 37 states,
"open meetings" in 29 states, and "confidential sources" in 12
states. In addition, a national "freedom of information" law has
taken effect amid cautious testing by government and news
media alike to determine what its long-range effect is likely to
be.[49]

However, the journalist is very far from achieving
the almost universal status of confidentiality for his sources that
is accorded to the lawyer for his client, the physician for his
patient, and the clergyman for his flock. Moreover, it is unlikely
that he will ever be given access to all public records or admitted
to all meetings having to do with public business. Nor are these
ultimate goals as desirable as some perfectionists believe they
are. For if the journalist is given such privileges, it follows as a
matter of public policy that he will be asked in return for some
such manifest of responsibility as the licensing that is required
of the physician, the examination and character study to which
lawyers must submit before admission to the bar, and submission to the higher ecclesiastical authority that usually regulates
the clergy. Put in the simplest terms, it will not work.

There are other disturbing elements about FoI.
What makes the campaign truly remarkable is that the supposed
beneficiary, the American public, seems to have shown no all-
consuming interest in the movement and certainly has done
little to support it. The burden has been carried almost entirely
by a comparatively small group of dedicated editors, plus a few
interested publishers and broadcasters. They have done the
hard—and often thankless—job of speaking, writing, and lob-

258   bying on behalf of such illustrious organizations as the American Society of Newspaper Editors, National Editorial Association, Sigma Delta Chi, Associated Press Managing Editors, American Newspaper Publishers Association, National Association of Broadcasters, and other groups of lesser renown.

A LONELY CRUSADE

It is no great secret that the prime movers for FoI have had to contend with an almost monumental apathy inside the profession as well as outside it. Frequently, they have complained of lack of support. However, they have persisted despite an increasing tendency to question the value of their total effort and slowly rising opposition within government and the legal profession. In effect, they hold that by incessant lobbying for legal enlargement of their rights they will surround the journalist with sufficient safeguards that will be a substitute for an aroused public opinion. The rationale for FoI, consequently, is thus almost entirely defensive.

J. Russell Wiggins, editor of the *Washington Post* and one of the most devoted FoI campaigners, recognized the danger of an apathetic public when he wrote: "The requirements of freedom are not satisfied in a climate where only the rich, powerful, resourceful and courageous dare assert the right to utter what is unpopular. There must be encouragement, in an affirmative way, for those who seek knowledge and desire to use it. The indifference, indolence and ignorance of great numbers of citizens will be a serious barrier to the full realization of mankind's greatness. Where a state is hostile and the population prejudiced against freedom of expression, this freedom and every other freedom will not long survive." [50]

If there were a latter-day John Wilkes or John Peter Zenger with a great cause around which journalists could rally in an appeal to public opinion, they might not have so much difficulty in arousing sympathy for their campaign of self-defense. But for the most part, the cases that have come to public attention in recent years are based on issues that do not readily make an impression either on the public or even the news media themselves. Such cases have been in United States courts since 1874. As early as 1896, Maryland recognized by law the journalist's right to a certain amount of professional secrecy. New Jersey became the second state to pass a law protecting the confidentiality of sources in 1933 and ten others have followed since.[51]

In most states of the nation, however, journalists who defy the courts by refusing to reveal their sources have to face up to the contempt power. One of the most celebrated in this century was Martin Mooney, a reporter for the *New York American*, who wrote a series about "policy racket" gambling operations in 1935. When he refused to tell a New York County Grand Jury who the gamblers were, he was held in contempt of court, fined $250, and sentenced to 30 days in jail. Upon appeal, his conviction was affirmed.

In a more recent case, a 20-year-old college newspaper editor, Annette Lesley Buchanan of the University of Oregon, was fined $300 for contempt of court in 1966 because she refused to reveal her sources for an article on campus marijuana smoking to the Lane County Grand Jury, Eugene, Ore. She won national publicity and sympathy for her appeal, making her for a brief time one of the minor heroines of American journalism.[52]

However, the courts have been careful not to create too many martyrs, or to make examples out of the illustrious except under extreme provocation. It is an easily observable truth that most reporters are not usually challenged for their sources, even in states where there is no legal immunity for journalists. In fact, the whole structure of investigative journalism is based on the assumption that law enforcement authorities will generally seek to cooperate with the press in the exercise of its "watchdog" function instead of trying to obstruct an inquiry.

In Illinois, for example, the lack of statutory protection for journalists did not stop George Thiem, a reporter for the *Chicago Daily News*, from unmasking thefts of state funds by Orville E. Hodge, the State Auditor, who was subsequently convicted and jailed. Thiem was never asked for the name of the young woman clerk in a state office who referred him to the necessary records on condition that she would never be identified.[53]

Nor was there any disposition in New York to question Malcolm Johnson's sources in his exposé of waterfront racketeering for the *New York Sun* in 1948, *Newsday*'s sources in its inquiry into political and labor shenanigans on Long Island in 1967 and 1968, or numerous other investigations that have yielded major results.[54] It would have been a rash official, indeed,

260 who would have challenged so formidable a reporter as Clark Mollenhoff of the *Des Moines Register-Tribune*, who also happens to be a lawyer. At one time, when Defense Secretary McNamara tangled with Mollenhoff, President Johnson sent the Pentagon's boss on a Swiss vacation, muttering, "He ought to know better than to tackle that ———." [55]

THE POSITION OF THE PRESS

It is curious that, despite the demonstrated ability of journalists to take care of themselves without legal protection in most cases, there should be so passionate a resort to the comparatively less effective FoI statutes where they exist. Furthermore, those journalists who have the best records for achieving success in gathering information by traditional methods are generally the ones who insist on new laws protecting confidentiality and access, as well, on the apparent presumption that every little bit helps. Mollenhoff, for example, argued in the Buchanan case that the prosecutor should have proceeded with vigor against narcotics peddlers instead of trying to "harass a journalist." But if the protest was intended to stimulate interest in an Oregon law to protect the confidentiality of journalistic sources, it failed.

Most lawyers, including a committee of the American Bar Association, have consistently opposed the extension of such confidentiality statutes. They argue that a policy of martyrdom by the journalist—of accepting punishment rather than to reveal sources—is likely to be a greater service to society, whatever the journalist himself may think of such a proposition. Basically, the legal profession doubts that freedom of the press actually is involved in most of the cases in which journalists shout from every conceivable platform that their liberties are being endangered. The lawyers also argue that the general principle governing the administration of justice in the United States, as elsewhere, is that judicial and legislative bodies have a right to demand and obtain complete information. Finally, they warn that laws protecting the confidential nature of journalistic sources might encourage some reporters, admittedly a minority, to fake stories on the basis of nonexistent, confidential evidence.

James E. Beaver, associate professor at the University of Washington Law School, wrote with particular reference to the Buchanan case: "Whether or not the 'special position' sought for newspapers is secure, reporters are going to continue protecting their sources of information, and judges continue to

deal very lightly with contemptuous journalists . . . The public's   **261**
interest is better served by the newsman's code which means
something to him, than by creation of a privileged status to
shelter him against standing on his own hind legs."

The contrary view was posed by Robert C. Notson as
president of the American Society of Newspapers Editors, who
concluded that any requirement that forced journalists to reveal
sources would seal off information which, if published, would be
likely to have a beneficial public effect. "The pledge of confidentiality is not to be made lightly," he wrote, "but, once made,
should be kept by the editor and respected by the court, barring
an overriding public interest . . ." [56]

Another view of the journalist's case was given by a
nationally recognized expert on the law of the press, Dr. Fred-
rick S. Siebert, dean of the College of Communication Arts,
Michigan State University, who wrote: "In the long run, society
will be more satisfactorily served if the various media of public
information are privileged to determine when a source should be
withheld and when a source should be revealed. Granted that the
instruments of government should have access to all relevant
information in the majority of cases, the relationship between
the journalist and his sources is of such importance to our society that it should be protected by law." [57]

Such arguments as Dr. Siebert's, however, have not
made a perceptible dent in the opposition of bench and bar to
expansion of the body of protective laws for the benefit of the
journalist. Nor has he swayed all the doubters in the ranks of
journalism itself; despite their somewhat reserved demeanor,
they do amount to a considerable minority and can make their
influence felt if they wish. Basically, they believe that the news
media are actually hurting themselves by repeatedly raising the
issue of confidentiality without sufficient cause and thereby
creating the public impression that they are continually sounding the alarm when there is no fire. If freedom of the press is
really in jeopardy, then the minority would like to apply Justice
Holmes's test of a "clear and present danger" before the FoI
crusade is whipped to greater intensity.

THE "OPEN RECORDS" CAMPAIGN

The same feeling, to an even broader extent, applies to the drive
for more access to public records and meetings by representatives of the news media. Not every journalist believes that he has

262 an inherent right to see everything and hear everything that pertains to the public's business. In fact, considering the breadth of the restrictions and the fairly obvious reasons for most of them, it is difficult to say exactly where the line should be drawn. For example, the confidential records of executive departments of government on a wide range of subjects from military secrets to diplomatic correspondence and law enforcement are generally held to be of a nonpublic nature. In addition, there are federal or state statutes imposing either mandatory secrecy or limited access at best to many nonjudicial records including data pertaining to criminal identification, fire prevention, industrial relations, narcotic drugs, juvenile delinquency, public welfare, health, and even motor vehicles in some cases. Some tax records, particularly income tax, also are not generally open for public inspection. Nor is there a uniform policy for so ordinary and useful a field as vital statistics.

As for police records and judicial proceedings, there are many instances in which there is no right of public inspection. A despairing reporter in the New York State Supreme Court, Manhattan, once exclaimed after learning that a judge had impounded papers in a divorce case: "There are more secret records in this place than there are in the Pentagon!" It has seemed so to many a reporter who was denied access to public records in instances that appeared to him and to his news organization to be both arbitrary and unreasonable.[58]

The responsible news media, in consequence, are torn between a desire to respect the processes of government that clearly demand a certain amount of confidentiality and to check the growth of such objectionable official practices as holding unnecessary executive sessions and maintaining unnecessary secrecy over public records. It is one thing for a President to insist on the right of executive privilege in his dealings with other branches of the government, or for other executives to safeguard government proceedings in the national interest. It is quite another for town councils and school boards to go behind closed doors primarily to spare themselves the inconvenience of public questioning of their decisions. In between lies the vast grey area in which there are interminable wrangles over whether secrecy is the best policy—or the worst. When in doubt, quite understandably, the press plumps for full disclosure and not even the moderates pose many objections.

Another reason for the outward strength of the

press policy on "open records" and "open meetings" is the disclo-   263
sure of misconduct in public office—sometimes even on the
bench itself. The government is not in a good position to defend
a policy of secrecy in public offices if it can be shown that either
wrongdoing or partiality may be possible by-products. Nor can
sympathetic editors be expected to champion the government's
cause in such circumstances. And when the press is able to
demonstrate that innocent persons have been convicted of
crimes they did not commit, as Gene Miller of the *Miami Herald*
did in 1966 when he helped free two persons who had mistak-
enly been found guilty of murder, the legal profession cannot
contend that all virtue resides in the courts. Sufficient human
error may always be uncovered to support the argument for full
disclosure.

In this extremity, the moderates of the bar have
sometimes appealed to those of like mind among the press not to
take the law too literally. When Stephen J. Roth was Attorney
General of Michigan, he once suggested to reporters: "I think the
less concern you have with what you're entitled to under the law,
the better off you're going to be . . . I think reporters . . . get a
lot more cooperation than the law requires public officials to give
them in the matters of automobile accidents, arrests, criminal
prosecutions, etc." [59]

Harold L. Cross, one of the foremost authorities in
the land on the law as applied to the press, argued that this was a
profoundly realistic view, although he conceded that the right of
access to public documents is not always adequate. "It indicates,"
he wrote, "the wisdom in the preponderant majority of cases and
circumstances of present newspaper practice in placing primary
and major reliance on the processes mentioned rather than the
'law.' Sugar, plus judicious admixtures of strength and determination, catches more 'police news' than vinegar." [60]

Here is where the FoI stalwarts have always parted
company with the moderates of the profession. Those who campaign under the slogan of the "People's Right To Know" are
seldom impressed with the notion of a compromise that leaves
the decision on access to public records entirely in the province
of government. One of the most ardent of FoI advocates, Virgil
M. Newton, Jr., managing editor of the *Tampa* (Fla.) *Tribune*,
argued: "Theoretically, an informed public opinion is supposed
to direct the people's representatives in their law-making. That is
the very lifeblood of free legislative government. But if the people

264   are uninformed, through bureaucratic secrecy, and confused, through bureaucratic propaganda, on the major issues of government, how can a citizen make an unprejudiced decision and let his Congressman know how he feels about any one measure?" [61]

THE FEDERAL LAW

This, basically, is the rationale that has resulted in federal as well as state legislation to support the continuing FoI campaign. No one can be sure of the eventual effectiveness of the federal "freedom of information" law which became operative on July 4, 1967, but every government officeholder is well aware of it. In form, it is an amendment of a 20-year-old Administrative Procedures Act (5 U.S.C. 22) under which federal records could be withheld "in the public interest" or if they related "solely to the internal management of an agency." In substance, it is similar to the state laws already enacted that limit official secrecy. But its comparatively untested procedures make it an uncertain quantity.

President Johnson's somewhat ambivalent attitude toward the federal legislation is an indication of the government's own strong doubts. For while the President expressed *pro forma* approval of the law, he also gave fair warning that it "in no way impairs the President's power under our Constitution to provide for confidentiality where the national interest so requires." This was a reference to the doctrine of executive privilege under which Presidents have repeatedly asserted the right to withhold certain types of information in the national interest, even from Congressional investigating committees. The Congressional sponsors of the information bill to date have never disputed the President on this point.

Even more bluntly, the President insisted that government officials "cannot operate effectively if required to disclose information prematurely or to make public investigative files and internal instructions that guide them in arriving at decisions." This, to some extent, took the edge off his rather routine statement of support: "No one should be able to pull curtains of secrecy around decisions which can be revealed without injury to the public interest." As always, it appears certain, the government and the news media are going to have differing estimates of what constitutes the public interest—and this is going to make for an interesting time.

Typically, lawyers and business people seeking infor-

mation on government contracts have been far more eager than 265
journalists to use the newly opened public reading rooms in
federal agencies to study various types of records. But the law
has also made possible some advances in the gathering of news.
At the Pentagon, for example, the Defense Department finally
dropped its system of monitoring all interviews granted to journalists—a procedure begun during the 1962 Cuban missile crisis. Moreover, on request, such information as records bearing
on federal pardons granted to prisoners in federal jails have been
granted to the *Cleveland Plain Dealer* and background on public
welfare operations in Mississippi have been made available to
the press of that state.

However, it is clear that the journalist will encounter dogged opposition in nine specific areas in which the new law
provides exemption from disclosure. These include such categories as national security, foreign policy data in which the government requires secrecy, trade procedures within the province of
government that should be kept secret, personnel files and medical data concerning government employees, bank reports, and
intergovernmental data that might be used in litigation against
the government.

As a practical matter, the most important part of the
new statute is its establishment of the principle of review by the
courts of any decision by the federal government to withhold
records. While this is in effect an open invitation to the press to
institute judicial action to pry records loose from reluctant federal officeholders, the courts—with voluminous internal records
of their own to safeguard—are scarcely likely to create a reporters' holiday.

Consequently, the press's customary attitude of
self-congratulation over the slightest indication of progress in
the FoI campaign is not really warranted. The ever aggressive
Clark Mollenhoff warned his colleagues soon after the adoption
of federal legislation: "The new federal records law will be
meaningful if it is understood by the press and the public and is
used as a device to force government agencies to produce documents. It will be meaningless if it is not used, or if political
appointees or career bureaucrats are permitted to twist its nine
exemptions into an unintended authority to withhold . . . To be
realistic, we must accept that a change in the law does not
change the attitudes of those bureaucrats who have tried to
claim personal proprietary interests over documents in their cus-

266   tody. Neither will it change the tendency of bureaucrats and political appointees to try to impose secrecy to avoid disclosures of corruption or mismanagement." [62]

The prospect, consequently, is for a continuing struggle. In some respects, the resort of the press to legal action to obtain more information is like swatting Uncle Remus's Tar Baby. The more legislation there is, the more involved the press is likely to become in expensive and time-consuming lawsuits which may make news in themselves but not the most desirable kind. Unhappily, a very large section of the public is even less interested in the press's legal adventures than it is in the inordinately dull accounts of how routine news must be gathered from a maze of sources. What the public wants, primarily, is the news; like editors, the people as a whole have scant patience with alibis or voluminous reasons why information is not available.

Eugene S. Pulliam, Jr., of the *Indianapolis Star*, was quite right in his lament before the American Society of Newspaper Editors about FoI: "We, as a profession, are improving but we still haven't convinced a majority of our readers that this fight is as important to them as it is to us." [63] And Creed Black, of the *Chicago Daily News*, was equally discerning in dissecting the attitude of the profession itself: "FoI is not a very sexy subject and it is sometimes hard to get even our own members interested. But . . . as bored as we get with it sometimes, I do think that the only way we are going to get anywhere is for every member, even if it is a chore, to interest himself in these questions." [64]

THE FUTURE OF FOI

If anything has been oversold inside and outside journalism, it is FoI. The symptoms are plain enough. The evidence of public and professional boredom with the issue is so apparent that it needs no further documentation. Despite Clark Mollenhoff and his cohorts, it is very difficult for most people to believe that the government at any level can successfully withhold for any appreciable time the kind of information to which the public is entitled. The very success of the reporters, as shown in the news media day by day, completely overshadows the FoI campaign in the public mind. For quite truthfully, a decent balance has been achieved between the government's legitimate effort to safeguard sensitive information in the public interest and the press's equally necessary function as the public's "watchdog" over the governmental process.

If the balance should ever shift appreciably in the direction of government, then the press will be in deep trouble because of the violent and—in some respects—premature appeals that have been made in the cause of FoI. Then the penalty for overselling will have to be faced. For it will be very difficult to appeal to an inert public, its senses dulled by an overreacting press, if there should be real danger of regulation of the news media. Then there will be no escape for those editors who yearn to remain impartial spectators in the never ending struggle for control over the news. Whether they like it or not, they are the central figures in one of the most important contests of the era and they cannot escape the consequences in time of crisis.

Necessarily, no one in journalism would want to see the FoI campaign abandoned, although some more appropriate symbol and more realistic nomenclature may be found. To drop the campaign after so much effort has been invested in it would be a confession of futility; whatever may be said of FoI, it is most certainly not a futile effort. What can and should be done is to scale the intensity of the effort to the needs of the news media and the times instead of crying "Woe!" on all occasions. It would also be helpful if the base of the activity could be broadened, relieving the handful of hardened press veterans and distributing the burden in more equitable fashion among all elements of the news media. Television, for example, should have a role commensurate with its responsibilities and its special problems should be attacked by the press with the same vigor that it uses to espouse its own cause. There can and should be no separation of the news media in such matters, for what affects one affects all.

But most important of all, the issues that affect the freedom of the press—which means all news media—should not be discussed in symbols and platitudes that obscure rather than enlighten. The blunt and hardheaded attitude with which the journalist approaches the news is equally appropriate for the consideration of his own fate. It will also help if he can abandon both self-interest and self-adulation, admittedly a difficult task for a journalist but not beyond his talents.

The private commercial organizations in the United States whose principal enterprises consist of the news media should never forget that it is their privilege, but not necessarily their inalienable right, to give the news exclusively to the American public. As long as the public is convinced of both their professional skill and their good faith, excesses and errors may

268   be forgiven and quickly forgotten. But once the news media fail to justify public confidence in their independence and their credibility, then the whole system of gathering and distributing news by private hands is in danger. This is the primary reason for abandoning crude caricature and overblown peril in discussing such things as FoI. For if the free press is to have more than a mere symbolic meaning to the American people, its problems are worth plain spoken and sensible discussion in terms that the mass audience will believe, appreciate, and understand.

MANY VOICES,

18

MANY MEDIA

At the height of his power, the first Joseph Pulitzer once exclaimed more in anger than in sor-
row: "Every reporter is a hope, every editor a disappointment!"
His grandson, Joseph Pulitzer, Jr., the editor-publisher of the *St.
Louis Post-Dispatch*, was less angry but more precise years later
in expressing the same basic notion: "When a reader knows before he turns to the editorial page exactly what will be said there,
his interest in it and his respect for it are bound to be low." [65]

This, unhappily, is the situation of many an American newspaper's editorial page today. If anything, the plight

270   among most of its magazine and electronic rivals is even worse. At a time when the American news media as a whole are enjoying unexampled prosperity, and therefore should not be afraid of exercising editorial independence, their many voices have appallingly little to say to the people of their era that is fresh or provocative or inspiring.

Now and then, a few devoted journalists of romantic bent will announce on occasion—usually before the National Conference of Editorial Writers—that the editorial page has at last aroused itself from its long sleep. But in the main, it is not really so. Any discerning reader may note at a glance, in most parts of the United States, that the spirit of Greeley, Pulitzer, and William Allen White is less in evidence on the editorial page of his daily newspaper than that of Rip Van Winkle.

Opposing points of view are often solemnly balanced against each other. Conservative and liberal columnists are carried on the same page, supposedly canceling each other out. In many a chain-operated newspaper, an editorial page may carry one shade of political view to win the approval of a particular community while a different political position is presented by the same chain for another newspaper only a short distance away. With the exception of a few score stalwarts out of the 1,750 daily and 8,000 weekly newspapers in the United States, there is little show of either principle or conviction on the editorial page. The same is true of most magazines, some of which do not even bother with editorials. As for the electronic media, all except a courageous few are still in the stage of mouthing editorials condemning crime, Communism, and the boll weevil and praising Sunday school, Arbor Day, and the sanctity of the American home.

THE CRITICAL EDITORIALIST

The editorial writers themselves are the first to testify to the shortcomings of the editorial page of the American newspaper. A. H. Raskin, assistant editor of the editorial page of *The New York Times,* wrote: "Most editorial pages are so predictable in position and so pedestrian in style that they seem to have become the first part of the paper to be completely automated." J. Russell Wiggins, editor of the *Washington Post,* sadly observed over a pile of editorials entered in a contest; "In the theatre, there are writers who can make words sing. Why aren't there more people on editorial pages who can make words sing?" Vermont C.

Royster, editor of the *Wall Street Journal*, demanded: "If we
aren't persuading our readers, why bother? Well . . . a good
many newspapers might as well not bother; their editorial columns are sheer boredom." [66]

A reformed editorial writer, Creed C. Black, the
managing editor of the *Chicago Daily News,* argued, "Too many
pages still seek the safe middle ground, using the same fuzzy
clichés that were in vogue 20 years ago." To prove his point, he
assembled this editorial, complete with headline, composed of
sentences snatched bodily from a dozen current editorial pages:

THE NEED FOR LEADERSHIP

The Blank report presents an opportunity for further
thoughtful re-examination. This carefully and thoughtfully considered proposal has been in the making for eight months. During
this gestation period all segments of public interest have been represented and heeded.

The current report adds weight to the previous findings.

On the other hand, we have something new.

Honest men may differ in answering these questions.
But the problems must not block progress. The time has come for
leadership on this long overdue reform.

It is a frightening prospect. What is being done to
meet the acute situation should have been done long ago because
the crisis was foreseen.

Bluntly put, some intelligent taxpayers are getting fed
up with this kind of performance. Whether that will be effective in
this case is problematical.

It is delusive to pretend that success will come easily.
Disrespect for constituted authority is widespread. But something
must be done. The only question is how to go about it. Not to do so
deliberately is to flout the public interest.

The time for action is now.[67]

There are some who have made earnest efforts to
restore the precision, grace, and eloquence of the English language to the editorial page. Two editors, newly appointed, decided on a policy of discarding any editorial that sounded like an
editorial, surely a sign of enlightenment. Knowledgeable laymen
were consulted and asked to serve as critics; one, Dean Thomas
H. Eliot of the Washington University College of Liberal Arts,
said after scanning 30 editorial pages that they were "not irresponsible, not very interesting and not very local." [68] But despite

272 these and other innovations, few have come along who can conform to Ralph McGill's prescription for journalistic vitality: "A newspaper . . . must make its news and, equally, its editorials, a part of the tangible issues of the daily lives of its readers. It may thereby make some angry. It may lose some circulation. But even those who are made angry will know what they read touched their lives." [69]

This is where many newspapers and their editors fail. On the basis of a deliberate policy decision, they seek to remove themselves from any commitment to become involved with the affairs of their community, their state, and their nation. The turbulence of the worst sections of our cities by day and the cold horror of their streets and parks by night are not for them. To avoid making anybody angry, they become detached observers, reporting and commenting loftily on the struggles, the failures, and the occasional successes of those who are not afraid to plunge into the turmoil of public affairs. But as for tearing their clothes or even soiling their own hands in the public interest, never!

THE CODE OF NONINVOLVEMENT

All too often, newspapers and their editorialists raise a wholly false standard, composed of the flimsy white gauze of objectivity and disinterest, behind which they retreat from participation in the things that demand a personal commitment—the affairs of the community. They pretend to be shocked when they are asked to campaign for funds for a charity, for a new school, or highway, or to serve on committees to improve race relations. They blandly argue—these editorial neuters—that this would be a betrayal of their journalistic commitment to be disengaged, to remain above the battle so that their precious commentaries will always be undistorted by one interest or another. Such viewpoints would have brought Olympian snorts of utter disgust from those like Joseph Pulitzer and Horace Greeley who never shirked a commitment in the public interest or flinched from the deepest involvement in the life of their times.

It should be made clear that not all the editors who cling to the pose of noninvolvement are cowardly or lazy—or worse. Some are first-rate journalists with a great potential for leadership; yet, either through inheritance or other circumstance, they have become heirs to an odd kind of journalism which often leads them to avoid even so minuscule a step as the

endorsement of candidates for political office. Their argument, if 273
it may be called that, grants the premise that a newspaper may
investigate conditions or even campaign in the public interest,
but they insist that the editor himself must never descend into
the public arena. Just how this can be done, of course, remains
an utter mystery. Under so hollow and fraudulent a code, William Allen White would be considered a traitor to the sacred
principles of noninvolvement because he led the fight to range
the United States on the side of the Allies in World War II. And
Edward R. Murrow, who gave distinction to television by opening
the battle against Senator Joseph R. McCarthy when most newspapers feared to do so, would be damned as a commentator who
took sides in the major controversy of his day. The direct extension of the philosophy of editorial nonalignment is, of
course, the ultimate extinction of the editorial page—something
that cannot be found today in more than 200 American dailies.

No matter how the proposition may be considered, it
is completely phony. In most cases, the pretense of noninvolvement is a convenient excuse for doing nothing. It contributes
heavily to the historic failure of the modern American editorial
page, with few exceptions, to attract either the confidence or the
support of many of the paper's readers. For the public quickly
recognizes noninvolvement for the pious fraud that it is. Where
editors have chosen to exercise their franchise as citizens, their
influence and their good works have increased their usefulness.
From national celebrities such as Erwin D. Canham and Ralph
McGill to suburban editors like Bill Caldwell of the *Record* in
Hackensack, N. J., with his widely read local column, the journalists who have elected a policy of commitment have never
lacked for either readers or excitement.

Shortly before his untimely death, Worth Bingham
of the *Louisville Courier-Journal* wrote that he was "easily seduced into working for civic, charitable and cultural endeavors."
He did not fear that he would be ignobly used as a mere source
for publicity—something any journalist quickly learns to sidestep. "A newspaper," Bingham wrote, "should be prepared to comment on the activities of almost any civic or charitable organization. The Community Chest and the Chamber of Commerce
certainly aren't immune, and yet we would be shrinking from
our responsibilities if we divorced ourselves from these organizations." [70]

It may be taken for granted that the editor who

274 divorces himself from his community, even for the highest of motives, will have little to say that will interest, enlighten, or mobilize public opinion. The attitude of nonalignment is just as counter-productive locally as it is internationally. Any such editorial page is bound to have a far lower readership than some of the advertising, and even less public confidence. Its editor cannot aspire to mold public opinion; he has abdicated. A major political figure, a shocking television sequence, an attention-arresting picture, or even a clever headline will have more influence. And this, unfortunately, may apply to many of the better editorial pages as well.

SOME GOOD PERFORMANCES

Despite these heavy handicaps, it is to the credit of the editorialist that he is able to number some in his ranks who are able to spread faith and hope in the land, and sometimes even a little charity as well. It was said of John B. Oakes of *The New York Times* that he had given his one-time dull grey page a reviving dose of elixir, a lot more muscle, and a crew cut. All this was true; for a Princetonian, the *Times*'s soft-spoken editorial page editor could be abrupt and ungentlemanly. He was not above swatting an opponent every day and hammering away at policies objectionable to the *Times* with the vigor of a Grady or a Watterson. Nor were such editors as Robert Lasch of the *St. Louis Post-Dispatch* or Lee Hills of the *Detroit Free Press* lacking in either courage or originality; in their respective communities, each was a participant, a leader and a fighter for progress.

It was heartening to realize that Thomas M. Storke, octogenarian though he was at the time, could tear into the supersecret John Birch Society in the *Santa Barbara News-Press* when mightier Californians were silent; that William J. Dorvillier, in the *San Juan Star*, could fight the power and influence of the Catholic bishops of Puerto Rico for trying to influence an election, and that Hazel Brannon Smith, in her small weekly *Lexington Advertiser*, held out for years against the threats and boycotts of the White Citizens' Councils in her native Mississippi. Just as Lauren K. Soth helped change a national policy by bringing a Russian farm delegation to Iowa with an editorial invitation in the *Des Moines Register-Tribune* and Ralph McGill used the columns of the *Atlanta Constitution* to bring American farm know-how to Pakistan, the influence of the more vigorous editorialists spread far beyond their own cities.

Younger men repeatedly demonstrated that even   275
on comparatively small newspapers, the editorial page did not
have to be a dull, mean thing filled with plugs, handouts, after-
thoughts, and apologies. The *Pine Bluff* (Ark.) *Commercial* (circ.
20,613) established a national reputation for its editorial page
through the work of a newcomer, Paul Greenberg; so did the
Riverside (Calif.) *Press-Enterprise* (circ. 68,348), with editorialists such as Timmy Hays and Norman Cherniss, and the *Day-
ton* (Ohio) *Daily News* (circ. 155,541) under the editorial direction of Jim Fain. The Gannett Group newspapers proved that
chain journalism did not have to be deadly by entering on a long
and difficult campaign to convince readers, in the face of an
appalling amount of negative evidence, that the integration of
the Negro into American society was a policy that eventually
would pay dividends. And in television, there were individual
stations that tackled the touchy subject of big city ghettos with
both courage and conviction.

Such performances as these, while all too rare, serve
to demonstrate that there is no need for weak and lackluster
editorial positions among the American news media. Primarily
because of the inadequacy of editorial leadership, the columnist
and the commentator have risen to extraordinary power—
particularly in the daily press. Between 1959 and 1965, for
example, a study of more than 700 daily newspapers showed
that the aggregate number of major columnists they published
had increased from 71 to 138. Nor is it unusual these days for a
single paper to have a dozen syndicated columnists; larger ones
have displayed as many as 20 at a time. The ill-fated *New York
World Journal Tribune,* in its first issue, boasted that it was
publishing at least 30 columnists—more than any other paper in
the world.[71]

In an impish moment at the 50th anniversary din-
ner of the Pulitzer Prizes, James Reston observed with due grav-
ity: "I ask you to think of the sweep of change of these 50 years:
in politics, from Woodrow Wilson to Lyndon Johnson; in world
affairs, from Lenin to Kosygin; in journalism, from Lippmann,
Krock and David Lawrence, to Lippmann, Krock and David Lawrence." *

* When Arthur Krock retired in 1966, his last line of his final column in *The
New York Times* was: "All right, officer; I'll go quietly." And when Lippmann
decided in 1967 to cut his output sharply and settle in France, he said he was
tired of the "necessity of knowing who said what and who saw whom and who is
listened to and who is not."

276 THE RISE OF THE COLUMNIST

It is not quite that pat, of course. A dozen syndicate executives, balloting on columnists they consider essential to a newspaper, once singled out (in alphabetical order) Joseph Alsop, Walter Lippmann, Drew Pearson, James Reston, Inez Robb, and Henry J. Taylor. With the death of George Sokolsky of King Features, the top man among the conservative columnists remained the venerable David Lawrence with William F. Buckley, Jr., as a challenger. Newcomers like the team of Rowland Evans and Robert Novak stirred up interest because, like Pearson, they gambled on short-range and long-range predictions—always an interesting exercise. When a forecast came to pass, it could be promoted as the work of genius; if it was wrong, it could be quietly forgotten.

Another factor that has increased the demand for columnists among newspapers is the fashion of "balance." One editor proudly announced to his colleagues, after a census of his daily columnists, that he published five liberals, six moderates, and eight conservatives. There was more than a suspicion, in some quarters, that such liberals as Marquis Childs and Ralph McGill actually benefited from the fetish for "balance" because the top-heavy favoritism for conservative columnists changed within five years toward something like a 60–40 conservative liberal ratio in the late 1960s. With top writers jumping into the $100,000-a-year or better category, this is clearly good business for the columnists; it is also fine for editors of average-size papers who manage to put together an attractive package of columns for just about what they would have to pay a first-rate reporter. With enough "balanced" columnists, for that matter, an editor does not even have to think.

The columnist, rather than the comic strip, is fast becoming the most important property of many of the hundreds of companies in the $100-million-a-year syndicate business. When the *New York Post* bitterly complained to the Department of Justice that it was denied such columnists as Lippmann, Evans and Novak, and the humorist, Art Buchwald, Buchwald cracked, "A columnist reaches his highest state of importance when he becomes the center figure in an anti-trust suit." [72] The demise of the *World Journal Tribune* gave the *Post* most of what it wanted without too much of a struggle. It was no wonder, in view of such competition, that the number of columnists of all kinds listed in the *Editor & Publisher* syndicate directory nearly

doubled in a quarter-century, going from 320 so-called serious   277
writers in 1940 to more than 700 in 1968.

Ben H. Bagdikian wrote in a study of columnists and their work, "Today, there are 45 syndicated columns with the word 'Washington' or a synonym like 'Potomac' in the title, though not all of them are serious or in politics. Of the 60 public affairs columnists, 42 live and work in Washington. 'Washington column' is the trade term for any column on politics or public affairs." [73] These, of course, are among the leading columnists; the hundreds of others vary in subject matter and importance in accordance with the demands of the trade. In any event, there is no prospect of a shortage in this overstuffed field.

By contrast with the average editorial writer—a grey shade flitting nervously about an odd corner of the average newspaper office—the columnist is a brassy and bumptious presence. One of the most popular and self-assertive, Drew Pearson, was published in 600 papers in his 70th year. He was read regularly and seriously by the President of the United States. Through his investigation of the financial background of Senator Thomas J. Dodd of Connecticut, the columnist became the central figure in a Pulitzer Prize wrangle—not because he won but because he lost. He made himself news by his enormous activity and his constant prying into places where the mere editorialist could not go even for a timid peek. The difference between his income, estimated at $200,000 annually, and that of the average editorialist, which was about 5 percent of it, strikingly illustrates the comparative status of major columnist and editorial writer. [74]

THE ROLE OF THE EDITORIALIST

True, the editorial page of a newspaper will always be one factor in the reflection of public opinion; in some instances, a most important influence. But the editorialist can scarcely contend at this late date that he is the sole representative of the public will, as he once did. Probably, this claim has never been valid; certainly, it is not today. One has to do more than publish editorials endorsing Newspaper Week and viewing with alarm the problem of Communism in West Bengal in order to compete with columnists like Pearson and television commentators like Eric Sevareid. And this is the problem of the editorialist who has to keep the brakes on because he has a timid publisher or is himself too fearful to take a controversial position.

It should not be assumed, however, that this makes

278 the commentator and columnist the principal oracles of our time. Far from it. The many voices of the news media, so bewildering in their diversity, can often be just as misleading as some polls of public sentiment; furthermore, they are often far more difficult to measure. It is for this reason that, on the national level, the public is usually inclined to follow strong and determined political leadership; at the state and local level, however, there is no gainsaying the influence that a respected editorialist may have on local and State officials, Congressional representatives, and United States Senators, and local civic, professional, business, and labor organizations. Yet, he is sometimes so beset by conflicting forces that he doubts he has any power at all.

This accounts for the comparatively modest view which the better editorialists take of their opinion-forming role today. It may not be calculated to impress the few old journalistic imperialists who still maintain a rather Napoleonic concept of the function of the press. But it is a practical position, far more entitled to respect than the barren editorial pages of so many newspapers that neglect their opinion-forming function. As Vermont Royster has phrased it: "An editor is no more entitled than anyone else to have his voice heeded; he has no inside track to wisdom. About all he can claim is that his major occupation is following the news and he may therefore be more familiar than most people with what goes on. His contribution is just to stir up his neighbors . . ." [75]

When the editorialist *does* stir up his neighbors, that is something. If he is able to persuade them beyond that to act in what he believes to be their best interests, he is fulfilling one of the most significant functions of journalism. There may be comparatively few in the press who can do this in the declining years of the twentieth century—and even fewer in radio and television. But when such voices are heard above the sometimes painful cacophony of democracy, they give dignity and meaning to the entire profession.

THE BASIS OF

19

PUBLIC SERVICE

In the five centuries that separate Gutenberg's adaptable wine press from the communications satellite and the computer, the public interest has not always been very high on the list of journalistic priorities. The requirements of the counting house and the needs of state frequently have intervened. It is all the more heartening, therefore, that public services should now be regarded as one of the most desirable activities of American journalism, even though not everybody agrees on precisely what it is or how it should be practiced.

At one extreme, tough-minded old newspapermen

280   insist that the best demonstration of the press's public service function occurs when it is able to throw crooks into jail. At the other, the cynical young sophisticates of television praise every triviality they utter, from routine weather forecasts to income tax deadline announcements, as a "public service by your public service station." In between lies a vast, undefined area of journalism that is often vitally necessary to the life of any community.

Some of this may be regarded as routine work which good news organizations are expected to do without creating committees to claim special credit for civic virtue. Much of it, clearly beyond the routine phase, depends on the vigor, imagination, and enterprise of the journalist and his organization in deciding what needs to be done and then attempting to do it in good conscience and good faith. At the highest level, when a campaign is successful, some demonstrable public service is performed although the public may be the last to appreciate it.

But certainly, a well-defined effort and usually a certain amount of extra expense and even risk are often necessary to the thorough-going practice of public service journalism. It is not enough for the news media to proclaim their allegiance to the public interest, to indulge in very large campaigns of self-promotion through the sponsorship of sports teams and contests and exhibitions in the arts, or to conduct a number of ten-minute crusades against everything from auto accidents to crime in the streets. The spurious crusade, in the long run, fools nobody—not even a dim-witted publisher who is given to self-delusion.

If there is uncertainty over the principles and practices of public service journalism, it is not particularly surprising in a profession that traces its development in the New World from Benjamin Harris and Benjamin Franklin to S. I. Newhouse, Henry Luce, and General David Sarnoff. Nor is it to be regarded as a bad thing. From the tiny single issue of *Publick Occurrences* to the seven-pound Sunday *New York Times* and from the static-cracked voice of KDKA in Pittsburgh to the bright hues of news on network television, the American journalist too often has displayed a smug self-satisfaction that is far from warranted. Over a large area of the press, which so often presumes to act without invitation as the leader of the news media, such an attitude has been particularly out of place.

Norman Isaacs, the executive editor of the *Louisville Times* and *Courier-Journal*, once exploded in a moment of irritation: "I've examined a good many newspapers . . . and I must say that most of them are totally undistinguished. In a great many newspapers, you can rip off Page 1 and . . . you have to struggle to find out what town [the paper] was published in. They all look very standard." [76] A British visitor concurred after a tour of the nation, saying: "The flow of ideas in the various newspapers seemed to radiate *out* from Washington and New York, seldom *in* from the various state capitals . . . I had expected a Babel of confusing voices, but in fact I thought I heard a choir . . . singing variations on a single theme." [77] And the author of a survey of local news coverage—the bread and butter of the daily press—found that on many papers it was a "vast grey monotony, lit only occasionally by a spark of interest." From Page 1 to the women's pages, he called it a "trip through Dullsville." [78]

With a considerable area of the American press bogged down in mediocrity, and self-satisfied mediocrity at that, it is understandable that the electronic media and the news magazines have been able to strengthen their positions as purveyors of news and opinion to the nation. However, this scarcely means that television and the news magazines between them are going to put the daily newspaper out of business in the foreseeable future, or even alter the current balance of the news media in any substantial manner. Local advertising is still too dependent on newspapers, with only a few exceptions, and newspaper profits outside some major metropolitan areas therefore continue to be better than the general level of performance. Moreover, television at present has neither the capacity nor the will to do a thorough day-by-day job of telling the news in some depth and the news magazines must always be thinking up new ways to make last week's news interesting this week. Eventually, with the evolution of different concepts of news media, this may change. But what newspapers now have to fear principally from the opposition is the possible loss of media leadership and the prestige that goes with it.

THE PUBLIC SERVICE PRESS

Consequently, the current revival of public service journalism among a significant segment of American newspapers, with power far greater than their comparatively modest numbers, amounts to something more than an expression of the press's willingness to serve the community, state, and nation. A broad

282 element of more or less enlightened self-interest exists here,
even among the comparatively few papers that have always
mounted large-scale campaigns in the public interest as a matter
of policy. Joseph Pulitzer and E. W. Scripps, among others,
championed such a philosophy on the assumption that a grateful
public would support a press that acted in its behalf. The modern
crusaders, disinterested though some of their works may be, are
similarly motivated in large part. For, with some notable exceptions, neither the magazines nor television thus far has been able
to match the press in such endeavors.

There are not many public service newspapers out
of the 1,750 in the daily press and the 8,000 weeklies—perhaps
a few hundred at best. They are widely diverse in size, location,
and political and economic orientation. Taken separately, what
they do has an impact on their communities, their states, and
sometimes their regions as well; only rarely does a local crusade
assume national importance although it has happened. Taken
together, the public service press forms a substantial and powerful group, progressive in its tendencies regardless of political
convictions. What such papers do, week in and week out, overshadows the products of the complacent, standpat majority. In
originality, content, and appearance they have a freshness,
drive, and public appeal that has not been known in American
newspaper journalism for almost a hundred years. If there is one
quality that is common to all of them, it is a conviction that they
are not a mere business or service organization but a public
trust.

Historically, this has been the motivating force behind such newspapers as the *Chicago Daily News, Louisville
Times* and *Courier-Journal, Milwaukee Journal, St. Louis Post-
Dispatch,* and others of the old stalwarts. From their earliest
years, they have specialized in effective and sustained attacks on
wrongdoing in public office, the suppression of crime, and the
strengthening of civil liberties. In the years immediately following World War I, campaigns such as that of the *New York World*
against the Ku Klux Klan and Florida peonage thrilled the young
idealists who gazed raptly at the crusading journalist through a
romantic haze. But what these hero-worshippers failed to notice
was that the crusaders were small in number and their support
was exceedingly slender—so slender that the *World* died. There
were, on the whole, more heroic newspapermen in the movies in
those days than there were in actual practice.

Those who persevered did manage to create, in the words of Joseph Pulitzer, Jr., "a tradition of conscience or, more specifically, a conscientious attitude toward the service of the press to the public . . . an instrument for promoting democracy." [79] Such high-sounding words have meant something only when publishers of courage have been willing to support their staffs in sometimes hazardous undertakings that go far beyond the coverage of the news. It is to the credit of American journalism, despite all the unwarranted self-adulation in the profession, that such publishers continue to flourish and that their numbers are slowly increasing today.

Since World War II, and particularly since the rise of television, these publishers have supported the revival of the newspaper crusade in its intensive modern form. It has attracted so much attention that it has stimulated interest in campaigning even among a few newspapers that saw little advantage, in former years, in accepting costly and often unnecessary risks. As for the magazines, with their tradition of muckraking at the turn of the century, it is truly surprising that not many have tried to emulate or exceed the work of the leaders of the daily press. And in television, the experiments with crusading in such cities as Chicago, New Orleans, Jacksonville, Salt Lake City, and New York City, while praiseworthy, have not yet begun to approach the standard of the free-swinging radio commentators before World War II and Edward R. Murrow's television campaigning shortly thereafter.

From its earlier preoccupation with the exposure of graft and corruption and other spectacular phases of crusading journalism, the newspaper campaign in its modern phase has broadened to cover newly significant areas of public affairs. Among them are the ever present concern with civil rights and the improvement of the situation of the Negroes as well as other minorities, the attack on water and air pollution, urban decay, problems of health, housing, traffic, education, and the tax structure and a host of other current considerations. It is perfectly obvious that such issues have not been explored in all cases because of a newspaper's overwhelming concern with the public interest. Some have been forced into campaigning because of the competitive new pressures of the opposing media.

But for those who scoff that the whole thing is just a circulation "gimmick," there is a ready reply. No newspaper has much to gain by campaigning for legislative reapportionment,

284   the propagation of birth control information, or the advocacy of a civic bond issue to improve schools, sewers, or the water supply. The most invigorating part of the performance of the public service press has come from smaller newspapers, which have everything to lose and very little to gain by trying to emulate the giants with their formidable resources.

A newspaper as small as the *Hutchinson News,* in a long campaign, has been able to force the equalization of voting districts in the State of Kansas and obtain true legislative reapportionment. The somewhat larger *St. Petersburg Times* has exposed malpractice in the construction of Florida's magnificent state highways, with a resultant saving to the taxpayers of millions of dollars. Statewide newspapers such as the *Milwaukee Journal* and the *Louisville Courier-Journal* have succeeded in obtaining laws to force private interests to cease polluting the air and water and stop destroying the nation's natural resources through strip mining. Such things are occurring in the United States today with greater frequency wherever news organizations have the courage of their convictions.

AREAS OF WEAKNESS

This, however, scarcely means that the journalist can demonstrate a line of unbroken success in his public service campaigning. Nor is he likely to run out of either issues to investigate or causes to support. Some of his longest, loudest, and most necessary crusades, such as the regulation of the sale of firearms, have dragged on for years. If indeed he has been able to report progress in this or other matters, it has often been because he has had the help of forces outside journalism that have produced a more potent impression on public opinion than his own.

A case in point is the automobile safety campaign. For years, the newspaper crusade against automobile accidents has been a weary staple of American journalism. The journalist, in his anxiety to make an impression, used editorial warnings not to mix driving and alcohol, published horror pictures of accidents, and made eloquent demands for stiff sentences against drunken drivers. Finally, Ralph Nader, a young lawyer, decided that the safety standards of the automobile industry itself might be worth examining and the result is now history. General Motors made the tactical error of having a private detective agency shadow the brisk young author of *Unsafe At Any Speed,* touching off an indignant explosion of publicity before a

Senate investigating committee. Thereafter, over the protests of
most automobile manufacturers who demanded more time for
changes, Congress voted into law the first significant advance in
years for the manufacture of safer automobiles.[80]

In the regulation of another widely advertised product, cigarettes, it has been the government health authorities
and the leaders of the medical profession who have crusaded
most effectively to give the public due warning that the cigarette
is a probable cause of many types of cancer and other ailments.
At first, only a handful of leading newspapers published the
details. But by the time the cigarette companies were obliged to
print cautionary labels on each package, it was a shoddy newspaper, indeed, that refused to publish at least a few paragraphs on
the subject. Among the television networks, CBS became the first
to present an hour-long program that discussed the link between
cigarettes and lung cancer but most news broadcasts continued
to cover the news with a quick sentence or two. It should be
noted that CBS also pioneered with an hour-long documentary
on the auto safety problem.[81]

In another vital area of consumer news, drugs, the
news media have scarcely distinguished themselves to any
greater degree. Generally, it has taken a first-rate newspaper to
publish on Page 1 the news of the mislabeling of a wide variety
of products including some low calorie foods and drinks, baby
formulas, multivitamin pills, and vitamin-fortified foods. The
same is true of ordinarily expensive brand-name drugs, such as
antibiotics, that can be bought very cheaply under their scientific
names. The first that was known of this matter by a considerable
section of the public came with the Federal Drug Administration's action against offending companies for making excessive
claims in 1966 and resultant legislation thereafter that required
widespread relabeling of products.[82]

Actually, under today's competitive conditions, the
news media have little excuse to be hesitant about publishing
news that reflects on advertisers. The leading newspapers have
not been backward about using this material and giving it the
display it merits. Nor have very many lost advertising because of
it. In most instances, the local advertiser needs the single prosperous newspaper in the community more than the newspaper
needs his patronage. As for national advertising, much of it has
gone to the magazines and television anyway; kowtowing to the
national advertisers will not bring them back into the newspa-

286   pers in any great volume. Furthermore, the news magazines have shown that it pays to publicize consumer news at face value regardless of what the advertisers may think. It is a lesson that most executives in television have yet to learn.

This is not to say that the newspapers today are totally free of advertiser influence. Even in some of the better ones, advertisers or agencies of little principle will take advantage of a persistent editorial weakness if they can in order to produce a certain amount of "news" favorable to a client and see that it is published with a large order of that client's advertising. Cervi's *Journal*, a weekly, made such an accusation against the *Denver Post* on the basis of an internal *Post* memo it had obtained, and the story was widely published despite the *Post*'s denials that it regularly condoned such practices. Canned "editorials," originating with a San Francisco advertising agency, have been run in some small California papers to support Detroit manufacturers' views of auto safety. In fact, any reader can easily observe for himself the ratio of favorable "news" of an advertiser that is published with or near his advertising, particularly in special sections, and draw some lamentable conclusions.

In an exposé of such conflicts of interests, the *Wall Street Journal* said: "All this hardly enhances the image of objectivity and fierce independence the U. S. press tries so hard to project. Yet talks with scores of reporters, editors, publishers, public relations men and others reveal that practices endangering—and often subverting—newspaper integrity are more common than the man on the street might dream. Result: the buyer who expects a dime's worth of truth every time he picks up his paper often is short-changed.

"All newspapers, including this one, must cope with the blandishments and pressures of special interests who seek distortion or omission of the truth. And no newspaper, again including this one, can ever be positive that every one of its staff always resists these blandishments and pressures."

One of the more recent scandals has been the case of Harry Karafin, a veteran investigative reporter for the *Philadelphia Inquirer,* whose strange inquiries led to his discharge shortly before the Philadelphia magazine published an exposé dealing with his equally strange activities in public relations. As a result, the *Inquirer* ordered all its staff to list their outside sources of income. Naturally, newspapers don't like to publicize such matters and relatively few do so. While there are instances of newspapers exposing other newspapers, they are comparatively rare. In addition to whatever practical considerations there may be, it is always difficult to get at the facts in such cases.

When a likely looking crusade fails for no apparent reason, there is always a lot of talk and some raising of eyebrows. If there is a suspicion of editorial interference, reporters very quickly signify their displeasure. In an abortive *Boston Hearld* inquiry into crime, for example, four investigative reporters left the staff under varying circumstances. And in Chicago, a civic group known as the Better Government Association shifted its support in a truck licensing inquiry from the *Tribune* to the *Daily News* when the *Tribune* seemingly lost interest.[83]

Certainly, in these and other difficult areas, no newspaper can expect easy going. Of course it is possible to do a serious and painstaking inquiry despite all pressures, but it requires time, talent, courage, and determination. Moreover, when a local editor decides he is going to go after a local gang with local headquarters in the absence of police action against them, it can be exceedingly dangerous. Don Mellett, a crusader in the old tradition, was shot and killed during such a campaign in Canton, Ohio, and few of his successors have forgotten it. That may sometimes account for the forthright editorial attacks on the New York families of Cosa Nostra from some remote area by a newspaper that overlooks the more important job of going after the no less obnoxious gangsters at home. No newspaper of character will tolerate this kind of sham battle.

Another ancient journalistic practice, that of using reporters as stunt men or disguised operatives in a campaign, no longer is as popular as it once was. There has always been a serious question about the ethics of a reporter who plays a false role and a newspaper that requires him to do so as a condition of employment. It is on this ground that many responsible newspapers have given up on this kind of activity, regardless of the instances in which it is occasionally useful. As one editor commented, "A lot of the goofiness has gone out of the business. The public has grown up and so, I hope, have we."[84] However, when Edgar May of the *Buffalo Evening News* became a case worker for the New York State Department of Public Welfare and thereafter produced recommendations that became the basis for wide-

288   spread reforms, he won a Pulitzer Prize. The incident proves only that no rule in journalism can be inflexibly applied.

THE RISKS OF CRUSADING

Still, the hazards of newspaper campaigning often exceed the rewards. A disillusioned editor once said, "Crusading is a rich man's game . . . You lose advertising, you lose circulation, you even lose prestige. People begin thinking you have a personal ax to grind, and that the publisher himself is working for some ulterior motive. And when you have thwarted the plans of scheming politicians and have saved the city or county millions of dollars, what happens? Nobody gives a damn." [85] It is characteristic of the journalistic crusader that the complaining editor kept right on campaigning.

Inevitably, all but the strongest and most secure editors must proceed with a sense of prudence in approaching an assignment that is likely to require the services of a substantial part of their staffs over a period of weeks. Few can blame them if they seek some assurance of success in an admittedly risky campaign before committing their major resources to it. And yet, how often is it possible for a reporter—or a group of reporters—to present an editor with such guarantees in advance of an inquiry? It is no wonder that a decent respect for the laws of probability—and the laws of libel—often become inhibiting factors in the preparation of campaigns that may involve attacks on leading citizens, respected private establishments, and the courts. No newspaper lightly plunges into such hazardous undertakings; when it does happen, it attracts widespread attention whether the newspaper wins or loses.

To a cautious editor who nevertheless wants his newspaper to acquire a reputation for public service, many options are open. For example, he may gain almost as much credit by attacking a dishonest slum landlord as by exposing a department store with a certain number of unpublicized building violations. A small-time usurer by all odds is easier to investigate than a bank president who may be involved in unexplained dealings, or a judge who is suspected of bowing to undue influence. There also may be many questions about the administration of justice in the average small or medium-sized city, but an editor usually thinks a long time before deciding to attack a mayor or a police chief. Caution, however, is not to be equated with cowardice. As the records of the various journalism awards demonstrate year

after year, mayors, police chiefs, wealthy merchants, judges, and
bank presidents are not sacrosanct.

Harry Ashmore, who defied the power of the segregationists in the South when he was editor of the *Arkansas Gazette* in Little Rock, put it this way when he once discussed the problem with a group of his fellow editors: "When you advocate something really important and you do it effectively, you are going to split your readers somewhere around the middle. You are going to outrage a good many of them and you are very probably going to outrage the most important and the most influential of them." [86]

In consequence, no sensible person expects any newspaper—or any other news organization for that matter—to plunge into public service journalism with a fresh campaign every week. Or even every month, under ordinary circumstances. Any crusade that is of vital importance to the community must be researched and planned with meticulous care. The time has long since passed when it is possible for a newspaper to break a campaign with a three- or four-part headline series and trust to tipsters, luck, and reportorial ingenuity thereafter. Consequently, it is probable that such efforts on the whole do not really provide the public with much stimulation or excitement; most of them, by their very nature, must be slow-paced. Months and even years may elapse before a newspaper is fairly able to claim some measure of success or, as sometimes happens, quietly give up a cherished project because it is beyond attainment.

There were long, arid periods between the questions that were first raised in the tiny *Pecos* (Tex.) *Independent* and the eventual conviction of Billie Sol Estes in the Texas courts of widespread agricultural frauds. Nor was John Frasca of the *Tampa* (Fla.) *Tribune* able to establish overnight that an innocent man had been convicted of a robbery and thus obtain his freedom. It took months of effort by Monroe W. Karmin and Stanley Penn of the *Wall Street Journal* to establish that American gangsters had moved into gambling operations in the Bahamas, thus contributing to the fall of the government there in a subsequent election. And before the *Boston Globe* could force the abandonment of a judicial nominee who was supported by the powerful Kennedys of Boston and New York, it had to conduct the most painstaking inquiry into his personal qualifications.

It can scarcely be said therefore that the campaign in its modern form lends itself to the kind of entertainment

290 values that are so popular in television. Nor is it a very easy way for a newspaper to build a reputation for public service. There are too many imponderables in the hard business of campaigning. The whole process often takes so long that the public only vaguely remembers the beginning and the middle, even if there is a spectacular end. Consequently, the rewards of public journalism are far from assured.

THE "ACTION LINE" COLUMN

These factors account in part for the swift rise of a relatively simple and popular device for attracting readers to newspapers through a variation of the concept of public service. It is the "Action Line" column, as most newspapers have labeled it, and its purpose is to service the complaints of readers against everything from department store gyps to malfeasance in public office. While the idea is far from new, the notion of the newspaper as a modern "Ombudsman," or public defender, has generated a wide appeal. Several score newspapers are using the feature, many of them on Page 1.

The ever ingenious William B. Steven began the remodeled question-and-answer column in 1961 under the title of "Watchem" in the *Houston Chronicle*. Telephone callers were connected with a small staff of college students supervised by a *Chronicle* reporter when they dialed these letters, which coincided with the telephone number of the office. The questions were then researched and answered in the column, which proved helpful to citizens in a number of cases and also supplied a few tips on local stories to the *Chronicle* city desk. However, Steven's career as an independent-minded editor did not last long in Houston under a conservative-minded management and he departed for Chicago, taking a good reputation for public service journalism with him.

Although "Watchem" attracted some interest outside Houston, not much happened until the *Charlotte* (N. C.) *News* began a similar question-and-answer column called "Quest" in 1965. Then, the movement really spread to cities across the nation from the *Washington Star*'s "Action Line" to the "Kokua Line" (Kokua means help in Hawaiian) of the *Honolulu Star Bulletin*. Some of the stuff in these columns was trivial and not really worth publishing. For example, an inquirer asked why garbage trucks had to operate so early in the morning and was told it would interfere with traffic if they began any later. Another, evidently a scary individual, wanted to know if any animals had ever escaped from the local zoo and was told, "No." [87] But in other instances, some discernible good was accomplished. In Detroit, the *Free Press* located a 17-year-old girl who had run away with a parole violator, helped them get married and found the bridegroom a job after the authorities decided to deal leniently with him. In St. Louis, the *Post-Dispatch* helped a storekeeper force the city to clean a clogged sewer that had been responsible for flooding his shop. In Washington, D. C., the *Star*'s Pulitzer Prize-winning Miriam Ottenberg, in checking on a complaint about a mortgage foreclosure, found that the deed to a house had been forged and thereby exposed a ring of forgers. [88]

Although the successful "Action Line" column may pull several hundred telephone calls and letters from readers every day in some cities, no editor contends that such a feature is the ultimate in public service journalism; it is not, in any sense, a substitute for worthy campaigns in the public interest or the development of in-depth investigative reports on subjects of wide public concern. But "Action Line" does give smaller newspapers, with modest resources, an opportunity to demonstrate their usefulness to the community. As for the larger ones, "Action Line" may provide a lead now and then in the development of more important material. It is, consequently, a helpful part of the organization of a public service effort and serves as a link between the reader and the press.

THE BALANCE SHEET

The total record of public service journalism in the United States has produced a number of accomplishments in matters large and small during the relatively few years of its current revival. Just how far it is going to progress from now on, however, is quite another matter. The departure of such editors as Bill Steven in Houston and Harry Ashmore in Little Rock, to name only two, should be sufficient warning that not all managements can sustain the work of fearless editors in the public service tradition. To be fair, it should be pointed out that the cases were totally dissimilar but the net result in each was the same. Another inhibiting factor is the passivity of the community, in many instances, when a newspaper has taken on a difficult battle in the public interest; no editor can be encouraged when he notes symptoms of mass boredom with his crusade and mass delight with some dim-witted comic or silly charade on television. As for

292   television itself, no more than a start has been made on the kind of public service that has distinguished the work of the press leaders; the electronic media could do much more.

The hard truth is that the public service movement, in this or in any other age, has not given great rewards to those who are the most active in it. But like the duties of citizenship itself, the public service press has a role to play in the increasingly difficult and even precarious process of self-government in the Western world. If the newspaper is to retain its leadership among the news media and develop a better identity as a strong and independent force for progress in an open society, then it has no choice but to continue the struggle in the public interest. The old ways may be easier and sometimes even more profitable. But time is running out on them.

THE FUTURE OF

20

THE JOURNALIST

Among the first things a journalist learns in the newsroom is that the organization matters more than the individual. It is to be expected therefore that when editors peer into the future of journalism, they customarily worry more about the changes that will come in time to the news media than they do about their own kind. If the worst does happen— an electronic newspaper instantly delivered to the family rumpus room in 100-page editions on microfilm—it will serve them right. For either they or their lineal descendants will have to stoke the computer input with such timeless intelligence as "U. N. Dead-

293

294 locked on Disarmament," "House Cuts Foreign Aid," "Stocks See-Saw In Dull Session," "Paris Raises Hemline," "Weather: Fair and Warmer," and "Giants, 3; Dodgers, 2."

This is not an entirely frivolous view of things to come. What it suggests is that the developing revolution in the news media will not really have much effect on the shape of the news itself unless something is done first about the journalist. For it is he, more than the computer and the other mindless gods of electronic science, who will continue to form the habits that lead the public to depend on particular news media, or a combination of them, for information, ideas, and advice. His attitudes of mind and heart, as well as his education, training, and background, will do more to determine what the public is to be told than any kind of tube, press, tape, or camera that carries his message. Always assuming, of course, that he retains a decent amount of independence to do the job.

The relationship of the journalist to the public, in consequence, becomes immediately relevant, as do the ideas that necessarily flow from it. To begin with, neither is particularly satisfied with the other because neither has a great amount of trust, generally speaking, in the judgment of the other. And this is not a new situation in the history of the republic, going back as it does to the opposing views of Thomas Jefferson and Alexander Hamilton on the nature of democratic government. Whatever may be said of the public's dubious estimate of the journalist, it is rather broadly duplicated by some of the leading journalists of the day in their evaluation of the public's capacity for self-government in the atomic age. The aristocrats of journalism, certainly, leave no doubt about their position.

THE JOURNALIST AND THE PUBLIC

In his Elihu Root lectures before the Council on Foreign Relations, James Reston of *The New York Times* soberly raised the question of whether the conduct of American foreign policy could in fact be left to the whims of American public opinion. Referring to the belief that "the people know best," he said: "This is undoubtedly sound doctrine for sinking a sewer or building a bridge or a school in a local community, but is it a practical way to conduct foreign policy? Are the people getting adequate information to enable them to reach sound judgments on what to do about South Asia or the Atlantic Community, or the balance of payments, or China, or outer space? Is there any such information and any such people? And would enough of them pay attention to sustain a commercial newspaper or radio or television station that concentrated on these fundamental questions? . . . Personally, I do not believe that the constitutional assumption that 'the people know best' is a very reliable guide to the conduct of American foreign policy today." [89]

Another distinguished neo-Hamiltonian, Douglass Cater, has an exceedingly unflattering view of the average newspaper reader. He is, Cater wrote, "the median man, destined, like Orphan Annie, never to grow an inch. His intelligence is such that he must have it explained day after day who is Secretary of State but, paradoxically, can be trusted to have highly complex issues described for him in a few terse sentences . . ." [90]

Even more devastating comments on the state of public intelligence are also a part of the journalists' record. When the *New York Herald Tribune* suspended publication, one of its cleverest critics, Judith Crist, mourned, "This was a very special paper. And there's no reason why it should disappear except for an asinine public." [91] And Clark Mollenhoff, the scourge of the wrongdoer in Washington, concluded almost in despair: "If the public doesn't care about its Congress—or doesn't show that it cares—and if it continues to shrug its shoulders over arrogant administration and shoddy favoritism, as well as outright corruption, then one day the house of democracy may fall." [92] As for the younger generation of journalists, the Hamiltonian urge is even stronger. Tom Wolfe, who considers it necessary to attract public attention with such beginnings as "Z-O-O-M!" and "W-H-E-E!," has concluded with magnificent finality on the part of a whole new generation of Americans: "For most people in this age group, there is absolutely nothing in the newspaper that is of any immediate interest." [93]

Such judgments have had no perceptible effect in bridging the gap between the journalist and his audience. Outside the articulate circle of intellectuals who take cheerful swipes at the journalist on all occasions, the public in the United States seems to have been as indifferent to his condemnation as it is to his infrequent praise. This is bitter medicine in a profession that is not inclined to be humble. For the journalist may interpret, advise, comment, report, and entertain either as critic or clown with at least an outward show of public acceptance, but he has not often been ordained in the United States to be a leader of men. Since the time of Benjamin Franklin, no Churchills, Clemenceaus, or Theodore Herzls have sprung from American soil to lead their people to the heights. It is perhaps symbolic that the

296 only editor who ever became President of the United States was Warren Gamaliel Harding, of Marion, Ohio. There has been no thought of running another ever since.

Not all journalists, of course, have been moved to denigrate the intelligence of their audience. With a quarter of the nation in school, and almost 4 percent in the colleges and universities alone, it is difficult for even the most cocksure of journalists to sustain the theory that he is dealing with a nation of bumpkins. True, it is the perennial weakness of the journalist to believe that he must address himself on occasion to the lowest common denominator. What seems to be indicated, as a first step therefore, is a change in his attitude toward the public at large.

Walter Lippmann, the most influential American journalist of his time, set a suitable example for his colleagues without in any way attempting to lecture them on their faults. During the mid-twenties, he himself became the first of the neo-Hamiltonians when he pointed out that the press alone could not create "a mystical force called Public Opinion" which would "proceed to lay down the law for everything all the time." He concluded, "It is not workable. And when you consider the nature of the news, it is not thinkable." [94]

However, on his 70th birthday, he returned to his theme with a somewhat broader view more akin to the Jeffersonian tradition which he presented to his fellow-journalists in the form of a dialogue with himself: " 'And you, my dear fellow,' I tell the critic, 'you be careful. If you go on, you will be showing how ridiculous it is that we live in a republic under a democratic system and that anyone should be allowed to vote. You will be denouncing the principle of democracy itself, which asserts that the outsiders shall be sovereign over the insiders. For you will be showing that the people, since they are ignoramuses, because they are outsiders, are therefore incapable of governing themselves . . . Do you not realize that, about most of the affairs of the world, we are all outsiders and ignoramuses, even the insiders who are at the seat of government?' "

He then summoned his underdeveloped profession to serve the governed through the news media so that they could "arrive at opinions about what their governors want them to consent to." His final words were: "In this we do what every sovereign citizen is supposed to do but has not the time or the interest to do for himself. This is our job. It is no mean calling. We have a right to be proud of it and to be glad that it is our work." [95]

Is this proposition, then, really more workable and more thinkable than it was when Lippmann was a young man? The neo-Hamiltonians argue volubly that it is not, pointing to the abysmal evidences of public apathy and ignorance in the polls. The argument is not impressive. In the first place, the polls are not beyond reproach. Samuel Lubell had no difficulty finding the fatal flaw in a poll that professed to show that 25 percent of the American people did not know a Communist regime ruled mainland China. "Only a single, poorly worded question was asked to arrive at this sensational statistic," he pointed out. "This 'finding' is not justified. The sooner this figure is buried and forgotten, the better." [96] In the second place, if it is true that 20 to 25 percent of the American public consists of "slobs," as one of the pollsters inelegantly contends, then it is an exceedingly powerful and determined 75 to 80 percent who are breaking down doors to get into schools, theatres, museums, art galleries, concert halls, and libraries and buying out book stores, as well. The thesis of the public's fatal incapacity to inform itself as a part of the process of self-government needs more documentation than its sponsors have been able to provide.

It is barely possible that if the public does not pay as much attention to the journalist as he thinks it should, the fault is more likely to be his than the failure of his audience to harken to his wisdom. For the hard truth is that the journalist does not take lightly to change in his own profession, although he is constantly advocating it for others. The myth persists, after more than fifty years of functioning journalism schools, that anyone can become a journalist, merely by declaring that he is one; in fact, the schools themselves still are regarded with suspicion by the hard-nosed editors of the land. Even worse, the academic community maintains a deep channel of separation between its own interests and those of the journalist which only a few are able to bridge. And this at a time when so eminent a figure as McGeorge Bundy, president of the Ford Foundation, has pointed out, "The professions of scholarship and of journalism are threatened with a requirement of merger. A cynic might say that the scholars should learn to write and the journalists should learn to think." [97]

THE EDUCATION OF THE JOURNALIST

Before the form and substance of American journalism can be shifted appreciably to become more attuned to the requirements of the day, the journalist will have to overcome his mistrust of

298   higher education and the educator will have to allay his fundamental doubts about the journalist. It is utter nonsense to pretend that a man can be given a liberal arts education, a year or
two in a newsroom covering everything from a police beat to Sunday sermons, and then thrust into the maelstrom of Washington,
a global conference, or a major war without the severest difficulties for all concerned. In any other profession, it would be unthinkable.

While heroes have been created through such haphazard methods, the result more often has been deep trouble for
the news media, the public, and quite often for the government as
well. The argument that only young men can stand up to the
tough regimen of the journalist is not entirely sound; if it were,
Ernie Pyle would have whiled away World War II on a night copy
desk somewhere and his supposedly superannuated colleague,
Leland Stowe, would have been drawing a tiny pension. Both
won Pulitzer Prizes for their work—a symbolic recognition of the
error of journalism's wasteful practice of considering most men
over forty (and nearly all women) to be doddering misfits.

Some of the excesses of reportage in current affairs,
both at home and abroad, are all too clearly the end product of
earnest efforts by relatively untried, untrained, and overly emotional journalists of tender years. It is no wonder that Keyes
Beech, the veteran war correspondent of the *Chicago Daily
News*, has protested repeatedly against the practice of permitting bright young journalists to gain experience in matters of
great moment, such as the Vietnam War, at the expense of both
foreign nations and their own. Of course, journalism needs the
brains, guts, and brimming vitality of youth, and it must pay
much more than it now does if it is to retain some of the greatly
talented young men who have proved themselves, but in all but
exceptional cases it is a mistake to rush the seasoning process. If
there is a greater need than that of youth in the profession today,
it is for mature judgment and experienced leadership, which is
even harder to come by.

While the flaws in journalism education are self-
evident, no great reforms appear to be in the making for the
present. Except for the beginners' courses in high school through
which so many journalists (including this one) first learned of
the fascination of what amounts to an impossible art, the principal burden of education for journalism today still rests at the
undergraduate level. It has long been known, however, that un-

dergraduate schools for many reasons cannot produce a sufficient number of journalists to meet the needs of the profession.
Nor can the effective graduate journalism programs, which are
still limited to relatively few institutions, be counted on to fill the
gap between the demand and supply of trained people. Therefore
journalism personnel experts have taken to recruiting college
editors or even rawer prospects from among the liberal arts
majors and even science students in the colleges and universities. These newcomers are then thrust into a species of training
program. The trouble is that few such operations last for very
long and all of them are necessarily and unashamedly offered up
to the trade school process of feeding bodies into a particular
industrial channel. The basic fallacy here is the notion that a
journalist can be stamped into shape like a cookie, thrust into a
preheated oven, and baked until ready at excessive pressure and
high temperature.

Instant journalism is seldom a conspicuous success.
Most journalists require as much as ten years to mature, although there have been a handful of brilliant exceptions. It is for
this reason that the promising midcareer program has been
offered to still youthful but established journalists at several
leading universities. Yet, despite the excellence of the concept,
some of the nation's major news organizations have participated
either reluctantly or not at all because of the fear, sometimes
justified, that their newly trained specialists would not return to
their old general assignments. Here, the problem is not so much
money, although newspapers in particular can still boost their
generally improved pay for seasoned professionals, but what
amounts to a lack of opportunity for a number of qualified
specialists. What often happens is that the well-trained specialist
leaves journalism for government, the universities, the founda-
tions, industry, or even public relations at the time of his greatest usefulness.

It is at this juncture that the business of journalism
and the profession of journalism have yet to work out a proper
accommodation. The superior performance of those trained journalists who have been permitted to develop a specialty indicates
the potential gain for the profession. As for the rest, who drop
out, they demonstrate the reality of the journalistic "brain drain"
at the midcareer level, which is in fact almost as serious as it is
in the university classrooms and immediately thereafter.

A change in journalism education, of course, could

300   come quite dramatically with the emergence of an entirely new type of mass news medium in the electronic age. Such miracles are always talked of in the wee hours at journalism conventions around a friendly bar. However, it is probable that the best hope of modernized journalism practice lies in a thoroughgoing re-examination of journalism education as it now exists.

There is little possibility of modeling the training of the journalist on the specifications set forth for lawyers, physicians, clergymen, engineers, or even sociologists, who are a kind of ersatz journalist in their own right. In years to come, it is desirable first of all for the journalist to complete a general education before he is called upon to specialize in a highly complex profession. For neither at the undergraduate stage nor at midcareer should he be so segregated from the varied world in which he is to move that he becomes ingrown, both professionally and socially, and confined very largely to close association with other journalists. There will always be some form of undergraduate journalism education for that reason, but it should be broadened to appeal to nonjournalists as well.

When the profession is able to support expanded graduate study, the journalist, upon completing his general education, should be immersed in his professional studies for no less than two years, and, if possible, three. The foremost theoreticians and practitioners of journalism should be recruited to instruct him in his responsibilities as well as his freedoms, his relationship to the public interest as well as his recognition of the needs of his own news organization, his background, and knowledge of the basic issues of his time. He should be familiar with something more than the techniques of journalism which, in some respects but not all, can be taught with greater facility on the job than in the classroom. The history and literature of journalism, its formidable communications practices, its legal problems, and its relationship to the government, the economy, the society, the arts and sciences, and the other professions all should be fruitful fields for instruction; more so, certainly, than they are today. But primarily, the journalist should be given more time to mature in the universities.

The journalism of the next few decades will have need of more highly qualified practitioners. Its role in a free society is likely to be far greater than it is today, if it can recover a good measure of public esteem. Without such support, it is scarcely likely to maintain either the independence or the affluence that are now so characteristic of the news media in large part. For immense changes are in the making, from within journalism and from without, entirely aside from the matter of techniques. The journalist of the future will need all the strength he can muster to survive the growth of constricting pressures. If it remains an economic impossibility to support a broader system of journalism education, the main handicap at present, then he will indeed be at a disadvantage to cope with the strange new world that is even now in its formative stage.

THE NEW JOURNALISM
Beneath the turbulence of the present, the shape of the journalism of the future can be dimly perceived. It will continue to be both a profession and a business, as it necessarily must, and its purposes and aims will remain the same even though its market and product are likely to be quite different. For the press will discover sooner or later that it is charging the subscriber too much and the advertiser too little, that its sometimes smudgy inks are as objectionable as its news presentation, and that its rigid format is not standard for all time. The electronic media are bound to force upon the daily press a certain amount of contraction, but Fred Friendly's prophecy that all bad newspapers will die in the process is not likely to be realized. For if the electronic media proliferate beyond the power of the advertiser to sustain, the same inexorable process of the survival of the fittest will take place within radio and television just as it has in the press. The government's first move into public television is a sign of the future. Bad television is not here to stay, regardless of what the rating systems say. It may well be that a few failures will be good for the soul of the electronics industry, just as they have speeded up the process of self-examination by the press.

No one knows today whether it will be economically feasible to support two or three national networks during the next 15 or 20 years. It is apparent, from the unhappy venture of the United group, that a fourth network even now is bound to encounter almost insuperable economic and technological difficulties. Moreover, there is even a serious question that three networks can operate today without an enormous intake of outside capital. If the cost of electronic advertising should rise so high that it is impossible for an advertiser to obtain an adequate return, then there may be only two independent networks in the United States—and eventually only one. Certainly, it is not fore-

302 ordained that the government will forever stay out of active participation in broadcasting if the independent broadcasters should fall out of public favor either through continued poor programming, new scandals, or sheer incompetence.

Throughout the news media, whatever the shape of the future, the public interest will continue to demand a sharp separation between the functions of business and advertising, on the one hand, and editorial news gathering and comment on the other. But one of the lamentable realities of our time is the blurring of the line between the two, and it is not really caused by the advertiser in most instances. He is the catalyst, the necessary component of an independent press and electronic news system, but he is not the force that drives the engine. However, in a segment of the news media, there exists a feeling that it would be better to remain beholden to the advertiser interest and not unnecessarily antagonize it—even though the better advertisers may do nothing to stimulate or even invite such support. Thereby, the profession of journalism is reduced in stature and debased by its own people.

The stronger components of the news media, though well able to give proper service to the advertiser while keeping him in his accustomed place outside the editorial function, have created an even greater hazard for themselves through the practice of diversification. When a railroad or a public utility or a copper company owned a newspaper or television station in the past, the public usually was able to conclude quite rightly that the editors and managers had to serve interests that sometimes were diametrically opposite to their own. Today, with some of the press and electronic leaders investing in so many enterprises with interests that could affect the presentation of the news, the process of diversification raises serious questions. If they cannot be answered boldly and forthrightly, then public uncertainty over internal influences on the news is likely to grow. Something like a journalistic Ombudsman is needed here to police the business of journalism in order to safeguard the profession of journalism.

The pressures from within that seek to regulate the flow of news, however, are demonstrably small as compared with the tremendous influence that often is brought to bear from outside journalism. All the prestige of the White House is centered on the propagation of policies for which a favorable hearing is sought in the news media. The various departments of the federal government, from Defense and State on down, each have special interests to promote and defend, as do the various units of state and local governments. In the courts, under the leadership of the United States Supreme Court, the news media have been placed on the defensive. Yet, it is evident that the public seems not to be excessively disturbed by the movement of the courts, the law enforcement agencies, and a substantial part of the legal profession to curb the performance of the news media on the dubious ground that injustices have occurred in the past. This is not a very good standard to apply in an admittedly imperfect and growing democratic society.

Seldom, since the passage of the Alien and Sedition Acts of 1798, has there been a time in American history when there have been so many encroachments on the flow of the news and the work of the journalist. If he blames the news management policies of the various branches of government, the pressures of private publicity and the hostility of the courts, he may have a point. But his own meek acceptance of the adulteration of the news, in some instances, as well as his unacknowledged censorship of much national and foreign news in large areas of the country, are also to blame. He has shouted throughout the history of the nation for freedom of the press, but usually for his own primary benefit. With good reason therefore the thoughtful citizen on occasion turns away from the news media after a particularly sticky job of reportage and wonders, "What can we believe?" Not even the editors at all times can be certain of the answers.

If it requires the prestige of a university and the investment of $300,000 in federal funds to seek national reassurance that the United States Air Force is not lying about "flying saucers," [98] what will it take to restore a decent respect for the credibility of a considerable section of the news media? Certainly, it is no longer possible for all American journalism to ride along in comfort—and occasionally in glory—behind a few hundred responsible newspapers and magazines that do merit a large measure of public confidence, and a stalwart handful of commentators and newsmen for the electronic media.

No sensible person wants codes, national authorities, or commissions that pass resolutions about matters which they do not faintly understand; nor is there much sense in discussing punitive measures for journalists who may displease a judge. There is a balance to be maintained between the forces of

304   government and the independent news media, which the public is bound to favor provided it is convinced of the good faith of both sides.

This is really the crucial point. Through the usual democratic processes, the American government and its elected officeholders periodically submit themselves to a test of public confidence at the ballot box. The news media and their directing authorities, fortunately for their peace of mind, do not. Whatever the aristocrats of journalism may think of the public's capacity, it has regularly distinguished itself by registering its will on Election Day with precision, efficiency, and often with a great deal of discrimination and judgment.

The news media on occasion have cited huge circulations, or high audience ratings, as a sign of public approval. But both magazines and newspapers with fabulous circulations have disappeared overnight. A record television audience for shows like "Batman" also has little meaning; one of the worst plays ever seen in the American theatre, "Abie's Irish Rose," ran for five years. Neither did very much for the prestige of their respective media.

THE MISSION OF THE JOURNALIST

When all the defenses are submitted and all the arguments are examined, two courses remain open to the American news media unless they choose merely to drift and hope, which is unlikely. The first course already is in process of development—a slow but inexorable tightening of the conflict between government and the news media over the control of the character and flow of the news. Just how far this will go depends as much on the determination of the news media to maintain their independence as it does on the operational processes of government. The manner in which the journalist conducts himself, in consequence, is likely to be crucial. Another Oswald case or another Sheppard trial, with all their journalistic excesses, may wear public patience with the news media to a dangerously thin level of support.

The other practical course that remains open is an effort at self-regulation that goes beyond the passage of pious resolutions and includes continued efforts to confer with physicians and public health authorities, bench and bar, government officials at various levels, and others who have an interest in softening conflicts of interest. Historically, the journalist has mistrusted such joint efforts as breeding grounds of restraint on his ability to act. However, he no longer can expect separate and preferred treatment in the United States merely because he is a journalist. It is the power of the government that is increasing in this era, as James Reston has so accurately observed, and not the power of the press.

Any thoughtful observer, reflecting on the public mood in this nation, is bound to conclude that the burden of proof is now on the journalist. Free journalism is a right only if it is not abused, a privilege only as long as the public sustains it in practice. If the journalist is therefore driven to seek a larger measure of public support than he can count on today, he will be well advised to abandon such disparate roles as the theoretically detached observer, the practically functioning philosophical anarchist, or the brisk and soulless representative of a prosperous business. If he is to continue to merit Constitutional protection for his work, his best resource is to concentrate on the practice of journalism as a public service. Merely saying that the public interest comes first in journalism does not make it so. A greater emulation of the deeds of the substantial journalistic minority who recognize their public obligation is called for from the rank and file of the news media.

In the world of the future, there will be increasing need of such an independent force to safeguard the public interest. In one area of American life alone, a wholesale assault on the rights of the individual already is possible through the growth of electronic eavesdropping devices that can be manipulated with equal facility for good or ill. Even more to be watched is the experimentation with changes in the human personality through drugs and surgery, supposedly for the benefit of those wretches inclined toward crime and other antisocial behavior (although nobody has defined the role of the Big Brother who will select the subjects for tests). Propaganda systems for inducing conformity in great masses of people, despite many failures, still have a fascination for a section of the intellectual elite as the answer to the problems of a troubled society. And even if resort to such dubious efforts is continually discouraged, that will not in itself be any bulwark against the creation of a whole new catalogue of injustices in a changing social order that could be worse than the ills they are supposed to eradicate.

For all his many faults, the dedicated journalist has a continuing role as a public defender in these and other important matters for as long as his freedom to think and to act is

306   preserved. Despite the guarantees in the Constitution of the United States, this is by no means certain. In a world conditioned to cherish security above freedom, the independent journalist has never been safe. His way is still lonely, obstructed, and dangerous in most of the nations of the earth. The halter is more frequently his lot than the laurel wreath. The temptation therefore is great to urge the journalist, at the expense of all else, to act with far greater caution and much more restraint than he has in the past in order to preserve the freedom he still enjoys in the United States and the prosperity that has come to the American news media.

It is, of course, true that the spirit of the times demands of the journalist a larger measure of self-regulation, and even self-government. And yet, if caution should turn into timidity and self-regulation into abject cowardice, then American journalism would indeed be irreparably damaged as a balancing force between the needs of government and the public good. The first requirement of the journalist is still independence—"drastic independence," in Joseph Pulitzer's phrase—and all else in American journalism flows from it. For if there is no resolution to uphold an independent point of view, even at the price of being wrong on occasion, then there can be no realistic effort to get at the truth in difficult situations and thus serve the public interest.

This is still the mission of the journalist. In his very independence and diversity—sometimes even his wrongheadedness—lie the public's best protection against his excesses. There will always be some who complain that he dares too much and says and prints too much and raises too much hell—and of course he must plead guilty to the charge. But if he did not do these things, he would not be a journalist. He would have little chance, in many complicated issues, of getting at the truth. Sometimes, indeed, it may seem impossible to find the truth, but it is in the nature of the journalist to attempt the impossible. That is his distinction in life. It is his badge of honor.

NOTES AND

COMMENT

PART I—GROWTH OF THE MEDIA: PROBLEM AND PROMISE

1. THE LIMITS OF POWER

1. James Reston, *The Artillery of the Press* (New York: Harper & Row, Publishers, 1967), p. 71.

2. *The New York Times*, April 4, 1967, p. 87.

3. UNESCO, *World Communications*, 4th ed. (New York: UNESCO Publications Center, 1964), pp. 165–174.

4. Newspaper statistics for 1966 from "Highlights of a Record Year," brochure published by the American Newspaper Publishers Assn., April, 1967; see also Jon G. Udell, "The Growth of the American Daily Newspaper," a research publication of the School of Commerce, University of Wisconsin, pp. 6–8; Peter Kihss, "Study of New York Newspaper Merger," *The New York Times*, March 22, 1966, and Kihss's summary of *New York World Journal Tribune* suspension May 6, 1967; *The New York Times*, "1966 profit report," April 24, 1967, p. 52; *Newsweek*, November 29, 1965, pp. 55–60, for magazines; Robert U. Brown, Sigma Delta Chi Foundation lecture at DePauw University, December 10, 1965, published in *The Quill*, March, 1966, pp. 16–19; American Newspaper Publishers Assn., *Information Newsletters* for May 3, 1966 and March 21, 1967; *Editor & Publisher*, July 23, 1966, p. 14, for results of survey of 111 newspapers; McCann-Erickson report for 1965 gives following comparative advertising totals: Newspapers, $4.4 billion; TV, $2.5 billion; magazines, $1.2 billion, and radio, $0.9 billion.

5. *Time*, August 12, 1966, p. 35; *The New York Times*, March 1, 1967, p. 33; *Wall Street Journal*, July 12, 1967, p. 1.

6. For material on Walter Cronkite, see *Newsweek*, October 14, 1966, pp. 56–63; for general considerations of television, see Fred W. Friendly, *Due to Circumstances Beyond Our Control* (New York: Random House, 1967), pp. 269–279; see also *Editor & Publisher*, March 11, 1967, p. 13; Val Adams, "Profits Increase in TV Industry," *The New York Times*, August 7, 1965; Robert E. Kintner, "Broadcasting and the News," reprinted from *Harper's* magazine by the National Broadcasting Co., copyright, 1965, by Harper & Row, p. 4. (Shortly after writing this article, Mr. Kintner resigned in one of several executive shakeups that shook the television industry and thereafter served as a Presidential assistant at the White House.) It should also be

308 noted, in connection with the statement of television profits, that *Time* reported on October 14, 1966 that the three networks would spend nearly $150 million a year on news alone. TV profits for 1966 were reported in *Time* September 8, 1967, p. 54. For further detail on the problem, see the American Society of Newspaper Editors' "Problems of Journalism," the *Proceedings of the 1965 ASNE Convention* at Washington, D. C., p. 36.

7. *Newsweek,* October 14, 1966, pp. 56–63.

8. ASNE, "Problems of Journalism," 1965, pp. 40–44.

9. Turner Catledge, Sigma Delta Chi Foundation lecture at the University of Kansas, *The Quill,* January, 1966.

2. A QUESTION OF PURPOSE

10. Renaudot quoted in Eugene Hatin, *Histoire de la Presse en France* (Paris: Poulet-Malassis et de Broise, 1859), Vol. No. 1, pp. 78–79.

11. Meyer Berger, *History of The New York Times* (New York: Simon and Schuster, Inc., 1951), pp. 107–108.

12. Still carried daily under the masthead on the editorial page of the *St. Louis Post-Dispatch.*

13. *The New York Times,* February 28, 1967, p. 27.

14. *The New York Times,* May 17, 1967, p. 37. For wire service background see *Newsweek,* January 15, 1968, pp. 46–47.

3. THE INTERLOCKING MEDIA

15. UPI *Reporter,* April 21 and July 14, 1966.

16. Ben H. Bagdikian, *Esquire,* March, 1967, p. 128. The figures may be checked by tabulating totals in the *Editor & Publisher Yearbook.*

17. Guido H. Stempel III, *Columbia Journalism Review,* Spring, 1967, p. 11.

18. Stempel, pp. 11–12.

19. Peter Kihss, *The New York Times,* November 10, 1965; AP *Log,* November 3–9, 1965; UPI *Reporter,* November 10, 1965.

20. R. W. Budd, Malcolm S. MacLean, Jr., and Arthur M. Barnes, "Regularities in the Diffusion of Two Major News Events," *Journalism Quarterly,* No. 43, pp. 221–230. The table is from research conducted in Iowa City.

21. A. M. Rosenthal, *38 Witnesses* (New York: McGraw-Hill Book Company, 1964).

22. Elmo Roper & Associates: "The Public's View of Television and Other Media, 1959–1964" (New York: TV Information Office, 1965), pp. 2–3. Newspapers were given by 56 percent as the first source of the news, since the total respondents' opinions exceeded 100 percent. The 2 percent difference is not much to arouse such a storm of controversy.

23. Walter Cronkite, "What TV Is Doing to Newspapers," Associated Press Managing Editors, *Red Book* (New York: The Associated Press, 1965), p. 18.

24. *Editor & Publisher,* "Gallup Poll Shows Papers Still Tops in
News," August 28, 1965.

25. *Editor & Publisher.*

26. "Nielsen Disputes Harris on TV Data," *The New York Times,* February 28, 1967, p. 74.

27. *Newsweek,* January 2, 1967, pp. 41–44.

28. For an elaboration of CBS operations, see Chapter 6, "Trends in Television."

29. For an elaboration of NBC operations, see Chapter 6, "Trends in Television."

30. *Washington Post,* March 14, 1963, p. A–2.

31. APME *Red Book* (New York: The Associated Press, 1965), p. 25.

32. Federal Communications Commission 67–743:2055. Docket No. 16828: "Opinion and Order on Petition for Reconsideration" in matter of application by ABC for assignment and transfer of station licenses, adopted June 22, 1967, pp. 33–34; see also "Dissenting Opinion of Commissioners Bartley, Cox, and Johnson," pp. 28–32.

33. See dissenting opinion, pp. 33, 73. ITT merger rejection in *The New York Times,* January 2, 1968, p. 1, 75.

4. NEW TIMES FOR NEWSPAPERS

34. "Daily Newspapers in 1966" (New York: The American Newspaper Publishers Assn., April, 1967), p. 7.

35. *The Bulletin,* American Society of Newspaper Editors, August 1, 1966, p. 9.

36. *Bulletin,* pp. 8–9; For data on "Failing Newspaper Act," see *Editor & Publisher,* August 19, 1967, pp. 9–10, 55–56.

37. *Editor & Publisher International Yearbook,* 1967; A. H. Raskin, "What's Wrong with American Newspapers," *The New York Times Magazine,* June 11, 1967.

38. Dwight E. Sargent, "The Flourishing American Daily," *Montana Journalism Review,* Spring, 1967, p. 3. Baron Thomson's rise is summed up in *Editor & Publisher,* September 2, 1967, p. 9; *Time,* September 8, 1967, p. 45, and *The New York Times,* January 1, 1968, p. 13.

39. *Editor & Publisher,* April 16, 1966 survey.

40. Reported to me by the publisher, who asked that no names be used.

41. *Newsweek,* June 20, 1966, p. 62. See also *Editor & Publisher,* June 4, 1966, p. 17.

42. *The Quill,* June, 1966, pp. 26–30; *Columbia Journalism Review,* Spring, 1966, pp. 29–31.

43. *Newsweek,* December 5, 1966.

44. *The New York Times,* March 3, 1967, pp. 1, 55. See also *The New York Times's* sketch of Newhouse on March 29, 1959.

45. *The New York Times,* May 6, 1967; *New York World Journal Tribune,* May 5, 1967.

310   46. A. H. Raskin, *Silurian News*, October 31, 1966, p. 1. See also Raskin's splendid account of the 1962–63 strike in *The New York Times*, April 1, 1963. Estimates of last circulation in *Editor & Publisher*, October 14, 1967, p. 108.

47. *The New York Times*, March 19, 1967, p. 33; *Columbia Journalism Review*, Winter, 1965, pp. 4–9. *The Times*'s announcement that it would not publish in the evening was on October 2, 1967. *Editor & Publisher* comment on October 7, 1967, p. 13.

48. Vermont Royster, *Nieman Reports*, March, 1967, pp. 3–6; Paul Miller, in *Editor & Publisher*, September 25, 1965, p. 15.

5. MAGAZINES AND THE NEWS

49. This material is based on interviews with knowledgeable sources.

50. *Editor & Publisher*, February 11, 1967, p. 11.

51. *Statistical Abstract of the U. S.*, 1966, p. 524, Table 730.

52. Magazine Advertising Bureau of the Magazine Publishers Assn., reporting as of January 1, 1965. *The New Yorker* reported on in *Newsweek*, January 1, 1968, p. 53.

53. *Time*, August 12, 1966, p. 35; February 24, 1967, p. 40.

54. *Columbia Journalism Review*, Summer, 1964, pp. 32–33.

55. *The New York Times*, July 25, 1966, p. 18.

56. *Time*, February 24, 1967, p. 40.

57. See July, 1966, *Cosmopolitan* and *Newsweek* comment, July 18, 1966, p. 60.

58. *Columbia Journalism Review*, Summer, 1964, pp. 32–33.

59. *The New York Times Sunday Magazine*, July 18, 1965. See C. Lasch, "Majority of Dissent Magazines Thrive On Unpopularity."

6. TRENDS IN TELEVISION

60. FCC Order on ABC Merger, p. 27. Text of ITT decision to drop merger is in *The New York Times*, January 2, 1968, p. 1.

61. *Newsweek*, February 20, 1967, p. 63. In New York City, the rating for the China program was a point behind "The Man From U.N.C.L.E."

62. FCC order on ABC Merger, p. 27. Despite the loss, ABC's news budget was put at $40 million for 1968.

63. *Time* cover story on Cronkite, October 14, 1966, p. 56.

64. *Columbia Journalism Review*, Spring, 1966, pp. 22–28.

65. Jack Gould, *The New York Times*, June 7, 1967, p. 95.

66. FCC Order on ABC Merger, pp. 42–43. An attempted fourth network, the United, lasted for a short time early in 1967 but collapsed of financial anemia.

67. *The New York Times*, January 29, 1967, p. D–19; *The New York Times* "A Program for Public TV," March 12, 1967; *Newsweek*, February 6, 1967, p. 89; March 27, 1967, p. 92. Summary of Carnegie report in *The New York Times*, January 26, 1967, p. 27; beginning of PBL experiment in *The New York Times*, November 6–7, 1967; Broadcast Act signed by LBJ, *The New York Times*, November 8, 1967.

68. *Time*, July 22, 1966, p. 76; see also William A. Wood, *Electronic Journalism* (New York: 1967), pp. 110–124.

69. *New York Herald Tribune*, April 5, 1966, p. 19.

70. *The New York Times*, October 2, 1966, p. D–19. Program was on Channel 5, October 2, 1966, at 9 P.M.

71. Minow text was published in *The New York Times*, May 10, 1961. See also *Columbia Journalism Review*, Summer, 1965, pp. 27–32, for reprint of Edward R. Murrow's 1958 speech to Radio-Television News Directors in Chicago.

72. *The New York Times*, March 22, 1967, p. 95.

73. *Newsweek*, June 5, 1967, p. 66; *The New York Times*, September 14, 1966, p. 63, and March 12, 1967, pp. 5–7.

74. *The New York Times*, October 9, 1966, p. D–21.

75. *The New York Times*, June 17, 1966, p. 91, and June 16, 1966, p. 95.

76. E. William Henry, statement before House Interstate and Foreign Commerce Subcommittee on HR 7072, July 16, 1963, p. 13.

PART 2—OF MANNERS AND MORALS: TRUTH OR CONSEQUENCES

7. THE MEANING OF THE NEWS

1. *Newsweek*, April 25, 1966, pp. 56–61.

2. *Time*, April 15, 1966, pp. 30–34.

3. *The New York Times Magazine*, June 12, 1966, p. 28.

4. *The New York Times*, August 22, 1966, p. 32.

5. *Indianapolis Star*, June 6, 1966, p. 22.

6. *New York Daily News*, August 12, 1966, pp. 8, 34.

7. *The New York Times*, August 18, 1966, p. 4; *Washington Post*, August 11, 1966; *The New York Times*, August 10, 1966.

8. *The New York Times*, June 7–8, 1966; *Editor & Publisher*, June 11, 1966, p. 13; *Time*, June 17, 1966, p. 62.

9. AP *Log*, September 14–20, 1961.

10. Clinton Rossiter and James Lare, eds., *The Essential Lippmann* (New York: Random House, Inc., 1963), p. 400.

11. A. T. Steele, *The American People and China* (New York: McGraw-Hill Book Company, 1966), p. 166.

12. *Newsweek*, May 22, 1967, p. 71. Bundy and Moyers stated their positions while they were in private life, having each completed a long term of service at the White House. Bundy later was called back for duty in the Middle East crisis, and Moyers was consulted from time to time.

13. *Wall Street Journal*, January 11, 1963.

14. *Newsweek*, May 22, 1967, p. 71.

15. *Editor & Publisher*, January 6, 1962, p. 9.

16. American Society of Newspaper Editors, *Bulletin*, March 1, 1964, p. 7.

17. *Wall Street Journal*, August 23, 1966, p. 16.

18. *Editor & Publisher*, January 20, 1962, p. 58.

312   19. Ralph McGill, *The South and the Southerner* (Boston: Little, Brown and Company, 1959, 1963), pp. 232–233.
    20. Personal letter from Harry S. Ashmore dated July 21, 1966. Quoted with permission.
    21. Theodore H. White, *The Making of the President 1964* (New York: Atheneum Publishers 1965), p. 200.
    22. *Newsweek,* August 8, 1966, p. 54.
    23. ASNE *Bulletin,* January 1, 1966, p. 14.
    24. *Bulletin,* p. 13. See also the *Bulletin* for January 1, 1968, with Ben Gilbert's p. 1 article, "Race Coverage."

8. THE CREDIBILITY GAP

    25. *The New York Times,* June 9 and 11, 1966, p. 1.
    26. Statements made to me during a survey of correspondents' opinion.
    27. *The New York Times,* August 8, 1966, p. 26.
    28. James Reston, *Foreign Affairs,* July, 1966, p. 565.
    29. *Editor & Publisher,* July 16, 1966, pp. 14, 51.
    30. *The New York Times,* August 7, 1966. *Editor & Publisher,* July 23, 1966, p. 6.
    31. General sources include James E. Pollard, *The Presidents and the Press* (New York: Public Affairs Press, 1964); John Hohenberg, *The New Front Page* (New York: Columbia University Press, 1965); Jonathan Daniels, *The Time Between the Wars* (Garden City, N.Y.: Doubleday & Co., Inc., 1966), and *The New York Times* and *New York Daily News* for August 12, 1966 on the FDR story.
    32. For details see John Hohenberg, *Foreign Correspondence: The Great Reporters and Their Times* (New York: Columbia University Press, 1964).
    33. *The National Observer,* March 18, 1963, p. 14.
    34. J. R. Wiggins, *Freedom or Secrecy,* rev. ed. (New York: Oxford University Press, 1964), pp. 101, 233.
    35. Allen W. Dulles, speech at Yale University, February 3, 1958.
    36. David Wise and Thomas B. Ross, *The Invisible Government* (New York: Random House, Inc., 1962).
    37. Wiggins, pp. 108–109.
    38. Maxwell Taylor, *The Uncertain Trumpet* (New York: Harper & Row, Publishers, 1959).
    39. For many years, Congressional committees did not question the minimal appropriation for public relations in the military budget, which totaled less than $1 million. The services as early as World War II "complied" with this unrealistic sum by specifying that only certain particular duties could be classified as "public relations." They even made out weekly slips giving the total number of hours spent in the "public relations" function—sometimes none at all, sometimes 30 or 45 minutes out of the entire week. It was not considered "public relations," for example, to answer "questions from the public," *i.e.,* respond to a newsman's query, or to draft statements, write speeches,

or do many of the things that are a normal part of a public relations
man's duty. The "budgetary limitation" thus stood up for more than
20 years, but it came nowhere near meeting the cost of the salaries
alone of the thousands of officers and enlisted men who were specifically assigned to public relations functions, regardless of how they
were described for budgetary purposes or what grandiose name was
assigned to them for purposes of concealment.

40. Sidney Warren, *The President as World Leader* (New York:
J. B. Lippincott Co., 1964), p. 415.

41. John Hohenberg, *The Pulitzer Prize Story* (New York:
Columbia University Press, 1959), pp. 212–214.

42. James Reston, *Foreign Affairs*, July, 1966, p. 558.

43. David Wise and Thomas B. Ross, *The U-2 Affair* (New York:
Random House, Inc., 1960), pp. 88–94.

44. Wise and Ross, pp. 110–113.

45. Clifton Daniel speech, *The New York Times*, June 2, 1966,
p. 14.

46. Jack Raymond, *Power at the Pentagon* (New York: Harper
& Row, Publishers, 1964), p. 48; Ben H. Bagdikian, *Providence
Journal*, March 5, 1961.

47. AP *Log*, February 2–8, 1961.

48. *The New York Times*, May 11, 1961.

49. Raymond, p. 280.

50. Raymond, p. 328.

51. Raymond, pp. 326–327; see also *Editor & Publisher*, July
16, 1966, p. 14; Charles Roberts, *LBJ's Inner Circle* (New York: Dell
Publishing Co., Inc., 1965), pp. 212–224.

52. *Washington Post*, February 22, 1966, p. B–1.

53. *The New York Times*, April 21, 1966, p. 26.

54. *Columbia Journalism Review*, Summer, 1965, p. 10.

55. Roberts, pp. 197–211; UPI *Reporter*, May 27, 1965; Elmer E.
Cornwell, *Journalism Quarterly*, Spring, 1966, pp. 3–9.

56. Wiggins, pp. 108–109.

9. WAR, TRUTH, AND VIETNAM

57. Richard Harwood, *Washington Post*, April 30, 1967, p. C–1,
recalls the Nixon episode. The stages of the United States shift from
denial to admission of the attack on the Soviet ship may be traced in
The New York Times from June 3–21, 1967.

58. Saul Pett, AP *File* for March 6, 1966, reported Opinion Research Co. poll for CBS on United States official announcements and
their credibility; *Newsweek*, July 10, 1967, p. 76, reported Louis
Harris poll on public confidence in news media.

59. Max Frankel, *The New York Times*, June 29, 1966, p. 3;
James Reston, *The New York Times*, June 29, 1966, p. 46; *Time*, July
8, 1966, pp. 11–17.

60. Arthur Krock, *The New York Times*, June 30, 1966, p. 38.

61. Allen W. Dulles, *The Craft of Intelligence* (New York:
Harper & Row, Publishers, 1963), p. 237.

314

62. Clark Mollenhoff, *Despoilers of Democracy* (Garden City, N. Y.: Doubleday & Co., Inc., 1965), p. 382.

63. W. H. Ferry, Harry S. Ashmore, *Mass Communications*, published by the Fund for the Republic, 1966, p. 6.

64. Attributed by several Washington correspondents to a Gaullist visitor to Washington in the 1960s.

65. *Editor & Publisher*, July 2, 1966, p. 46.

66. J. R. Wiggins, *Freedom or Secrecy*, rev. ed. (New York: Oxford University Press, 1964), p. 235.

67. John Mecklin, *Mission In Torment* (New York: Doubleday & Co., Inc., 1965), p. 100. See also Malcolm W. Browne, *The New Face of War* (Indianapolis: The Bobbs-Merrill Co., Inc., 1965).

68. *Letter from* Beverly Deepe, January 7, 1965.

69. UPI *File*, September 9, 1964. See also Charles Roberts, *LBJ's Inner Circle* (New York: Dell Publishing Company, 1965), p. 23.

70. *The New Leader*, October 10, 1966, pp. 3–5.

71. Salisbury series in *The New York Times*, December 25, 1966; January 10, 1967. Also see his book, *Behind the Lines* (New York: Harper & Row, Publishers, 1967).

72. *Time*, June 10, 1966, pp. 54–59.

73. Private correspondence.

74. *The New York Times*, August 2, 1966, p. 3.

75. *Time*, July 21, 1967, p. 23.

76. Private correspondence.

10. COVERAGE BY THE HERD

77. *Newsweek*, July 24, 1967, p. 69.

78. Curtis D. MacDougall, *The Press and Its Problems* (Dubuque, Iowa: W. C. Brown, 1964), pp. 332–333.

79. Herbert Brucker, *Saturday Review*, January 11, 1964, pp. 75–77.

80. Brucker.

81. *Time*, February 26, 1965, p. 52.

82. ASNE *Bulletin*, May 1, 1965, pp. 5–7.

83. *Editor & Publisher*, August 7, 1965, p. 9.

84. *Editor & Publisher*, p. 9. See also Stan Opotowsky, *The Nation*, September 30, 1961, pp. 203–205.

11. JUNKET JOURNALISM

85. "Activities of Non-Diplomatic Representatives in the United States": Hearings before the Senate Committee on Foreign Relations, 88th Congress, 1963, Parts 1–13, U. S. Government Printing Office; *Editor & Publisher*, June 22, 1963, pp. 11, 51; August 24, 1963, pp. 9, 52.

86. Francis Pollock, "South Africa's Lobby; A Bid for New Friends," Master's Thesis, Columbia Graduate School of Journalism, 1966.

87. *The New York Times*, August 18, 1966, p. 4.
88. *Wall Street Journal*, February 14, 1966, pp. 1, 12.
89. I have received assistance from sports writers, reviewers, editors, and others who, for obvious reasons, prefer to remain anonymous. See also *Newsweek*, October 9, 1967, p. 60.
90. *Editor & Publisher*, September 1, 1958, pp. 3–5.
91. *Wall Street Journal*, February 14, 1966, p. 12.
92. *Newsweek*, June 30, 1958, p. 48.
93. John Hohenberg, *The Pulitzer Prize Story*, pp. 60–64; *The New York Times*, April 4, 1963; *Editor & Publisher*, April 13, 1963, pp. 13, 62; Peter Bart in *Harper's*, August, 1963.
94. *Nieman Reports*, October, 1963, pp. 18–23.

12. UNDERDEVELOPED JOURNALISM

95. *Saturday Review*, August 6, 1966, p. 38.
96. *Honolulu Advertiser*, July 27, 1967, p. C–1.
97. ASNE, *Bulletin*, March 1, 1963, p. 4.
98. *Columbia Journalism Review*, Summer, 1966, pp. 5–6.
99. *Columbia Journalism Review*, p. 8.
100. *Time*, March 31, 1967, p. 66.
101. *Time*, May 19, 1967, p. 55.
102. Marylin Bender, *Red Book*, August, 1967.
103. ASNE *Bulletin*, March 1, 1963, p. 3 is source of remark on product plugs. For discussion of women's pages, see APME *Red Book*, 1963, pp. 15–21.
104. *Chicago Daily News*, June 7, 1966, p. 23.
105. *Boston Globe*, June 3, 1966, p. 26.
106. *The New York Times*, September 7, 1966, p. 42.
107. APME *Red Book*, 1965, pp. 100–102.
108. APME *Red Book*, 1964, pp. 120–122.
109. APME *Red Book*, 1965, pp. 65–67.
110. Quoted in Gerald M. Loeb, "Flaws in Financial Reporting," *Columbia Journalism Review*, Spring, 1966, pp. 37–49.
111. Loeb.
112. *Time* cover story on Sylvia Porter, November 28, 1960, pp. 40–44. Survey by Timothy J. Hubbard in *Journalism Quarterly*, Winter, 1966, pp. 703–708.
113. A personal experience.
114. *Time*, April 8, 1966, pp. 82–87.
115. *The Quill*, December, 1964, p. 22. The author, Gene I. Maeroff, was on the staff of the *Akron* (O.) *Beacon Journal* at the time.

13. THE AMERICAN CULTURAL REVOLUTION

116. Louise Bruner, art ed., *Toledo Blade, Editor & Publisher*, November 15, 1958, p. 52.
117. Only 310 book columns or pages were listed for 1,761 newspapers in *Publishers' Weekly Literary Marketplace* for 1966.

316

118. *Editor & Publisher,* March 24, 1962, p. 13.

119. *The New York Times Book Review,* July 6, 1958, p. 2.

120. *Editor & Publisher,* March 24, 1962, p. 50.

121. *The New York Times,* March 25, 1962.

122. Such authors as Alexander King and Harry Golden were materially assisted by TV promotion on NBC's "Tonight" show. Art Linkletter, a TV personality, sold more than 2 million copies of his *Kids Say the Darndest Things.*

123. *The New York Times Book Review,* February 9, 1964, p. 30.

124. W. K. Zinsser, "Seen Any Good Movies Lately?" (Garden City, N. Y.: Doubleday & Co., Inc., 1958), pp. 135–136.

125. Ezra Goodman, "The 50-Year Decline and Fall of Hollywood" (New York: Simon and Schuster, Inc., 1962), p. 144. His Chapter 4 discusses the weaknesses of movie reviewers.

126. *The New York Times,* January 1, 1967, p. D–13.

127. ASNE *Bulletin,* September 1, 1965, p. 4.

128. From the Television Information Office of the National Association of Broadcasters, published in W. H. Ferry and Harry S. Ashmore, "Mass Communications," a pamphlet issued by the Center for the Study of Democratic Institutions, Santa Barbara, Calif., 1966, p. 30.

129. ASNE *Bulletin,* September 1, 1965, pp. 1–2.

130. ASNE, p. 5.

131. Private correspondence.

132. ASNE *Bulletin,* February 1, 1967, p. 13.

133. *The New York Times,* March 19, 1967, p. D–1.

14. THE ILLS OF PHOTO JOURNALISM

134. Stanton remarks in ASNE *Proceedings,* 1960, pp. 119–120; newsphoto survey in APME *Red Book,* 1965, pp. 165–166.

135. APME *Red Book,* 1963, p. 143.

136. ASNE *Bulletin,* August 1, 1958, p. 13.

137. Vincent S. Jones: "Are These Pictures Necessary?" ASNE *Bulletin,* June 1, 1962, pp. 1, 5.

138. J. D. Warren and L. D. Brandeis, "The Right to Privacy," *Harvard Law School Review* 4 (1890), p. 193.

139. *Columbia Journalism Review,* "The Cruel Camera," Spring, 1965, p. 5.

140. *Columbia Journalism Review,* p. 6.

141. *Columbia Journalism Review,* Fall, 1964, p. 7.

142. Ralph McGill to author.

143. Quoted by Vincent S. Jones, ASNE, *Bulletin,* June 1, 1962, p. 5.

144. Arthur Sylvester, "TV Covers the War," *Dateline: 1966,* publication of the Overseas Press Club, pp. 66–67.

145. Morley Safer, "TV Covers the War," *Dateline: 1966,* p. 71.

146. APME, *Red Book,* 1965, p. 166.

PART 3—THE SHAPING OF PUBLIC OPINION: 317
THE ENDLESS STRUGGLE

15. POLLS AND POLLSTERS

1. William H. Honan, "Good Case of the Poll Sniffles," *The New York Times Magazine*, August 21, 1966, p. 34.

2. It would be a violation of confidence to disclose the author.

3. *The New York Times*, August 28, 1966, p. 1. Gerhart D. Wiebe, in *The Journalism Quarterly* (Winter, 1967), criticized *The New York Times* for handling this faulty poll on p. 1 with a "misleading headline, inadequate treatment of the facts, and faulty editorial judgment as to the significance of the story."

4. *Newsweek*, July 10, 1967, pp. 36, 38.

5. APME *Red Book*, 1964, pp. 28–29.

6. *Columbia Journalism Review*, Fall, 1965, p. 3.

7. *The New York Times Magazine*, August 21, 1966, p. 60.

8. Samuel Lubell, "The New Technology of Election Reporting," *Columbia Journalism Review*, Summer, 1964, pp. 4–8.

9. APME *Red Book*, 1964, pp. 17–20.

10. ASNE *Bulletin*, February 1, 1958, pp. 1–2.

11. APME *Red Book*, 1965, p. 30.

12. ASNE *Bulletin*, February 1, 1958, p. 1.

13. *Editor & Publisher*, September 3, 1966, p. 42.

14. *The New York Times*, August 16, 1966, p. 26. See Murray Schumach's article, "The Last Years Downhill to Disaster."

15. Samuel Lubell, *Columbia Journalism Review*, Summer, 1964, p. 6.

16. *The New York Times*, September 11, 1966, p. E–11.

17. John Strohmeyer, ed., *Bethlehem* (Pa.) *Globe-Times*, in ASNE *Bulletin*, November 1, 1962, p. 1.

18. *Newsweek*, May 18, 1959, p. 66.

19. Richard K. Doan, *Philadelphia Inquirer*, March 13, 1967, p. 21.

16. FREE PRESS AND FAIR TRIAL

20. Text of address by J. Edward Murray, chairman of Freedom of Information and Press-Bar Committee of the American Society of Newspaper Editors, before the 90th meeting of the American Bar Association, Honolulu, August 4, 1967, p. 13.

21. Standards Relating to Fair Trial and Free Press, recommended by the Advisory Committee on Fair Trial and Free Press, Paul C. Reardon, Chairman; David L. Shapiro, Reporter; revisions of tentative draft dated July, 1967, and submitted to 90th meeting of American Bar Association at Honolulu, p. 16. (Hereafter this document is referred to as the *Reardon Report*.)

22. *The New York Times*, February 24, 1967, pp. 1, 18.

23. Text of address by Arthur B. Hanson, general counsel, American Newspaper Publishers Association, before the 90th meeting of

318   the American Bar Association, Section on Judicial Administration, Honolulu, August 4, 1967, p. 1.

24. Warren Report, as published in *The New York Times*, September 28, 1964, p. 19A.

25. Herbert Brucker, *Saturday Review*, January 11, 1964, p. 75.

26. Anthony Lewis, *The New York Times Magazine*, October 18, 1964, p. 31.

27. ASNE, *Proceedings*, 1965, pp. 222–228.

28. Curtis D. MacDougall, *The Press and Its Problems* (Dubuque, Iowa: W. C. Brown, 1964), pp. 400–402; Wiggins, pp. 57–58.

29. Wiggins, pp. 55–56.

30. ASNE, *Proceedings*, 1964, pp. 222–228.

31. ASNE, *Proceedings*, 1965, p. 120.

32. *The New York Times*, November 17, 1964.

33. *The Quill*, March, 1965, pp. 12–17.

34. Estes v. Texas 381 US 532 (1965).

35. Anthony Lewis, *The New York Times Magazine*, October 18, 1964, p. 94; John Hohenberg, *Foreign Correspondence: The Great Reporters and Their Times*, p. 416.

36. Seymour v. U. S. 373 F. 2d 629 (5th Cir. 1967) 631–632.

37. Hanson text, pp. 1–2.

38. AP *Log*, February 2–8, March 23–29, 1966; ASNE *Bulletin*, April 1, 1966.

39. *The New York Times*, June 7, 1966, pp. 1, 43; June 8, 1966, p. 11; *Editor & Publisher*, June 11, 1966, pp. 11, 76; *Newsweek*, June 20, 1966, p. 64; foreign comment in OPC *Bulletin*, July 23, 1966, pp. 4–5.

40. Text of address by Robert C. Notson, president of the American Society of Newspaper Editors, before Georgia Press Institute, February 24, 1967. This quotation is typical of what a number of press leaders had said ever since the issuance of the Warren Report and is not necessarily limited to the time at which the speech was delivered.

41. *Chicago Tribune* and *Chicago Sun-Times*, *Chicago's American* and *Chicago Daily News* for July 13, 1966; *Time*, July 22, 1966, pp. 20–22; July 29, 1966, p. 56; *Newsweek*, August 1, 1966, p. 76; *Editor & Publisher*, July 23, 1966, pp. 6, 9, 44.

42. Statement of the Freedom of Information Committee of the American Society of Newspaper Editors, published in the *Honolulu Advertiser* in connection with the American Bar Association convention, July 30, 1967, p. B–2.

43. *Honolulu Advertiser*, July 30, 1967, p. B–2.

44. Jack Ruby reversal reported in newspapers of October 6, 1966 (see *The New York Times* and *Washington Post* in particular); Ruby death reported in *The New York Times*, January 4, 1967, p. 1.

45. These observations are based on the record of proceedings at the 90th meeting of the American Bar Association in Honolulu, Section on Judicial Administration, August 4, 1967. See also report of Reardon committee in *The New York Times*, October 2, 1966, pp. 1, 81; report of *The New York Times* press survey on subject October 9, 1966, p. 89; see also discussion in *Time*, October 7, 1966, p. 96,

and October 14, 1966, p. 72; *Editor & Publisher*, October 8, 1966, pp. 9–10.

46. Murray text.

47. *Toledo Blade* code commented upon in *The New York Times*, August 22, 1966, p. 35.

48. *Reardon Report*, Appendix A, pp. 29–33.

17. RIGHT TO KNOW VS. NEED TO KNOW

49. The national "freedom of information" law was approved by Congress and signed July 4, 1966, by President Johnson, taking effect a year later. Data on state laws from University of Missouri.

50. Wiggins, p. 166.

51. International Press Institute Report, *Professional Secrecy and the Journalist* (Zurich: Frederick A. Praeger, Inc., 1962), p. 174.

52. *The Quill*, August, 1966, pp. 12–17; *The New York Times*, June 29, 1966, p. 23.

53. IPI *Report*, pp. 177–182.

54. John Hohenberg, *The Pulitzer Prize Story* (New York: Columbia University Press, 1959); see *Newsday*, November 8, 1967, for reaction to exposé of scandals on Long Island.

55. *Time*, August 12, 1966, p. 35.

56. *The Quill*, August, 1966, p. 15.

57. IPI *Report*, p. 184.

58. Harold L. Cross, *The People's Right to Know* (New York: Columbia University Press, 1953), Chs. 6–10.

59. Cross, cited on p. 95.

60. Cross, p. 96.

61. V. M. Newton, Jr., *Crusade for Democracy* (Ames, Iowa: Iowa State University, 1961), p. 19.

62. Clark Mollenhoff, *The Quill*, August, 1966, pp. 22–23; *The New York Times*, June 21 and July 5, 1966; *Editor & Publisher*, July 9, 1966, pp. 6, 13; see also issues of June 11 and 25, 1966.

63. ASNE, *Proceedings*, 1960, p. 23.

64. ASNE, *Proceedings*, 1965, p. 25.

18. MANY VOICES, MANY MEDIA

65. *Editor & Publisher*, October 21, 1961, p. 14.

66. A. H. Raskin, *The New York Times Magazine*, June 11, 1967, p. 5.

67. ASNE *Bulletin*, October 1, 1966, pp. 2–5.

68. *Editor & Publisher*, October 21, 1961, p. 14.

69. Ralph McGill, *Nieman Reports*, January, 1961, p. 6.

70. *Editor & Publisher*, July 9, 1966, p. 68. See also *The Masthead*, Summer, 1966, publication of the National Conference of Editorial Writers.

71. B. H. Bagdikian, "How Editors Pick Columnists," *Columbia Journalism Review*, Spring, 1966, p. 42.

72. *The New York Times*, September 15, 1966, p. 1.

320   73. B. H. Bagdikian, *Columbia Journalism Review*, Fall, 1965, p. 29.

      74. *Newsweek*, June 27, 1966, p. 87.

      75. Vermont Royster, ASNE *Bulletin*, October 1, 1966, p. 3.

19. THE BASIS OF PUBLIC SERVICE

      76. APME *Red Book*, 1965, p. 27.

      77. Stephen Hearst, "Itinerant Impressions of the American Press," ASNE *Bulletin*, September, 1, 1959.

      78. ASNE *Bulletin*, May 1, 1966, p. 3.

      79. Joseph Pulitzer, Jr., "A Tradition of Conscience," address at the Columbia Graduate School of Journalism, February 10, 1956.

      80. *The New York Times Magazine*, June 12, 1966, p. 32; *Columbia Journalism Review*, Summer, 1966, p. 23.

      81. *Columbia Journalism Review*, Spring, 1967, p. 33.

      82. *The New York Times*, June 18, 1966, p. 1.

      83. *Columbia Journalism Review*, Summer, 1966, pp. 10–11. A five-column *Wall Street Journal* article on "Ethics and the Press" was published July 25, 1967, p. 1.

      84. ASNE *Bulletin*, December 1, 1961, pp. 1, 7.

      85. Oxie Reichler, speech before New England AP Editors, Boston, May 19, 1958. He referred to Harry B. Haines, ed., *Paterson* (N. J.) *Evening News*.

      86. ASNE, *Proceedings*, 1965, p. 39.

      87. *Honolulu Star Bulletin*, August 21, 1967, p. 1.

      88. *Time*, February 3, 1967, p. 58; *The Quill*, September, 1966, pp. 24–25, a reprint of a *National Observer* article by Jude Wanniski. For an estimate of electronic progress in public service, see W. A. Wood in *Columbia Journalism Review*, Spring, 1966.

20. THE FUTURE OF THE JOURNALIST

      89. *Foreign Affairs*, July, 1966, p. 554.

      90. Douglass Cater, *The Fourth Branch of Government* (Boston: Houghton Mifflin Company, 1959), p. 171.

      91. *Newsweek*, August 22, 1966, p. 170.

      92. Clark Mollenhoff, *Despoilers of Democracy* (Garden City, N.Y.: Doubleday & Company, Inc., 1966), p. 386.

      93. ASNE, *Proceedings*, 1966, p. 170.

      94. Walter Lippmann, *Public Opinion* (New York: The Free Press, 1922), pp. 362–363.

      95. Rossiter & Lare, eds. *The Essential Lippmann* (New York: Random House, Inc., 1963), pp. 533–534.

      96. *Columbia Journalism Review*, Summer, 1966, p. 42.

      97. ASNE, *Proceedings*, 1967, p. 81.

      98. *The New York Times*, October 7, 1966, p. 4.